Courtesy of the author

About the Author

Clay Travis writes a popular sports column, titled "ClayNation," for CBS SportsLine. He has been profiled in *Sports Illustrated*, the *Washington Post*, and *Time* magazine, and has been featured on ESPN, *Good Morning America*, CNN, and NPR. A graduate of Vanderbilt Law School, Travis lives in Nashville with his wife, Lara.

DIXIELAND DELIGHT

DIXIELAND DELIGHT

A FOOTBALL SEASON ON THE ROAD IN THE SOUTHEASTERN CONFERENCE

CLAY TRAVIS

itbooks

AN IMPRINT OF HARPERCOLLINS PUBLISHERS

All photographs courtesy of the author.

HarperCollins books may be purchased for educational, business, or sales promotional use. For information, please e-mail the Special Markets Department at SPsales@harpercollins.com.

FIRST EDITION

Designed by Ruth Lee-Mui

Library of Congress Cataloging-in-Publication Data is available upon request.

ISBN: 978-0-06-143124-1
ISBN-10: 0-06-143124-9

HB 12.21.2017

To my parents,

NORM AND LIZ TRAVIS,

who always got me the next book

And my grandparents,

HENRY CLAY TRAVIS AND RICHARD K. FOX,

who gave me a name

CONTENTS

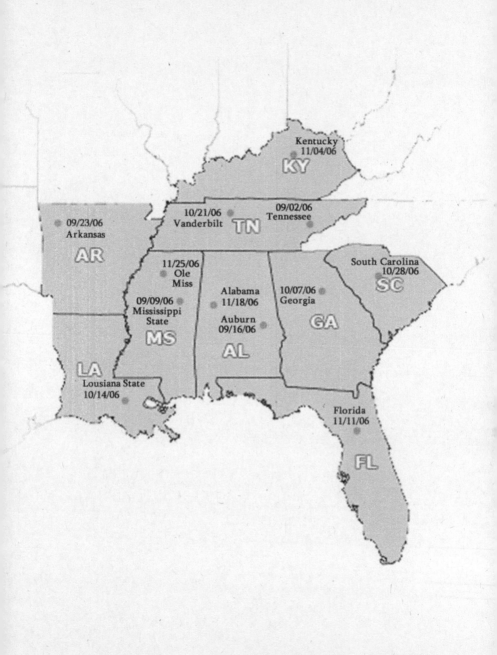

DIXIELAND DELIGHT

INTRODUCTION

I went to my first University of Tennessee football game at the age of six. It was the opener of the 1985 season, and it signified that my next-door neighbor Matt and I were finally old enough to be trusted with our dads in Neyland Stadium. I remember three things very well from this game:

1. An older man behind us had an air horn, which he would set off every time a big play happened for UT. (It's too bad these are now banned, because, to a six-year-old, being able to push a button and double over every adult within sight was the height of first-grade accomplishment.)

2. UT ended up with a tie score, 26–26, on a late UCLA touchdown. The concept of a tie was particularly deflating to my six-year-old mind, because it was far more complicated than a win or a loss.

3. Every time my dad, my next door neighbor's dad Tim, and every-

one else around us talked about the team they used the word *we*. As in, "We can't seem to keep our feet underneath us," or "We almost had a big play there." Around halftime I asked my dad why everyone was using the word *we*, which heretofore I'd only heard applied when the speaker himself was actually involved in a pursuit. After all, I was not a team member and neither were any of the other men sitting in the lower-bowl end zone of Neyland Stadium. "Because," said my dad, "this means so much to most people here, they want to make themselves a part of it."

This adoption of the pronoun *we* troubled me for most of my first year of fandom. After that year, my trepidation quickly disappeared, and I became a member of the *we* college football family that echoes across the geographic regions of our country. My particular *we* was the University of Tennessee. My orange-colored tribal band so initiated, I have never looked back.

Now, I'm a grown man with a home and a wife and a law degree. No one cards me at R-rated movies. If I wanted to, I could drive to the smutty gas station and load my trunk with pornography and beer. I even have a beard, a spotty and poorly maintained beard, but a beard nonetheless. To all who see me, I am indisputably an adult. However, some small part of me has never moved beyond the way I felt when I was in elementary school, watching University of Tennessee football games. I know I'm not alone in this. Across the South, there are countless men and women just like me: People who face serious decisions at very important jobs, life-threatening illnesses, and bone-crushing stress yet, each weekend in the fall, revert to the rhythms of their preadolescent life. As the coming crispness of autumn reveals itself in the coolness of early mornings and late evenings, we all become, once more, eternally the children we no longer are.

There's something about the pageantry and passion—the way sunshine comes later and departs earlier behind the colored leaves of the trees, and the pounding of drums in an onrushing band on a Southern campus—that stirs your heart. People who otherwise would not speak to you exchange high fives as you stand as one on a fall afternoon and scream in unison with blood-curdling fury. A feeling comes over you in these moments that is impossible to explain. Football time in the South has arrived.

One spring day, in the midst of an employment investigation designed to determine whether or not a coal mine pit boss had offered $19.75 to his fat coal mine secretary to give him a fully clothed, yet nonetheless lascivious, lap dance, it occurred to me that my life could be spent on more enjoyable endeavors. That, just maybe, there might be something more fun than interviewing people without teeth in an office filled with the fine, gray dust of disintegrated rock.

That's when I had my first vision of the Dixieland Delight Tour. Instead of breathing gravel, I could spend a few months traveling around the Southeastern Conference, watching a football game in each of the twelve SEC stadiums. Fortunately, my column at CBS SportsLine offered the perfect platform to make my vision a reality. And, most importantly, I knew it would be fun. Amazingly fun. All my life I'd wanted to be able to see a game from the stands of every SEC stadium. Even better would be to tour the circuit during a single season. So, I set about crafting a schedule that would allow me to travel to every SEC campus and attend a single game in each stadium. I branded the quest the ClayNation Dixieland Delight Tour;

"The DDT" for short, in honor of Jake "The Snake" Roberts, my favorite wrestling star from the 1980s whose famous finishing move was called the DDT.*

The DDT schedule called for me to begin in Knoxville, Tennessee, on September 2 and finish in Atlanta, Georgia, for the SEC Championship on December 2. In between, I'd have three months on the road to immerse myself in the game-day rituals and ironic excesses of the common fan. I was to become one with the rabid passion, the redneck braggadocio, and the cultural individuality of the South on football Saturdays.

It was to be a holy pilgrimage of sorts, a journey to all twelve Southern Meccas. From Nashville, Tennessee, to Columbia, South Carolina; from Lexington, Kentucky, to Gainesville, Florida; from Super Wal-Marts in Mississippi to the Bill Clinton Presidential Library in Arkansas to the riverboat gambling docks in Louisiana, the length and breadth of the South would be my home for the fall. And experiencing the Southeastern Conference as no one had ever done before would be my quest.

---

* For the uninitiated, the DDT is any wrestling move during which the wrestler falls down or backward, to drive a held opponent's head into the mat. The classic DDT is performed by putting the opponent in a front facelock and falling backward, so that the opponent is forced to dive forward onto his or her head (Wikipedia). Wrestling fans across the country hypothesized about what exactly the DDT stood for until Jake "The Snake" Roberts famously replied, "The end." At age ten, I considered the DDT to be the greatest thing on earth. Now that I'm older, I can honestly say it is the third best thing on earth. The first two are sex and SEC football.

THE QUEST

On doctor's orders, my maternal grandfather, Richard Fox, was not allowed to watch University of Tennessee football games. That was because my grandfather, a former Tennessee player, watched the games with such ferocious intensity that his doctor was afraid he might have a heart attack. So, for most of my youth, at halftime of each Tennessee game, my grandfather would call my uncle and inquire as to the score. If UT was comfortably ahead, he would begin watching the taped game. If it was a close game, he would wait until the end of the game to find out the final score before watching. If UT lost, he would never watch the tape. At no time did I consider this to be abnormal.

My grandfather also blazed a trail for modern athletes by being one of the first University of Tennessee football players to leave school without a degree. In the early 1930s, he played for General Robert Neyland while living in a dorm beneath the football stadium. When I was older, and the two of us visited Knoxville, my grandfather pointed out where he had lived as a student under the looming steel supports. The windows of those rooms were filled with cardboard boxes, and it was unbelievable to me that my grandfather had ever been so young or that his grass-stained cleats had once hung outside the door. On that day, as I stood with my grandfather and gazed at the gridiron on which he had played, it seemed impossible that I could ever root for another football team. My bloodlines ran orange.

Only once in my life did my grandfather ever break his doctor's orders and watch a live University of Tennessee game with me. It was in 1990, and I was eleven. It was the third Saturday in October. For University of Tennessee fans this meant one thing and one thing only: Alabama week. UT was heavily favored that year over a mediocre Alabama football team, and this was supposed to be the year that we would break Alabama's four-year winning streak over us.

On the day of the game, Grandpa bought me candy at a gas station outside Chattanooga whose sign had GO VOLS written alongside the gas prices. In so doing, he had chosen to drive past the gas station that had GO DAWGS written on its sign. "That man's from Georgia," my grandfather said with evident disgust. Georgia was, after all, at least ten miles away from where we stood. Consequently, my grandfather never bought gas from that station and that Georgia Bulldog fan. In the South, you learn at a very young age that small geographic differences can be the deciding factor between friend and foe.

On the way home, I begged Grandpa to watch the UT game that day, and he was unable to resist me, his only grandson, thanks in no small measure, I knew, to the fact that my grandmother was going to be shopping with my mom all afternoon. And that, if doctor's orders in regard to watching football were going to be broken, they should be broken to watch a Tennessee–Alabama game. Once home, I carefully chose my spot on the floor in front of the television. My grandmother loved clocks that tolled the time and, as we sat awaiting the start of the game, all around us the clocks began to chime in succession. As they chimed, I remember staring into a large mirror on the wall and seeing my reflection alongside my grandfather's. I saw myself, seated Indian-style, wearing my favorite orange T-shirt, my small hands jittery with excitement. I saw my grandfather seated in his favorite brown recliner just a short distance away, neck bobbing due to the bone spurs on his vertebrae, his bald head lightly sweating, large hands clenched tightly on his injured knees. His eyes were already locked on the television.

I remember thinking that this moment was perfect, a moment I would always remember. Kickoff between Tennessee and Alabama was just moments away, and I was going to be watching it for the first time with my grandfather. And then, suddenly, above the sound of the clocks chiming, the sound of the UT band playing "Rocky Top" echoed across the generational divide and sent the pulse racing in us both. At that moment, my grandfather seemed younger than he ever had before.

"Whatever you do, don't tell your grandma," he said.

"I won't," I promised.

On the television, Alabama's crimson clad team raced onto the field, and the orange crowd hissed. Then, the UT band formed a giant T on the field and the players rushed through, raising their index fingers skyward amid a raucous and jarring medley of sounds. Grandpa had played on this very field. His arms shook as he tightly gripped his injured knees. We were both so excited for the game that we were literally trembling. "They aren't excited enough" he warned.

I turned and felt a chill run down the length of my spine. "They look ready to me," I said.

"They aren't. It's Alabama and they aren't ready," Grandpa said.

The game was close all the way, even though UT was heavily favored. Finally, late in the fourth quarter as the game neared its end, the score was tied at 6–6 and UT lined up to attempt a fifty-yard field goal to seal the victory.

Grandpa leaned forward in his recliner, head bobbing, brow sweating. I sat with my fists clenched so tightly that my fingers ached. With hardly any time remaining, the ball was snapped . . . and one of Alabama's players blocked the field goal. There was a mad scramble as the ball rolled around on the sunlit field, and Alabama recovered the blocked kick. Now, Alabama set up for their own forty-seven yard field goal to win the game. Neither Grandpa nor I said a word. The scene was repeated in reverse. The ball was struck and sailed through the uprights. The kick was good and, just like that, the game was over. Alabama had won.

Grandpa leaned back in his recliner and slowly exhaled his breath. The overhead fan was still spinning. The mirror was still reflecting. It was still the third Saturday in October. But UT had lost. "Sonny boy," he said, dragging out the two words until they seemed to fill the expanse of the room.

I did my best to keep from crying because, after all, I was eleven years old and eleven-year-olds weren't supposed to cry. But when you are young and your team loses, it stings far worse than any bee. It seemed possible to me on that day that we might never play Alabama again. An entire year seemed an infinity of days, each of which would taunt me with the loss. It seemed that, for the rest of my life, Tennessee was going to keep losing to Alabama and there would be nothing I could do about it. Despite my best efforts not to, I began to cry.

My grandfather frowned. "Is Johnny Majors crying?" he asked, pointing to the television. Looking at the field, I could see that the UT coach, Johnny Majors, was not, in fact, crying. My grandfather continued. "Men don't cry about football games," he said.

I was tempted to respond, "You're right, they just watch them on tape after they already know who is going to win." But, then, I didn't say anything at all.

For the rest of his life, my grandfather never watched another live UT game.

I was born and raised in the South, a place where, on Saturdays, the uncertain path of a football in the air seems to float on the collective breath of a region. If you don't care who wins between Alabama and Auburn, you aren't from Alabama. If you don't cringe when you hear the first strident chords of "Gator Bait," then you aren't from Georgia. And if you don't speckle your sentences with y'all, fixin', and reckon or still call your dad Daddy even when you are seventy and he is ninety, then you're probably not going to be familiar with everything I write. That's okay. After all, not everyone can eat at Waffle House, or never get tired of whiskey, or turn in every direction on a football Saturday and see a gorgeous woman standing in sunlight wearing a sundress, replete with heels. But almost everyone can appreciate a road trip into the heart of a region and the exploration of football passion.

Football in the SEC is a religion founded on cleats, grass,

pads, sweat, spite, and the bountiful colors of the trees in autumn. It's a lifestyle embraced by millions of sun-drenched be-
sotted fools. Above all else it is a passion linking generations.
Each weekend, you see kids all over the South, throwing wob-
bling footballs with their fathers, grandfathers, or drunken un-
cles as the hours before kickoff wane. If you're like me, for just a
moment, you relive the youth you've left behind. And you
know that the cycle of football in the South will never fade
away because it's embedded so deeply into our culture. Every
Saturday another eleven-year-old boy sitting alongside his
grandfather becomes an SEC fan for life.

The Southeastern Conference is the most popular college
conference in America. Founded in 1932 with thirteen schools
(since its inception Tulane, Georgia Tech, and Sewanee have
left, and Arkansas and South Carolina have been added), the
SEC is now made up of twelve schools: Arkansas, Alabama,
Louisiana State, Auburn, Mississippi, Mississippi State, Tennessee, Georgia, Florida, South Carolina, Kentucky, and Vanderbilt.

For most of the SEC's history, there were no NFL teams in
the South, so college football was the one and only football
show in the region. Even now that the nine SEC states are
home to the New Orleans Saints, the Tennessee Titans, the
Atlanta Falcons, the Jacksonville Jaguars, the Tampa Bay Buc-
caneers, and the Miami Dolphins most locals view the NFL as
simply the place where former SEC college football stars go to
continue plying their trade.

The roster of former SEC greats who, during my lifetime
alone, have gone on to stellar NFL careers is legion: Bo Jackson, Herschel Walker, Peyton Manning, Champ Bailey, Em-
mitt Smith, Hines Ward, Jamal Lewis, Eli Manning, Reggie

White, Shaun Alexander, and Derrick Thomas. More than any other fans in the country, Southerners root for these NFL players on the basis of where they played in college rather than on the NFL teams they play for afterward. No matter what he does for the rest of his life Peyton Manning is, eternally, in the mind of Southerners, a Tennessee Vol. It's the same with all the other players listed. In the mind of a Southerner, professional football team allegiance is a business decision predicated on the NFL draft and money, while collegiate allegiance is personal. Very personal. When a high school athlete chooses to play for your school, you bequeath him your allegiance for life.

In 2006, the twelve schools of the SEC collectively brought in more than 6.5 million fans, and these were just fans who actually attended the games. Across the South, tens of millions of additional fans spent their Saturdays in front of the television watching their favored team do gridiron battle on CBS, ESPN, and the horrific regional broadcasts of Jefferson Pilot Lincoln Financial Sports. Many other SEC fans passed out on the trunks of tailgates outside the stadium.

Like no other region in the country, the rhythm of Southern life is predicated on the uncertain and tremulous flight of a football that could, at any moment, bound in any direction.

In addition to being the most popular conference in the country, the SEC is also the most competitive. Since 1992, Alabama, Tennessee, LSU, and Florida have all won national championships. Auburn has twice gone undefeated, yet had no opportunity to play for the national championship, and Georgia has finished third in the nation. Most conferences in America have one or two teams who can compete for a national championship; each new season in the SEC, six or more teams and their fans legitimately believe they can contend for college football's ultimate prize.

SEC football is also big business. In 2005, total football revenues for SEC athletic departments hit $350,193,187. That's just football. This figure dwarfed the revenue of the next closest conference, the Big 10, by over 73 million dollars. Indeed, of the ten highest grossing football teams in America, five are in the SEC. In the fiscal year ending in June 2006, Georgia made a football profit of 44.1 million on revenue of 58.7 million and Auburn made a football profit of 31.5 million on revenue of 51.6 million. In terms of profitability as a percentage of revenue, the top teams in the SEC share more in common with Google than they do with other collegiate athletic teams. For good measure, the two coaches in the 2006 NFC Championship Game, Sean Payton of the New Orleans Saints and Lovie Smith of the Chicago Bears, earned salaries less than seven of the head football coaches in the SEC.

These salaries are due in no small part to the fact that SEC football is a religion in the South. Shortly after Bill Curry was hired as the new coach at Alabama, his wife received a telephone call from her minister who was inquiring as to how they were doing in their new home. "Well," she said, "you know football is a religion down here." There was a pause on the other end of the line. "Oh, no," said the minister, "it's much more important than that."

Positioning myself as the most devoted of worshippers, I knew better than to visit SEC campuses and stadiums on the Dixieland Delight Tour without someone who has been there before as a fan. To that end, accompanying me on these forays into the wilds of Southern football I had alumni or friends as guides from each school except Mississippi State. (I did not exclude Mississippi State to ridicule the school but, rather, because I'm not sure anyone has actually ever graduated from Mississippi State.) Most of these friends and alumni I met in Vanderbilt Law School, which incubated some of the fiercest SEC debates in the country during my three years there. (A lot of people think law school is a place where the most seminal issues facing our country are debated, analyzed, and refined by our nation's young leaders. They are wrong. At least in the case of Vanderbilt, it was a place where some of the finest minds of the South spent hours inventively thinking about why your team sucked. I miss those days to no end.)

Like all great quests and religious pilgrimages, my DDT road trip necessitated a number of canons. These are the seven most important ones:

1. I would travel as a fan. This meant I did not have tickets provided and would be responsible for somehow finding a way to get into each game.
2. I would meet fans of each SEC team, tailgate with them, and find out what made their particular school unique.
3. I would have no hotel reservations and, because I'm a fool, would not even travel with a map in my car.
4. While I would be an acknowledged fan of the University of Tennessee, it was my goal to treat each school equally—well, almost equally—and apportion ridicule and plaudits even-handedly. I believe this is called *objectivity*. Of course I am not objective. For instance, I hate Florida. So, if you are reading this book and are a fan of a particular SEC team, inevitably I have written some-

thing that makes your blood boil. Take several deep breaths, work on your sense of humor and know that if this anger persists I may be reached at JimNantz@cbs.com.

5. I would employ a digital camera to record my travels. This is despite the fact that it's altogether possible that I am the worst photographer on earth. Not to mention that I have no idea how to transfer the resulting pictures to my computer.

6. I would wear the 99 cent aviator sunglasses my friend Tardio purchased for me from Mapco Express. I looked a bit like Goose from *Top Gun* before he drowned. (Given that I lose sunglasses with an uncanny regularity, if you happen to come upon a pair of classy Sunclassics brand sunglasses trodden in the dirt of a Southern football field, they are likely mine. Treat them with the honor and respect they so richly deserve.)

7. In games not featuring the University of Tennessee, I would attempt to wear at least one article of clothing that was popular with the home crowd to further legitimize my fandom experience. Early leaders for Florida were jean shorts ('*jorts*'), for Georgia those atrocious tight red pants, and, for Kentucky, I planned to carry a minibasketball.

Basically, I designed the DDT to be a road trip into the pigskin passion of the South that would allow me to experience SEC fandom as no one had ever done before. And these seven rules would ensure that, at all times, I remained a fan first and foremost. The DDT was to be a running cannonball into the heart of the SEC pool. And on September 2, 2006, I was off.

TENNESSEE

The DDT gets off to a rousing morning start on Saturday, September 2 at nine-thirty when my law school friend Junaid, my wife, and I leave Nashville, Tennessee, and head 180 miles east in the direction of Knoxville and the University of Tennessee's home opener against California.

Actually, it may have started in the late-night hours of that Friday when Junaid arrived on our front door from Memphis. Once he was inside, Tennessee quarterback Erik Ainge immediately became the topic of our conversation. Junaid, a UT grad, spoke for the state of Tennessee when he said, "I just have no idea what he (Ainge) is going to do tomorrow." There was a long pause as we both contemplated what might happen; then, he continued, "I hope we don't have to call a timeout on our first offensive play." Yep, UT's offense was so bad last year we were actually debating whether we could get lined up in a proper formation before the snap.

Junaid and I met at Vanderbilt Law School over a shared need to defend Tennessee football from the derisive comments of other SEC fans. Junaid (pronounced Ju-nyde) is a Tennessee poster boy—a tall, thin, black guy born and raised in Memphis, who attended undergrad in Knoxville, then law school in the center of the state at Vanderbilt. He has a tremendous recollection of sporting facts relating to the University of Tennessee and, of our conversations, 95 percent relate to sports.

Being aspiring lawyers, we both picked up golf shortly after law school commenced, and spent a ton of time on the links in the middle of the day while the rest of the world tried to make a living. We were living on school loans and it seemed like everyone else at Vandy already played golf or was learning to play. There was a rumor running through the law school that if you could play golf well, you got to practice law less. None of us were even qualified to practice law at that point, yet we were already working hard at avoiding it. Junaid could kill the ball off the tee, but we never had any idea where his ball was going to land. Come to think of it, Junaid in the tee box was sort of like Erik Ainge in the quarterback pocket.

Erik Ainge is the junior quarterback of the University of Tennessee. He is twenty years old and from Hillsboro, Oregon. As SEC football is roundly considered the best in the nation, young men from across the geographic expanse of the country make their commitments to play college football in the South. So, too, with Ainge. After a freshman year during which he evoked fond memories of former University of Tennessee quarterback Peyton Manning, during his sophomore year Ainge evoked horrifying images of the worst quarterback in girl's powder-puff football history. This horror clarified itself during a road game at Louisiana State University in 2005, when a back-pedaling Ainge threw an underhanded interception which was returned by an LSU defensive player for a touchdown. Mention this pass to any Tennessee fan and, inevitably, that fan will still wince. It was the worst interception I have ever seen. (As interceptions go, for me, it was the equivalent of elementary school corn dogs. Yep, the memory of the interception makes me nauseated.)

After the fatal interception, a shell-shocked Ainge seemed incapable of performing even the simplest of plays. He was replaced as starting quarterback, and spent the next several weeks on the bench bearing much of the criticism for an atrocious 5–6 Tennessee season—the worst in nearly two decades.

During the entire off-season Ainge has been the primary topic of conversation among Tennessee Volunteer fans. On his right arm, most feel, will rest the foundation of the Tennessee football season.

It is well after midnight before Junaid and I stop talking about Erik Ainge and his likely performance in the upcoming season. Tellingly, we have spent hardly any time at all worrying about our opponent, the California Golden Bears, and instead have ruminated upon our own team's woes. By the time I go to bed, my wife turns over and looks at me, "You're about to cover a lot of miles," she says, and then we sleep.

The next morning, I attempt to wake up from a nightmare. Erik Ainge has thrown five interceptions and a fan from California is sitting behind me screaming insults about me not being able to read and not owning shoes. Somewhere in the recesses of my mind I'm aware that I am dreaming, and that the game has not been played yet but, even still, I'm steaming mad, angry beyond compare.

My eyes open. I take a deep breath and convince myself that I've just had a bad dream. It's the opening Saturday of the SEC football season and my stomach is so tight I can't even bear the thought of eating anything. Neither can Junaid. When my wife, Lara, asks whether we want breakfast, I merely shake my head. "Oh, no," Junaid says, "nothing for me. Not on game day."

Junaid and I depart for Knoxville in separate cars. Lara accompanies me and, before we even leave the outskirts of Nashville, Junaid and I are involved in a three-person conference call with our law school friend Weatherholt, who is confidently predicting a 31–14 California victory. "You're a 5–6 football team until you serve notice otherwise," he says. Junaid and I disagree loudly. I do not mention my nightmare from the night before. "Erik Ainge is going to play superbly," I say with a confidence I don't really feel. My wife rolls her eyes as we carry on this three-way conversation across the state. "You do realize," she says, "that you are talking on the phone to someone you can see in your rearview mirror."

Eventually, our football conversation ends and I hang up, much to Lara's relief. Unfortunately for her, she now gets drawn into a conversation with me.

"If you were guillotined do you think you could see for a fraction of a second even though your head wasn't attached to your body?" I ask. She shakes her head in my direction. "I think you could," I say, "like when a snake gets its head cut off. Just for a fraction of a second." She sighs and then replies, "No. It's like when a computer cord gets yanked. Nothing at all." I continue debating this question for the next fifteen minutes. Riding in cars with me is great fun.

We are traveling in the direction of Knoxville in the DDT Mobile: a 2002 Mercury Mountaineer that I won during a Tennessee Titans football game. Seriously. But in case you don't believe me, here's the back story:

On the opening weekend of the 2002 NFL season, the Tennessee Titans were playing the Philadelphia Eagles. My dad and I were sitting in the north end zone of the Titans' stadium in Nashville. It was hot and I was wearing a T-shirt, khaki shorts, and flip-flops. A few minutes before halftime a Titans employee came down our aisle and tapped me on the shoulder.

"Would you like to be in the halftime contest?" he asked.

Of course, I immediately answered yes. Even though I had no idea what the halftime contest was. It could have been wrestling tigers for a prize of three Sonic Slurpees, and I still would have competed. Because here's the deal: When you get asked to be in a halftime contest, you do it. Period. The Titans employee beckoned me to follow him, and so down into the bowels of the stadium we went. Another contestant was already waiting there for us; we both signed waivers and were instructed that we would be participating in the halftime punt-catching contest sponsored by Logan's Roadhouse, a Nashville-based restaurant. Evidently, participants were supposed to have filled out cards in the restaurants, then have their name drawn to qualify for the contest, but somehow I was selected because they only had one contestant and they needed two. Even today, I still think that someone who was selected got cold feet and didn't show up for either the game or the contest that day.

In the contest, we would each be given the opportunity to

catch two punts, a twenty-five yarder and a forty yarder. If we caught the first punt, we received a gift certificate to Logan's Roadhouse and an autographed football from Titans coach Jeff Fisher. If we caught the second, we would be invited to come back months later on the last game of the season for a chance to win an SUV and a boat. I could barely swallow upon being informed of these details. Suddenly the flip-flops I had on seemed like a poor decision.

We were supposed to wear football helmets (which would have been the first time in my life I ever put on a football helmet), but the other guy's head was too big to fit in his helmet, so we were instructed to leave the helmets behind. I silently thanked the heavens that my halftime competitor had such a huge melon, because I was concerned that wearing a helmet would make catching the footballs harder.

With the waivers freshly signed, we were led out into the bright sunshine of the football field. The Titans and Eagles were playing the remaining minutes of the second quarter just a few yards in front of us, and I blinked in the sunlight and looked up into the crowd. Then I leaned over and touched the grass— primarily because I'd always wondered what an NFL field feels like. For the record, it feels just like normal grass.

When the half ended, the other contestant and I were hustled onto the field and introduced on the Jumbotron. When I heard my name echo throughout the stadium, I waved and marveled at how far away all the fans seemed from the center of the field. In front of us was a Juggs machine (like an automatic pitching machine, only for footballs) that had been modified to shoot footballs into the air as if they were punts.

Just before my first opportunity to catch, I was wracked with uncertainty as to whether or not I should kick off my Adidas sandals and go barefoot. My brain considered all the odds. Then I leaned over and tightened my flip-flops as tight as they could go. Thank God for Velcro. As I did this, it occurred to me that I was probably the first person on an NFL field to ever tighten his flip-flops in an effort to improve performance.

By the time I lined up around the twenty-five-yard line, I could think of nothing but the machine firing the ball into the air. I don't remember being cognizant of a single sound or of even where I was or how many people were watching me. I just saw the football rise into the air and I followed its arc until it nestled comfortably in my arms. One for one. The signed football and the dinner for two were mine.

The contest announcer smiled at me, gave me a handshake, and led me back to the forty-yard line, which seemed much farther than fifteen yards from where I had just been. Toes poised in the flip-flops I prepared to react to the football. Just before the Juggs machine let loose the second football, I took a few steps back, because I knew it was always easier to advance on a ball in the air than retreat on one. Thank God for Little League Baseball instruction: "When you hear the ball hit and you can't find it in the air or judge the distance, your first step should always be backwards." So too with the punt.

The ball soared into the air and, once again, I wasn't aware of anything but the ball and its flight. The football seemed to hang for a long time in the sunlit sky, then it came down once again into my arms. The crowd roared its appreciation, which I finally heard for the first time. I may or may not have pointed into the crowd and pumped my fist. Two for two. I was coming back three months later, on December 16, for a chance to win the car and the boat.

In the immediate days after my performance, I was a law

school demigod. Total strangers approached me and said they had watched me make the catches. My law school friends Hinton (my companion on the DDT to Arkansas) and Kumar (my host on the DDT stop in Georgia) had me repeat the performance in minute and exquisite detail. When I was done they asked questions. "So, did your flip-flops catch at all on the grass?" No. "Were you worried about the Velcro coming undone?" Yes. "Do you think any hot girls will recognize you at bars?" No. "Had I thanked God in my postperformance interview?" No, although I had been tempted.

For the next three months, everyone around me discussed my chances to win the car. For each of the seven remaining Titans home games two people had a chance to qualify for the final showdown. In the end, five other guys qualified alongside me.

So, during the final game of the season, a Monday Night Football telecast between the Tennessee Titans and the New England Patriots, I returned to the field for the finals of the contest. I was allowed to bring one guest and brought my dad. The two of us watched the warmups from the field and were then seated on the sideline for the entire first half. I remember thinking that at the very least watching an NFL game from the field was pretty cool.

At halftime, the contest was broadcast on the Jumbotron. A local sportscaster, Skip Baldwin, who was the reporter in the famous coin-flip tie-break story in *Friday Night Lights*, made jokes and we all smiled gamely. All the contestants were nervous and excited. The final contest had nothing to do with athletic ability. Instead, all six of us were to draw a key from a Titans football helmet; whoever's key started the car was the winner. I selected first, as I was the first contestant to qualify, and drew key number five. Everyone else picked on down the line until we each had a key.

We were lined up in the order of our keys and listened as the announcers revealed the prize. Not only would the winner be able to choose the SUV of his choice, but there was also a huge pontoon boat included. All the cars and the boat had been pulled out onto the field and were parked on the sideline in front of us. According to Skip Baldwin, the prize was valued at over sixty thousand dollars.

Each of us was required to climb into an SUV and attempt to turn the ignition. If your car started, you were the winner. I fiddled with the key in my hand and figured that I was in a pretty good place with key five. No way was the suspense in this contest going to end with keys one, two, or three. At least I didn't think so.

Keyholder number one's name was announced and he stepped forward to try his key in the ignition. "Did it start?" exclaimed Skip Baldwin. No dice. Same with keyholders two and three. Each of the men emerged from the car and shook their heads ruefully. We were down to the final three. After each nonsuccess I calculated my probability of success. Suddenly, my chances for a sixty thousand dollar prize were one in three.

Keyholder number four advanced. At this point, I figured it was going to be either key number four or number five that started the car. The contest sponsors would want to have the key ignition work. If both number four and my own key number five didn't work, then number six would know he'd already won even before he had to turn the ignition. Nope, plainly, that wouldn't do. Suspense dictated it was number four or me.

Number four sat behind the wheel. Attempted to turn the

key. Agonizing seconds ticked by. I could hear nothing but a dull roar from the crowd. If the car had blown up on ignition I probably would have barely heard it. Then . . . number four shook his head and climbed from the car. It was my turn. I walked forward to the car and sat down behind the wheel. Reached out and pushed the key into the ignition, turned the key and . . . it started.

I sprang out of the driver's seat with my fist held high in the air. Skip Baldwin rushed over and interviewed me on the Jumbotron. I have no idea what I said, but I said it loudly. It was, and still is, the luckiest day of my life.

Several weeks after my triumph, I picked out my prize and appeared in a local television commercial, in which I stood beside my brand new red Mercury Mountaineer and twirled a football outside the Tennessee Titans stadium. As I drove away, I rolled down the window and shot the camera with the index finger and thumb gun while I winked. I was a star, but not as much of a star as my new car. My dad recorded the *Monday Night Football* game and managed to find a shot of the car I would win behind Al Michaels and John Madden as they talked during halftime. For several months, he liked to pop in the tape, pause the screen, and point at the car on the football field. "Well," he'd say, "there's Clay's car."

And that's how I came to be driving a 2002 Mercury Mountaineer on the DDT. Yep, I won the car on a football field. So, I can legitimately say I've made a play on an NFL field. And there's never been a more appropriate car to rely on for a football road trip across the South.

Nor has there been a better travel partner than my wife. Lara and I met during our first year at Vanderbilt Law School, when

I had the good fortune to be recruiting members of the coed softball team. My recruiting methods had absolutely nothing to do with perceived softball skill and everything to do with the fact that she looked good in a sundress.

Lara is well-acquainted with football, having attended games at Michigan while she was an undergrad, and also having spent a season as a cheerleader for the NFL's Tennessee Titans.

During one of our first dates, she had the audacity to suggest that Michigan's Charles Woodson deserved to win the 1997 Heisman Trophy over Tennessee's Peyton Manning. Somehow, I forgave her.

As we drive, Vanderbilt is playing Michigan in football. Even though we are only about a hundred miles outside of Nashville, the Vanderbilt game is nowhere to be found on the radio dial. "Unbelievable," says Lara, an alum of both schools. We do, however, manage to find approximately fifteen radio stations discussing the UT–Cal game, which will start in about six hours.

Lara has never been to a University of Tennessee game before. She is filled with trepidation about what the SEC fan experience will be like, since she attended a game at Georgia several years ago and hated the fans there. Since that visit she has taken to saying, "I hate Georgia," any time any Georgia athletic event is featured on television. Incidentally, this hate of another SEC school, alongside an occasional drawl of her vowels, was the first clear sign that my midwestern-born wife was embracing the South.

We are traveling along I-40 East, which is like a huge Vol fandom slide ending in Knoxville. We pass car after car bedecked with Tennessee flags, Tennessee stickers, and orange-clad drivers. On game day in Tennessee, there is nothing orange that can't be placed on a car or worn on one's body. And, if you were heading to the game and driving less than seventy miles per hour, I didn't see you. I-40 East on a Tennessee game day is like a noncircular Daytona track.

On game day, Neyland Stadium's population would qualify it as the fifth largest city in the state of Tennessee. The state of Tennessee has a modest 6 million residents and, come Saturday, 106,000 of them gather in Knoxville to watch the Vols. Of course, this doesn't impress the Michigan Wolverine grad who shares my bed, "I mean," Lara says as we speed along, "one hundred six thousand people is a lot less than one hundred eight thousand people (the University of Michigan's announced seating capacity). It's really not that many."

We arrive in Knoxville at a little after one, eastern time. Somewhere, we have crossed into the eastern time zone which, when I was a kid, always made Knoxville seem like a strange and foreign land. Everyone wore orange and even their time was different. The state of Tennessee is so geographically wide that the distance from Memphis to the eastern edge of Tennessee is greater than the distance from Nashville to Canada. Yet, each season, Junaid, along with countless other UT grads, make multiple drives to Knoxville to see the Vols play. Distance, when it comes to SEC fans, is rarely an obstacle to seeing one's favorite team play in person. Now, Junaid has returned home to Memphis, where he is a practicing attorney. He describes Memphis as a hotbed of conflicting SEC fan bases, "We've got Alabama and Ole Miss and Mississippi State and Tennessee and Arkansas. All pushed closely together. God, those other fans suck," he says.

We park just off the Strip for ten bucks and commence our walk to the stadium area. The Strip is a collection of bars and restaurants that border the Tennessee campus. It is around one-thirty eastern time and the temperature is in the low seventies without sunshine. The bars on the Strip are packed with revelers awaiting the late-afternoon kickoff. The entire campus is swarming with Tennessee's orange colors.

Upon being reunited with Junaid, I ask him my guillotine question. "I think you could see for a second, too," he says. My wife stews alongside me. "You're both fools," she mutters.

We have our picture taken alongside the Rock (the Rock is, not surprisingly, a large rock that is freshly painted before every UT game) and meet Mark Nagi, without a doubt the funniest sportscaster in Knoxville who brought home the popularity of Tennessee Basketball Coach Bruce Pearl in a single

The Rock gets painted for every game. Junaid and I . . . not so much.

sentence: "I firmly believe if Bruce Pearl instructed the UT student body to invade Chattanooga, twenty-five thousand students would be driving down I-75."

We discuss the temperate weather and the fact that it will
not be to the Vols' advantage. UT fans have spent all summer
griping about the oppressive heat and, yet, now that we are
playing a team that is not from the South, we would prefer if
the grass were replaced with hot coals and the temperature
were approaching 150 degrees. Anything for a football advantage.

We run around making stops at a few different tailgates. At
one of these, I meet an actual Mississippi State grad, Ty Williams. Ty does not have his diploma in hand, but I accept his
word that he graduated from Mississippi State's School of Architecture in 2000. So, I've already learned the first of many
lessons on the DDT: Mississippi State has actual graduates.
Who knew?

Everywhere you turn, "Rocky Top" is being played. If you
gave someone directions that included, go to Philip Fulmer
Way (the street running outside Neyland Stadium) and walk
toward the "Rocky Top" soundtrack, that person would have
to walk north, south, east, and west at the same time. I have yet
to see a fan base fonder of their unofficial fight song. As we
stand beside the Tennessee River, the verses of the song echo
around us:

> Wish that I was on ole Rocky Top
> Down in the Tennessee Hills.
> Ain't no smoggy smoke on Rocky Top,
> Ain't no telephone bills.

Once I had a girl on Rocky Top,
Half bear the other half cat;
Wild as a mink as sweet as soda pop,
I still dream about that.

Rocky Top, you'll always be,
Home sweet home to me.
Good ole Rocky Top,
Rocky Top Tennessee.

Yep, "Rocky Top" is the song William Shakespeare would have written if he were drunk, from a mountaintop in Tennessee, and, you know, not that smart. Even still, like Tennesseans everywhere, I can't hear the song without immediately breaking out in chills. For a time in college, I had my alarm clock set to play "Rocky Top" in the morning. This drove my northern roommates crazy, but helped make the mornings somewhat palatable for me.

The popularity of the song is all the more surprising because in the tradition-bedecked SEC, the song is comparatively new and is not even UT's official fight song. Written in ten minutes in Gatlinburg, Tennessee, in 1967 by Felice and Boudleaux Bryant, "Rocky Top" rapidly attained almost universal popularity among the Tennessee undergraduates. This popularity led to UT's "Pride of the Southland" band playing it at a football game for the first time in 1972. Thirty-four years later, the song is perhaps the most recognized in the SEC, despite the fact that the first verse of the song deals with the lament of a lost love and lifestyle, and the second verse pays homage to moonshining and the implied murder of a pair of federal law enforcement agents. Yet, so popular is the song among bar crowds that a North Carolina band called the Red Clay Ramblers attained a measure of prominence for their song, "Play 'Rocky Top' (Or I'll Punch Your Lights Out)." It's possible that if "Rocky Top" were taken away from Tennessee fans, the National Guard would have to be called in to quell the riots.

From Ty Williams' tailgate, the song carries in every direction. Below us, I can see members of the Volunteer Navy who are tailgating in boats on the Tennessee River. Across the city of Knoxville, legions of Vol fans are preparing for the game on cars and boats. Somewhere, I am sure, Vol fans are preparing for the game in jets and on trains. Basically, if it moves and can get you to Knoxville, tailgating Vol fans are surely aboard.

Tennessee is known as the Volunteer State, based upon the number of Tennessee natives who volunteered to fight in the War of 1812. Many of these soldiers fought under Tennessee's own General Andrew Jackson at the Battle of New Orleans. So, the Tennessee team is known as the Volunteers. At some point, ingenious UT fans shortened this to the Vols. Most people who aren't from the SEC react with uncertainty when they hear this. Such as my wife. "What the hell is a Vol?" she asked a few months after arriving in the state. So now you know, consider yourself educated.

As I head for the Vol Walk to watch the UT football team, as mandated by tradition, walk down from their athletic dorm at Gibbs Hall to the stadium entrance, I run into Adam Duritz of the Counting Crows. Well, of course, I did. Adam and I have a very serious talk. He tells me, "I've been a Cal fan all my life." I tell him I am in the midst of the DDT and will be traveling around to all the SEC football stadiums.

He looks at me for a moment and then nods his head and confesses, "I love Jake the Snake."

If only.

Actually, he looks puzzled and asks, "What?"

When I leave him all I can think is: This fat dude with crusty dreadlocks dated both Jennifer Aniston and Courteney Cox?

By the time we arrive at the Vol Walk, we can only see the final vestiges of the team being swallowed in a huge onrush of orange-clad fans. Apparently, they started the Vol Walk early. The dull roar subsides and, all around me I hear people discussing how quarterback Erik Ainge looked in his walk. "He had his eyes up and was looking around. Not looking at his shoes or anything," says one man. His companion nods as if the first fan had just returned from the Oracle of Delphi. "That's good," he solemnly intones.

It was about to be a long September for Adam Duritz.

We find Junaid talking to several of his friends who are, predictably, all discussing how Erik Ainge looked in the Vol Walk. Sometimes, I think Ainge's biggest issue is just that he's from Oregon and didn't grow up around SEC football. I find it hard to imagine that very many people in Hillsboro, Oregon, assessed his readiness for a high school game by how he looked walking into morning al-gebra class.

Amidst a huge crowd, we stand awaiting the arrival of UT's Pride of the Southland band. The sun has come out and the temperature has begun to rise a bit. I notice I'm sweating. An older man in an orange polo standing beside me turns to his companion and says, "I wonder what the arrest rate is for the band compared to the football team."

We hear the first dull thump of the drums. The band is com-ing. The crowd begins to stir. On come the drums. As the band comes near, the sound of their instruments becomes overpow-ering. Catches you in the chest and makes your torso shake and tingle. All around me, men and women of all ages begin to raise their voices in a loud cheer. The police escort comes through, and even the officers on motorcycles are smiling. Then the band is upon us and all the shards of "Rocky Top" that have been breaking upon us all day are crystallized into one huge and overwhelming rendition. The band files into the stadium and so does the crowd. Kickoff is still over an hour away.

In the comparative silence after the band's passing, Junaid turns to me and says, "Last year at this same place, I had tears in my eyes on opening day. I couldn't help it. When you hear the band coming down the road, it just gets to you when you realize how much you care." He pauses and looks out over the sea of orange. "Probably too much," he admits.

All day Junaid and I have been pretty much abstaining from alcohol. This is because we both adhere to the same non-drinking-before-games-featuring-our-teams policy. For me, this boils down to the fact that I like to have all my faculties prop-erly working when the game actually arrives. I care too much to not be able to properly analyze the game situation. On some absurd level, I have to be ready in case head coach Phil Fulmer, offensive coordinator David Cutcliffe, or defensive coordinator John Chavis suddenly buzzes my cell phone on a crucial third and eight to ask my opinion on a play call. I can't slur when I'm talking to Phil.

Phil Fulmer is a stolid former offensive lineman for the Vols who has been Tennessee's head football coach since 1993. He is a fifty-six-year-old Tennessee native whose weight is often lampooned by opposing fans. He speaks in a slow drawl and is capable of using the word *heck* as verb, adjective, and noun. Indeed, it's exceedingly rare he gives any interview that doesn't feature the word *heck*. Only six SEC coaches have ever won more league games than Fulmer, and three of those coaches have stadiums named after them.

In 1998 Fulmer cemented his reputation by winning his second consecutive SEC title and a national championship. As a result, among other plaudits, the street outside Neyland Stadium was renamed Philip Fulmer Way. Last season, his team went 5–6, and it was Fulmer's worst ever as head coach. It got so bad that Tennessee lost at home to Vanderbilt for the first time in twenty-four years. This victory prompted the Vanderbilt athletic program to release a DVD entitled, *Victory in Knoxville*. The losing season also broke an eighteen-year record of winning seasons, and for the first time since the 1986 season UT didn't play in a bowl game. Shortly thereafter, Fulmer publicly apologized to Tennessee fans and announced that the 2006 season would see a return to winning football. This opening game against California would be the first to test Fulmer's promise to, predictably, "Work like heck to become a better football team."

. . .

There are lots of California fans around us, but the UT fans and the Cal fans seem to be amicable enough. This is not a blood feud SEC rivalry. There are no bad memories between the two. No sleepless nights or angry cursing to be found in this history. These are visitors not enemies. In short, unlike SEC rivalries, it's impossible to find a grown man anywhere who's ever cried as a result of any game between these two teams.

Junaid and I break our fasting vows. All day the two of us have had, between us, a single small package of peanut M&Ms that I purchased at a gas station en route to Knoxville. "I don't like to eat near game time because my stomach gets all twisted up," Junaid says. I am the exact same way. Suddenly, the heat and the excitement and a relatively late five-thirty kickoff have overwhelmed us. We head for food in the UT Student Union.

While eating a burrito, my wife discusses the difference between the game-day environment in Knoxville and at Michigan. "It's crazy here," she says, "really crazy. At Michigan there were people who cared a ton about the game but we just made fun of those people and thought they were weird." She pauses, "Here, everyone is like that."

Neyland Stadium rises high into the sky alongside the banks of the Tennessee River. The playing surface is at ground level, so fitting in 106,000 fans in a closed bowl requires a tall stadium and, consequently, a long skyward hike when you are sitting in the upper deck. As we walk up the concrete walkways on the outside of the stadium I almost lose my breath. All around me, Vol fans of all ages make the trek up the ramparts of the stadium. Our seats cost fifty dollars each, the cheapest face value available. Multiply this by the number of available seats and we're talking a bona fide money-making machine.

As I'm coming up the aisle of section MM, there is a sudden pause in movement. All around me the loud voices and cheering of the stadium fade, and slowly word is passed down to the back of the line in the aisle, "The prayer is going." Every man, woman, and child's hat comes off—even in the causeway where the field is not visible. Movement ceases. Drunken men who moments before were screaming at the top of their lungs become absolutely silent. Then, the prayer ends and people move again.

My wife tells me that included in the prayer was the line, "Thank God for the joys we can share together in life like football." It's possible the people from California have never been more shocked in their lives.

We are seated in the upper deck of the end zone beneath the Jumbotron. From row 28 in the upper deck, there are exactly five rows behind us in the entire stadium. It almost seems as if I am closer to the Tennessee River behind me than the field in front of me. There are over 106,000 people in the stadium today. At least 105,500 have better seats than we do.

If you are not thirty minutes early for an SEC game you are late. Seriously. When I went to college on the East Coast I was amazed that people at George Washington University basketball games didn't fill their seats well before the ball was tipped. I remember asking another student from the Northeast where all the fans were before one game and he looked at me like I was crazy, "The game hasn't even started yet," he said. The game hasn't started yet? Please. In Knoxville, this game started over nine months ago, when the 2005 season ended. The stadium is full.

The Tennessee band covers the field and the anticipation is building around me. When the band turns and begins its march toward the other end zone, where the Vol team is waiting in the tunnel, the crowd's roar commences. The Tennessee band forms a large T on the field. For just a moment the band is still in their formation. Then, the T splits and the Vols come rushing out onto the field between the members of the band. There is just one large sound. It is so loud it almost seems as if I can hear nothing at all.

At five-thirty-one eastern time, Tennessee's James Wilhoit sends the ball spinning into the air. Everyone in the entire stadium is standing. All around me, I hear the sound of a large breath being exhaled by 106,000 people at once. If a blimp were flying above the stadium, I envision it rising on the sudden upsurge of air.

Neyland Stadium is literally shaking beneath me. This would be more enjoyable, if, you know, I wasn't five rows from the highest point in the entire stadium. There are steel benches without backs for seats, and your knees press up against the person in front of you while you feel the knees of the person behind you on your back. This is not climate-controlled personal-seat license football.

The first Cal pass gains about forty yards. Vol fans everywhere groan. What if the entire off-season has brought no changes at all?

But, then, the Vol defense stiffens and the crowd's tension is lessened. We force Cal to punt.

Erik Ainge, who earlier had managed to walk down the street with his head raised, gains forty yards on his first throw of the season, a completed pass to wide receiver Robert Meachem. All around me I'm sure psychologically acute street savants are telling their friends, "I told you he looked good on the walk."

On their second possession, UT scores on an Ainge touch-down pass to tight end Chris Brown. The crowd explodes. Jun-aid turns to me and says, "Do you think David Cutcliffe* could be elected governor right now?" Before I can answer, a delirious whiskey-breathed man sitting in front of us turns around and exclaims, "Oh, God, yes!" There is a solid chance that this man has no idea who the current governor of Tennessee is. And why should he when the governor has such a comparatively minor job? It's 7–0 Tennessee.

During a television timeout, scores from other SEC games around the country are announced, "Southern Miss 7, Florida nothing," says the announcer. The crowd roars with glee. There is currently no team that the University of Tennessee hates more than the University of Florida. Okay, maybe Alabama. But a loss by either makes for a great day in Tennessee.

Late in the second quarter, Oklahoma native Robert Meachem turns a short curl pass into a forty-two-yard touch-down. As he is streaking toward the end zone in our direction, the entire crowd, young and old, male and female, of every race and creed, rises in one gigantic leap with upraised arms. It's 14–0 Vols at the half.

On the second play after halftime, Robert Meachem strikes again. He breaks a tackle and races eighty yards down the side-

---

* David Cutcliffe was the offensive coordinator during the late 1990s when Tennessee football ran off a 44–5 four-year record under his partial direction. Yep, that was one less loss in four entire seasons than Tennessee had in 2005 alone. Then, Cutcliffe left to become the head coach at another SEC school, the University of Mississippi. While there he engineered modest success, including a 10–3 season with Eli Manning, before he was fired. Now, having spent a year recovering from a heart illness, Cutcliffe is back in Knoxville as the returning offensive coordinator. It appears he has brought the offense with him. At this very moment in the game, there is no man more popular in the entire state of Tennessee.

line for a touchdown. Around me complete strangers are hugging one another. High fives are exchanged with wild imprecision. I am surrounded by a sea of flinging limbs moving in rapturous celebration. Junaid and I break out the rare double high five. I lift my wife into the air. We are winning 21–0, and it seems possible that our offense might no longer be offensive. All across the state of Tennessee, husbands start lobbying their wives to name their forthcoming son Meachem.

God bless Robert Meachem.

The Vols get another stop and then, three plays later, Erik Ainge uncorks a perfect pass to a streaking Jayson Swain and, unbelievably, the underdog Vols are leading 28–0. Just that fast. Junaid and I are both speechless. The crowd is a roiling mass of orange excitement. The largest Southern mosh pit you have ever seen.

The Vol defense gets yet another stop and, then, redshirt freshman Montario Hardesty breaks about fifteen tackles en route to a forty-five-yard touchdown run. This seals the deal. Delirium descends in a veil of orange madness all around me. All is bedlam. In six plays, the Vols have scored three touchdowns of forty-five or more yards.

It is 35–0, and the Vols pull their starters, including Erik Ainge, midway through the third quarter. If you had told every Vol fan in the country that Erik Ainge was going to be pulled from the game midway through the third quarter, there probably would have been five who would have believed it was because the Vols were routing Cal. My nightmares of the previous evening have been exorcised.

Once the starters come out, Cal scores a couple of late touchdowns, via their West Coast offensive pyrotechnics and the game ends with a final score of 35–18. But it doesn't matter; on this day, the Pacific Ten Conference has been no match for the SEC. The crowd is stomping their feet, clapping their hands, and chanting, "SEC, SEC, SEC. . . ."

There is no other conference more proud of itself than the SEC. SEC fans from rival teams hate each other with a passion bordering on the pathological, but when success arrives, it is embraced not just for the winning team but for the conference at large. I suspect there are many reasons for this, not least the feeling among Southerners that the rest of the country just doesn't understand our lifestyle and seeks opportunities to malign us.

If you think about the other major collegiate conferences in America—the Big 10, ACC, Big 12, the Pac-10, and the Big East—you realize these football conferences seem distinct from their geographic locales. The ACC stretches now from Boston to Miami, the Big 12 from Texas to Iowa State, the Big 10 from Penn State to Iowa, and the Big East from Connecticut to Louisville. From such disparate landscapes come fans with literally nothing in common except their shared league. These conferences don't have a unique geographic cohesion or a tradition of lasting history, and football is nowhere near as important across the scope of these schools.

The SEC is the South, period. And the South takes more shots, jokes, and derision than any other region in the country—to such an extent that, unlike any other region, Southerners of all races and creeds circle the proverbial wagons to defend against outside antagonists. So, too, with football. When an SEC team wins a football game against another conference it isn't just a football team that gains vindication; it's an entire region. Ultimately, the SEC is the most dominant conference in the nation, but the fans still see themselves as huge underdogs.

So, on this night, as the SEC cheer rises into the darkened skies and washes down upon the orange-clad masses like the most refreshing shower imaginable, Vol fans are not just cheering for themselves, they're cheering for the length and breadth of the South. The losses of 2005 are behind us and another football season has begun anew.

Later, as I drive home through the night and Saturday becomes Sunday, I will listen to the postgame radio with my ears still ringing from the noise of the game. All around us 106,000 people return from whence they came. Junaid and I will have ample discussion about what this game means for our season, and my wife and I will stop for a late-night dinner at Shoney's where

I load myself up with Mello Yello to ensure that I stay awake for the remainder of the drive home.

Finally, when I arrive in Nashville well after midnight, I will step outside of my car and inhale the sixty-two-degree air, the coolest night in months. There will be no doubt in my mind: I have driven into fall.

EULOGY FOR JEFFERSON PILOT SPORTS

As I prepare for the second stop of the DDT, the Auburn-Mississippi State game in Starkville, Mississippi, I realize that this will be the first all-SEC football game to be covered by Lincoln Financial, the sports telecast outfit that is taking over local broadcasts of SEC sports from Jefferson Pilot Sports, after purchasing the latter's parent company. Ergo my eulogy for the dearly departed Jefferson Pilot (1992–2006), known to all who live below the Mason-Dixon line simply as JP.

> Shut the door to your office so your coworkers can't see you cry. Get the box of tissues and place it next to your keyboard. If you're at home, make sure your wife is watching DVR'ed episodes of Grey's Anatomy before you read any further. Put the kids to bed—they don't need to see you like this. They're too young to know the pain of loss. It's going to be that painful. Okay, deep breath . . . deep breath . . . here it comes: Jefferson Pilot's SEC sports telecasts are no more.
>
> It got you right in the solar plexus, didn't it? Your wind is gone. Easy there, hombre, the world as you know it has not ended. You're still here. The sun is going to rise and set; the world will still spin; Pluto may or may not still be a planet and JP Sports is gone. Sometimes, you have to ache just to know you're alive.

Okay, two paragraphs of false pain is about as much as I can stomach. Let's be honest: There has never been a worse American-produced sports telecast than Jefferson Pilot's coverage of SEC sports. JP Sports' SEC coverage answered the following question: "What would happen if you gave the guys who

never left the audio-visual room at your high school the production rights to a major college telecast, and approximately
three cameras?" Except JP was not as good as those guys would
have been. How bad were they? JP is the only sports production
company whose name is preceded at least 80 percent of the
time by an expletive. "Fuckin' JP" should have been the
company's slogan. It would have had total recall in the South.

Since 1992, JP's eleven-thirty in the morning central time
zone SEC football telecasts have been responsible for more
early morning Southern drinking than any other single event
not involving NASCAR. JP's ability to turn an otherwise pleasant evening game into an early morning slugfest at a temperature approaching 110 degrees remains unparalleled in the
annals of modern sports history. As the early morning beer
flowed, JP's name was cursed to high heaven.

Walk into any Southern living room, watch a JP telecast,
and you could tell in about five seconds that you were witness-
ing utter incompetence. The telecasts reeked of error, ill preparation, and horrible decisions. It was not uncommon for JP to
misspell a team or coach's name. JP's announcers forgot which
game they were calling; their cameramen filmed the center of
the field for a few plays while the team advanced beyond the
scope of the lens.

Yet, for all of these flaws, JP attained, at times, a certain
measure of transcendent beauty like only things that are incredibly ugly can manage. Remember the World's Ugliest Dog,
and how people, eventually, convinced themselves that he was
cute? Or what about the right fielder in Little League whose
play was so atrocious he became the team's mascot? Ultimately,
JP became a cultural connection that was distinctly Southern.
They say the French initially hated the Eiffel Tower because it

was considered garish and indiscreet. All of Paris seethed. But then, slowly, its grotesqueries came to represent Paris, and the French embraced their erstwhile eyesore. Someday, I thought in the back of my mind, the absolute atrocity of JP's sports telecast was going to lead to a similarly unexpected devotion.

Alas, this was not to be. JP is no more. Now, our fifth-tier SEC games are going to be brought to us by the cold and unwelcoming folks at Lincoln Financial. I think they're probably even Yankees. I write now not to bury JP, but to honor it. So, without further ado, here are twelve classic moments, characteristics, and memories that defined the Jefferson Pilot sports viewing experience for SEC football fans:

1. Ineffectual, delayed sports scores. Jefferson Pilot shunned fancy contraptions and communication fads like the telegraph, Morse Code, and the Internet in favor of more reliable methods of communication, such as carrier pigeons. JP's sports score motto might as well have been, "There's never a finished game we can't give you a first quarter score for." So terrible was JP at keeping its viewers up to speed that, if the telecast had also covered current events, midway through last year's UT-Kentucky game, this would have scrolled across the bottom of the screen: "Neil Armstrong walked on the moon today . . . one small step for man, one gnat lap for mankind." Moments later, this score update would have trickled by: "Georgia Tech 126, Cumberland 0 (Halftime)."

2. The yellow-dominated color scheme and graphic accompaniment that made Nintendo's Tecmo Super Bowl look advanced. I halfway expected JP to steal Tecmo Super Bowl's graphic of the player running out of the hospital to accompany players returning from injury. Put it this way, if you put a live telecast of a JP football game up against a basketball game from the 1980s on

ESPN Classic, you'd be hard pressed to tell which one was current, based on the quality of the picture.

3. Somehow, JP could have a silk purse and end up giving you a sow's ear. Amazing touchdown pass of ninety yards? Sorry. JP was blocking the screen to update you on breaking news about Georgia Tech leaving the SEC. Huge goal line fumble? Tough luck. JP has already put the score on the board and gone to commercial. JP's incompetence was almost an art form. Meet abstract footballism.

4. Dave Rowe, Dave Neal, and Dave Baker. Say hello to the two announcers and sideline reporter for JP. Yep, all three have the same name. If you haven't experienced this announcing triumvirate of tomfoolery, consider yourself fortunate. Just imagine, it's like having three Bob Davies calling one game. And the Dave humor. My God, if one more joke was made about them all sharing the name Dave, I felt like their producer was going to attempt suicide by jumping out of the broadcast booth with a noose tethered to a boom mike that was, inevitably, not working.

5. The purple pill Nexium first down line. This was just way too much technology for JP. First of all, the line was never in the correct place. A player would cross the line by a yard and it would be fourth down, or a player would come up about a yard short and get the first down. Second, the purple line always ended up bisecting someone. That Nexium was the sponsor was strangely appropriate, however, since the JP telecast inevitably caused heartburn among everyone who watched it.

6. The musical accompaniment. Who didn't love the JP music? It was like something from a Las Vegas variety show in 1958. JP resolutely refused to leave behind the buildup to the climactic clash of the cymbal in the song. It was like every chord of their theme song had its very own punch line.

7. The you've-got-to-be-kidding-me face at a sports bar outside the South when you inquired if they would be showing the JP game. Any SEC fan who has ever tried to watch a JP game on satellite outside the South knows exactly what I'm talking about. The bartender looks at you like you've just asked him if they serve cherry martinis. J.P.? the non-Southerner would ask turning the station's initials into a drawn-out question that had no answer. Yep, JP, two letters that only a Southerner could string together and know what they meant.

8. The special bond of JP spectators. When I moved to the Virgin Islands immediately after law school, I met Jeff, a fellow lawyer, and Florida grad, clerking in the Caribbean. This was one of our first conversations: Me: "Yeah, I've got the college football package on Dish Network so you can come hang out any Saturday and watch games." Jeff: (Eyes aglow with hope) "Does that package get the JP games?" Me: "Oh, yeah." Jeff: "JP, awesome." (Multiple fist pumps) "Yes, JP." We're still friends.

9. How every game was "an upset in the making." JP always got about the fifth choice in televising games, after the more established networks had made their picks. And some weeks, there are only five SEC games. This meant that inevitably, JP chose one of two types of games: A perennial champ tramples a perennial lightweight (think Florida vs. Kentucky) or two teams no one cares about battling for fifth place in their respective divisions (think Vandy vs. Mississippi State). Without a doubt, when a favorite played an underdog, there was an "upset in the making." At the beginning of each game, JP would latch onto the most innocuous plays as evidence of a brewing upset. Uh oh, Florida's starting the first drive of the game at their own 17. What a tackle on special teams! Cue the JP music and

cymbal clash, then: "We've got an upset in the making." It was uncanny.

10. Dave Rowe (so atrocious he gets mentioned twice). My dad is the most affable fellow on the planet. If a nuclear attack happened, he'd be whistling through the nuclear winter while picking up charred branches. It is almost impossible for him to dislike anyone. Yet he hated listening to Dave Rowe so much he chose to watch all JP telecasts in silence. Even in the middle of summer, if you mention Dave Rowe's name, his face turns into an absolute scowl.

11. The camera angles. Instant replay review was a complete joke. If there was, for instance, a question about whether the ball had broken the plane of the goal line, JP's three cameras would feature the following footage: Sideline reporter Dave Baker making faces at Uga, the Georgia Mascot, in his doghouse, the Berlin Wall coming down, and the end zone as viewed from the opposite end zone. It was almost like JP was willfully trying *not* to show the game, much less the play in question. The instant replay officials would have been better served getting the feed from an undergrad's camera phone in the student section than trying to make a determination off JP's feeds.

12. The split telecasts. When the JP B-team would get to call a game, it was like a national holiday for awkwardness. This was the rough equivalent of handing a microphone to a random guy gambling in Tunica, Mississippi, giving him a suit and tie, telling him to watch a television monitor that was cutting edge when Nixon was impeached and having him talk about football. It was horrible . . . and spectacular.

To sum it all up, I vividly recall my then-girlfriend and now wife (Michigan born and raised) sitting down on my couch during law school while Vandy was playing Ole Miss on JP television. She scrunched up her face, looked over at me, and then sort of looked at the television screen quizzically before she asked, "What is this?" I think she summed up JP better in three words than I have in a couple thousand. What is this indeed? Join me in bidding JP goodbye.

MISSISSIPPI STATE

Almost nobody in the United States has any idea where Starkville, Mississippi, is. In the days leading up to the second stop of the DDT, here were the different ways people suggested I get there from Nashville: Through Atlanta, through Birmingham, through Memphis, and via something called the Natchez Trace Parkway. The latter sounded like an entirely made-up road, similar to the circuitous trail Ponce de Leon traced when he went in search of the Fountain of Youth. For some reason, I pictured Spanish doubloons occasionally sprinkled along the route and believed, if the road existed, that many people were still scalped in transit.

Plainly, these suggested paths to Starkville could not all be correct. So, I outsourced the directions hunt to my friend Shaw, who was one of four big-city George Washington University grads I had persuaded to accompany me to the Auburn-Mississippi State game. I did this because Shaw has his PhD in mathematics, and it was my belief that his mastery of various theorems, stratagems, maxims, and *Lost* arcana would get us there efficiently. Also, I was willing to overlook the fact that he had once demonstrated a degree of directional futility by managing to get himself locked inside a bathroom during a college party for over an hour. Even now Shaw still runs into occasional GW grads who stop him and say, "Wait, I know you, you were that guy who got locked in the bathroom."

Shaw called me later that night, presumably not locked in any bathroom, and said that Google Maps indicated that, from my address, Starkville was 330 miles away, a distance that would take six hours and nineteen minutes to drive. This was roughly three hours more than I had told him the drive would be when I convinced him to come, but his primary point was not to deride me for shortening the trip to ensure he came, but to discuss how complicated the directions were. Not convinced that the Google directions were correct, Shaw then searched Yahoo, which said it was 320.4 miles to Starkville from Nashville and would take six hours and thirty minutes. Finally, MapQuest said Starkville was 331 miles away and would take five hours and nineteen minutes. So, we decided to save time and follow MapQuest's directions and make a shorter trip by driving more miles.

Beginning at five-forty-five Friday evening, my friends Cliff, Shekhar, Shaw, and Krishna begin to arrive in Nashville. They came from San Francisco, Philadelphia, Washington, D.C., and Albuquerque, respectively. They all shared a common lifelong dream of visiting the state of Mississippi. Okay . . . maybe not. I lived with Cliff, Krishna, and Shekhar as roommates for two years in Washington, D.C., and Shaw lived next door to me when we were freshmen.

Cliff is Jewish and for most of college reacted to any setback by responding, "Oy vey," and throwing up his arms. For a time I picked up this vocabulary, which, considering the large Jewish population at GW, helped me fit in quite well. Now, Cliff is an insurance adjuster in San Francisco. As a Californian, he spent our entire college career defending the Pac-10 conference against constant assaults. He was, of course, unsuccessful in said defenses because the Pac-10 is a conference made up of pansies.

Krishna and Shekhar are Indian. When Shekhar arrived at GW, his mother had sewn his name and dorm room number into all of his socks. Seriously, every pair. Whenever we had a mess in the dorm room it was easy to determine whose socks were left behind. Also, during our sophomore year, Shekhar purchased those strength shoes that were designed to make you jump higher—the ones third-person Jimmy from *Seinfeld* sold. It was Shekhar's goal to dunk and he would put himself through workouts wearing these ridiculous shoes in the GW gym.

Krishna is the only doctor I know who has been thrown face first by a bouncer into a wall outside a club. Perhaps this explains why his father, an emergency-room doctor, used to tell us each time he visited, "Do not go on the outside after midnight. Nothing good happens. You will die."

When Krishna interviewed for residencies after graduating from George Washington Medical School he was consistently asked what he could have done differently to have improved his already solid medical school performance. His response? "If my friend Clay hadn't still been in Washington, D.C. during my first year of med school I would have gotten better grades. I would have drank less and played video games less and my grades would be much better." So, Krishna sort of blames me for ending up in Albuquerque, New Mexico. On the plus side though, his alcohol tolerance and *Madden* football skills are much better than they would have ever been without me.

We can't leave for Starkville until Krishna arrives at nine-forty-five Friday evening, roughly four hours before Lincoln Financial's first SEC football telecast kicks off in the middle of the very early morning while it is still dark. This means it's going to be altogether impossible for us to make Krishna's father happy and be in bed before midnight. Krishna cannot come earlier because he is a doctor and, "My patients are more important than SEC football games, Clay." In this he is, of course, entirely wrong.

We're on the road at exactly nine-forty-five, after picking up Krishna at the airport. Krishna immediately requests a stop. "I couldn't bring my contact-lens solution because they thought it was a bomb," he says. Krishna is also hungry. I refuse to stop.

After much whining about how he will be unable to see in the morning and that he is hungry, Krishna finally prevails upon me to stop in Pulaski, Tennessee. No one else is aware that Pulaski is the birthplace of the Ku Klux Klan. So, I inform everyone. Krishna is undeterred, "I'm going to have to wait a long time at McDonald's then," he says.

When he returns to the car after a long wait at McDonald's, Krishna says, "You were joking about that, right? This isn't really where the KKK started."

"Nope," I say, "it was born right here."

Krishna visibly shudders. "Fucking Tennessee," he says.

"Don't worry," I say. "we're going to Mississippi."

Once we return to the car, I inform my friends that many a Mississippi State fan is waiting to kick my ass upon our arrival.

They are angry that I have sullied the academic reputation of their illustrious university ("the Harvard of mideastern Mississippi") by writing in my CBS SportsLine columns that I did not believe anyone actually *graduated* from Mississippi State. Naturally, my friends are delighted to have me as their host.

At this point, we enter into a debate about whether two people named Krishna and Shekhar have ever taken a vacation in the state of Mississippi before. After at least half an hour of back and forth, we agree that we are probably making Mississippi Indian history. Suddenly, the drive is cloaked with the import of the Lewis and Clark expedition. Only there is no one easy analogized to Sacagawea.

Shortly thereafter, we cross into Alabama. Everyone in the car admits to never having been to Alabama before. Except Shekhar. For a couple of minutes, Shekhar is conspicuously silent. Then, he says, "I went to Space Camp in seventh grade at Huntsville." We erupt into laughter, and the thought of Shekhar in space camp entertains the car for the next forty-five minutes. Krishna backs up his brown brother, "Indians all wanted to go to Space Camp," as Shekhar tries to defend himself. "Space Camp was cool because you got to climb up and walk around in planes other people never even got to see," he insists. Unfortunately, Shekhar did not get a spacesuit, but apparently one kid in his group came all the way from Japan with his own spacesuit and was the coolest kid in Space Camp. "Everybody was real jealous," Shekhar said. Based on his voice, it sounds like Shekhar is still jealous.

We arrive in Mississippi some time after midnight and roll the windows down. It is cool and comfortable in the September night. A group vote decides my plan of proceeding directly to the tailgate at two in the morning is a bad idea. So, instead, we spend the next two hours driving around in Mississippi trying to find a hotel. We end up at a Best Western in Aberdeen.

It's about three-thirty in the morning and Krishna and Shekhar assert that they will take over negotiations for the hotel room because, "We're Indian and this guy is Indian." This is the kind of heavy-handed negotiating that distinguished every one of our late-night beer runs to 7-Eleven's in college. I accompany both Indians inside to perform the role of their awkward white cohort. The Indian motel owner is wiping sleep from his eyes. He has to unlock the door to the motel. Somewhere in the distance, behind the counter where he lives, I believe I can hear a baby crying.

"Hello," Krishna says, "Hello," Shekhar says, "Hello," says the Indian man. Then there is silence for a few seconds. "How much is the room?" Shekhar asks. "Seventy-nine dollars," the Indian man tells us. All is silent again, "Do you have an hourly rate?" Krishna asks to break the awkward silence with an even more awkward question. The Indian man looks at Krishna as if he has just raped his wife alongside the river Ganges. "No," he says with a piercing gaze. Then we take the rooms. It's a good thing I'm traveling with such adroit Indian negotiators. We go to bed sometime after four in the morning.

At eight-thirty, we get up. I feel like I've just survived a decapitation by guillotine. Especially because my law school friend Weatherholt called at seven-thirty in the morning, sending Shekhar and me into convulsions of cursing. Outside, it is overcast and even a bit cool. We stand in the parking lot surveying Aberdeen, Mississippi, which is one of those towns that looks completely the same either in the day or the night. Except in the night you sort of think you might be missing something, and then the day comes and you realize that you weren't.

We arrive in Starkville just before ten. There is literally no-where in town that is considered off limits for parking. People are pulled onto the shoulder of the highway as far as we can see, parking underneath highway overpasses, on sidewalks, and scrunching into any space they can find. It's like Mexico City in rural Mississippi. We park on the side of the highway and walk to Davis Wade Stadium. I hear my first cowbell. The sky remains overcast, but the temperature is still comfortable, which is a relief. When I was ten, I came to another September game at Mississippi State with my dad. The most prominent memory I have is that the crowd in our section cheered the loudest when the baking sun mercifully slid behind the light tower and brought a few moments of shade. It's still the only time I've ever heard a light tower cheered.

We walk over to the Junction (the name of the tailgating area at MSU) and watch the Mississippi State band march into the stadium. Compared to the Tennessee band, the State band looks weak and uninspiring. Members of the State band wear matching maroon polos and khaki shorts of varying hues and styles. This brings home the fact that there are approximately 432 different shades of khaki, each of which is represented in the band. Couldn't the school spring for matching shorts as well?

The guys playing the cymbals walk by us. Do the cymbal guys get band scholarships too? If so, isn't this the greatest scam ever? Or could someone legitimately be a better cymbal player than someone else? The group is uncertain. Although every-one asserts that if I were given a cymbal they would be able to pick me out as a bad cymbal player.

We make the rounds meeting Mississippi State fans. Many of the surrounding State fans are wearing stickers that say, BEAT AUBURN and almost everyone is tailgating in the Junction. The Junction is a flat expanse of open fields that abuts Davis Wade Stadium. There is an almost military precision to the orderly row of tents and revelry. The general mood is tamped down by the early start of the game. If you didn't know it, you'd never think a football game was about to be played. I hear no pregame radio call-in shows or other game-related sounds. The mood is friendly and social but not football crazy. Compared to Knoxville the weekend before, State seems more like a large and friendly gathering at a family reunion.

We head to the Internet Bulldog Boosters Club, a large collection of Mississippi State supporters with a substantial Internet presence, where I am to meet Sonya Baird. Sonya was one of the first MSU fans to e-mail and let me know that people *did*, in fact, graduate from her school. Upon our arrival, Sonya becomes the first of many to completely welcome us. "Help yourselves to whatever," she says and begins to introduce us to many members of the IBBC.

I talk with IBBC member Kevin Kalinowski about the controversy surrounding the cowbell. The NCAA allows so-called artificial noisemakers, but the SEC has banned them since 2002, provoking undying consternation among the MSU faithful. First, there is the legal argument of what officially constitutes an artificial noisemaker. "I mean, a zipper could be an artificial noisemaker," Kalinowski says. Second, if SEC officials deem the noise from artificial noisemakers to be significant, they give a verbal warning to the fans. It's common knowledge that warnings from referees only serve to make the crowd louder. If the fans do in fact get louder with their artificial noise-

makers, officials may enforce a five-yard penalty against the offending institution. On the third, and any subsequent penalty,
the offending institution will be penalized fifteen yards. So the
penalties, if enforced, could have a substantial impact on the
actual game. Much more impact than the cowbells do as noisemakers.

The cowbells have been associated with MSU ever since a
Jersey cow wandered onto the football field in the early 1900s,
disrupting a game. Following the interruption, MSU went on
to win the football game and, not unlike in many indigenous
cultures, the cow became a symbol of good luck. At some point,
the cow was replaced by just the cowbell. Handles have since
been welded onto the bells to make ringing easier, and these
special cowbells are now manufactured and sold specifically to
MSU fans.

Kalinowski explains that State fans have reacted to the
SEC ban by ignoring it and simply smuggling cowbells into
the games. Asked how, Kalinowski responds, "I put mine in
the front of my pants." I nod. "They don't pat in certain areas,"
he says by way of
further explanation.
"At least not here.
I've heard they do at
visiting stadiums."

I talk with Rich
Baird about life in
Starkville. He's a
State fan and profes-
sor who has lived in
a variety of South-
ern locales. "I love

Cowbell-ringing practice was surprisingly simple.

it here," he says. "Starkville is a good place to live. I've lived
[in] other places in the SEC, like Georgia, but I like it here best
of all." I ask him what he thought of Athens. "Let me just say
I'm living here for a reason," Baird says.

Everywhere I go there is evidence of the profound hatred
people at State feel for their biggest rival, Ole Miss. My final
stop on the DDT campus tour will be to Ole Miss, to see MSU
and Ole Miss battle in the year-end Egg Bowl. State fans hate
Ole Miss and their fans because they consider the other university to be pretentious and arrogant. State is thirty years
younger (established in 1878 to Ole Miss's 1848) and was initially founded as an agricultural college. One State fan approaches me and says, "My favorite shirt I've seen today says,
'You can't spell dumb without UM.'" Conversely, no one
seems to bear any particular animus toward today's opponent,
Auburn.

We head to the Barnes & Noble bookstore, which is about
fifty yards from Davis Wade Stadium. I'm sure half of you just
did a double take. No, I didn't screw up that sentence. There is
indeed a bookstore . . . in Mississippi . . . next door to the football stadium. The bookstore is packed, although no one seems
to be buying books. On the far wall, a flat-screen television
plays ESPN's *College GameDay*. I'm going to go out on a limb
and say this is the only Barnes & Noble playing ESPN's *College
GameDay* in the country.

My friends and I ride the escalator to the second
floor. When we come back down, we have traversed the only
escalator in Starkville. There's probably a decent chance
the Starkville elementary schools have taken a field trip to
see the escalator. "No, Jimmy Ray Lee, you don't sit down
on it."

I buy a maroon cowbell for twenty-five dollars. This seems like an outlandish price for a cowbell. Particularly for someone, like me, who has no cows. On the positive side, the handle on my cowbell is soft plastic and has ridges for a better grip. I think that perhaps I got the deluxe cowbell version. The lady checking me out in the store asks whether I want a receipt. I say that I do. She nods, "You don't want to be

You know what they call an escalator in Mississippi?
Magic stairs.

the first person caught for stealing a cowbell," she says. So true.

We walk outside and I practice ringing my modified cowbell. All around me cowbells are ringing, and people smile and nod in our direction. Even accompanied by brown people, I've entered a secret Mississippi club; the cowbell is the key that opens a door to a newfound social prominence. While I ring the cowbell, I am Starkville high society.

We buy thirty-five dollar seats from the ticket office, as the game is not sold out. Cliff points out that my cowbell costs almost as much as my seat. He is correct, but you cannot rustle cattle with a football ticket.

The Lincoln Financial production van is parked outside

the stadium. The relative modernity of their equipment is a mild disappointment; I was expecting an Amish buggy with a large roost for the carrier pigeons and maybe a butter churn.

At this moment I am currently embroiled in a feud with the entire Lincoln Financial network over one of my CBS SportsLine columns, which featured a eulogy for the Jefferson Pilot network not unlike the one in the previous chapter. I received the following angry e-mail from Lincoln Financial Senior Director of Marketing Matthew J. Van Ormer:

Mr. Travis-

I was recently forwarded a copy of your "column" in which you ridiculed and mocked Jefferson Pilot Sports nearly 15 years of production of SEC Football. In your column you lamented of "false pain" due to the pending loss of Jefferson Pilot's SEC football production. Well here's some late breaking news that should remedy that "false pain" . . . Lincoln Financial Sports IS Jefferson Pilot Sports. Though our parent company's name has changed our staff, crew, and yes, our announce team remains in tact. [Note to the JP/LF brain trust: *intact* is one word.] I was actually surprised that such a fine website "columnist" such as yourself was not able to establish this on your own, given the fact that it has been posted on our website homepage for nearly 6 months and that dozens of news stories have mentioned it during that time. But who needs research when you have a poorly thought out opinion written with bad comedic timing, right?

As for your assessment of our game coverage, you are certainly entitled to your opinion. However, I think it's worth noting that Lincoln Financial Sports (JP Sports) SEC Football and Basketball are the MOST WATCHED regional college football and basketball networks in the country. Over 1.2 million viewers in the southeast tune into our SEC football game each week. Not bad for a company that airs only the "5th choice" games, eh?

Don't worry, though, maybe your mean-spirited, one-sided rant will be enough to cause our viewers to turn their sets off this fall. That way our producers, announcers, and staffers can go back to selling insurance full-time. (It's not like they do this for a living or anything.)

For the record, I have no idea whether the Lincoln Financial/ Jefferson Pilot announcers also sell insurance or whether this was a poorly disguised attempt at sarcasm. If the three Daves are just random insurance salesmen who have been recruited to call football games, this explains a ton.

Upon receiving this e-mail, I drafted an itemized response to Mr. Van Ormer explaining that the fact that 1.2 million viewers watched JP Sports was a testament to what great fans the SEC had and not in any way an endorsement of their network. I also suggested that if they put me in the broadcast booth with a poorly behaved orangutan, ratings would double. And that Dave Rowe in the broadcast booth with a cobra would lead to a quintupling of ratings. But I was called off on escalating the feud by CBS editors, who explained that I had "hurt the feelings" of LF/JP and their crew. So now I'm going to make amends by reporting a promising development. Rumor has it that LF/JP is attempting to purchase the owls from Harry Potter to improve the timing of their score updates.

When I spot the brand new Lincoln Financial production van in Starkville, I get my picture taken alongside it with my thumbs pointing down.

After hanging out by the butter churn at the LF production van, I return to the Junction where I talk with MSU fan Ken Conerly. He informs me that a relative of his, former NFL All-Pro quarterback Charlie Conerly, played football for Ole Miss in the 1940s and later spent fourteen seasons with the New

When I knocked and asked about the Harry Potter owl rumor,
someone opened the door and said, "No comment."

York Giants. He talks about Charlie's career and the fact that
he played at State's biggest rival. Conerly goes on for some
length while I write. Then he looks down at me and says, "You
can't print that. My family will kill me." Maybe blood is thicker
than SEC football rivalries after all.

There are lots of Auburn fans milling around. As Conerly
says, "When your team is number four in the country, people
come watch them." Shaw is standing beside us. "How far do
Auburn people come?" he asks. Conerly looks at Shaw askance.
"They come from everywhere," he replies. Shaw had meant to
ask where Auburn's campus is located, but Conerly's point is
well taken. On SEC game days, fans make pilgrimages, traveling hundreds of miles from every possible direction.

I hide my cowbell inside the front of my pants to better
smuggle it inside. Kalinowski is correct . . . I am not patted

down. Clearly the gate checkers at State are sympathetic to the cowbell arrival. The sun is now out, and it has gotten warmer, which leads me to the revelation that cool metallic cowbells feel pretty nice in your pants on hot days.

Davis Wade Stadium, the second oldest in the country, seats 55,082 and each end zone is open. Inside, cowbells ring in every direction. It is thirty minutes before the start of the game and we take our seats. At Tennessee, if you are not thirty minutes early to a game you are late. Here at Mississippi State . . . not so much. There are clusters of sad-looking empty seats as the stadium clock ticks down the final twenty minutes before kick-off. The MSU student section is barely half full by the time the whistle blows, and the seats we have purchased at the box office on the day of the game are only twenty-eight rows up from the field.

There are lots of Auburn fans in attendance. The orange color of the Auburn fans mixes with the maroon of State throughout the stadium. I have witnessed zero hostility between the two fan bases, most likely because State's fans have already accepted that they will lose to Auburn, and Auburn's fans have not even considered that they might lose to State. The cheerleaders and the MSU bulldog race onto the field to the lyrics of "Bad to the Bone." This is an uncomfortable double entendre for the ill-fated State team.

The MSU team enters the field accompanied by the clanging of cowbells. Dry ice climbs into the sunshine around the sprinting team. Hasn't the dry-ice trend been going on for long enough? Is anyone really impressed by this anymore? What is dry ice even supposed to signify? I ask Shaw. "I think maybe they are just trying to recapture the timeless feeling of *Wrestlemania II*," he says. The MSU bulldog is not leashed and yet he never runs onto the field or needs to be restrained. I've never seen such a well-trained SEC mascot. Good for State. Now, if only they could work on the offense.

State coach Sylvester Croom strides onto the field, wearing his trademark oversized wristband with the offensive plays written on it. Presumably, some of them are forward passes. Currently, Croom is one of only six black head coaches in the 119 Division 1 programs; in 2003 Croom became the first black head football coach in the history of the SEC. On the day of the press conference announcing his hire, Croom strode to the microphone and said, "I want to make sure everybody understands, I am the first African-American coach in the SEC, but there isn't but one color that matters here—and that color is maroon." The Mississippi State fans present exploded in cheers. Thirty-eight years after the first black student was admitted to the school, an African-American head coach would lead its football team.

Croom rose to this position after a youth spent in the segregated South. Born in Tuscaloosa, Alabama, in 1954, with a preacher as a father, Croom starred as a tight end and linebacker in high school before becoming one of the first blacks to play football at Alabama. Croom's first season at Alabama, 1971, was the first year that Alabama fielded a mixed-race football team. Croom went on to star at Alabama as an All-American center from 1972 to 1974, winning three SEC championships and a national title in 1973. In 1974 Croom was the senior captain of Bear Bryant's Alabama football team.

After playing one season in the NFL, Croom coached at Alabama for eleven seasons before moving on to the NFL, and spending the next seventeen years coaching in the professional ranks. In 2003, Croom was almost hired as head coach of Alabama before Mike Shula was chosen. At the time, Croom was disappointed that Shula, who had ten years less coaching experience was hired instead of him, and believed his race had been the deciding factor. But, in late 2003, Croom joined Mississippi State seeking to turn the program around. His first two years at State have produced identical 3–8 records, but his impact has been far more lasting than that of wins and losses.

In Mississippi, a state with a larger percentage of blacks (37 percent) than any other in the nation, Croom looms large. Moreover, Croom's success in the Magnolia State is even more striking when one considers the complicated racial dynamics of life in the twenty-first century Deep South. Despite its large black population, in 2001, the residents of Mississippi voted by a 65 to 35 percent margin to retain the Confederate battle flag in the top left corner of their own state flag. What was most intriguing about this outcome is that many counties or voting districts with substantial majorities of black voters were evenly split on the resolution. When it comes to Mississippi and race, there is no simple formula.

Croom seems to recognize this. Soon after his appointment, he told the *Washington Post*: "There's much more at stake here than football. The fact that I'm African-American, that I'm the State football coach—well, I think it will have a positive impact on race relations in the state of Mississippi, and how the rest of the country views Mississippi. The place has changed a great deal. I don't know how many people outside here understand that. But they're about to find out."

Indeed, as head coach of Mississippi State, Croom serves as a source of both pride and hope to State fans. Pride for what he has done by becoming the first black coach in SEC history after a career spent overcoming obstacles; hope for what his on-field success could mean for both the football team and the state. But, ultimately, Croom knows that in the football-crazy South, the color of his skin is much less important than the number of wins he can string together in the SEC.

Although State may be the most progressive team in the SEC, that doesn't mean it has a chance in hell against Auburn. As soon as the whistle blows, Auburn sets about a deliberate and straightforward pummeling of State. There is nothing particularly fancy about the way Auburn is winning, but their dominance of the game is unquestionable by the time the first quarter is over.

There are two plays in particular from the first half that sum up State's fortunes on this day. The first occurs right after MSU narrowly prevents a Tiger touchdown by recovering an Auburn fumble at their own one-yard line. Still trailing by only a touchdown the State fans stand and loudly cheer in tandem with their ringing cowbells. My friend Shaw, standing beside me, claims my cowbell and is shaking it violently in support of the State team. "Who knew that shaking a cowbell was so much damn fun?" he asks. But then, three plays after squelching the Auburn drive by getting a turnover, State fumbles and Auburn retakes possession where they had originally lost the ball. State fans curse and cowbells go silent all around us. Auburn then scores to take a 14–0 lead. Shaw morosely returns the cowbell to me.

Then, as the first half winds to a close, Auburn attempts a fifty-yard field goal. The kick is five yards short and flitters harmlessly to the turf. But Auburn has not gotten the play off in time. So, Auburn is backed up five yards for a delay of game penalty. Auburn's kicker then drills a fifty-five-yard field goal. Ouch. It's 17–0 Auburn at the half.

Once the second half begins, we see injured MSU quarterback Michael Henig restlessly pacing the sideline with his arm in a sling, watching his team get licked in its home stadium. Anyone who watched State's opener against South Carolina ten days ago in an opening ESPN Thursday night game, couldn't help but witness Henig's emotional reaction to his injury. For the entire second half of the game, his eyes were red-rimmed and his desire to play was palpable. Each time the camera alit on Henig, I expected to see him making a wild dash for his team's huddle, even without a helmet or pads on. For me, Henig's frustration summed up in a single image why college football is better than pro football. Your average NFL quarterback would have been grinning and slapping fives with his teammates; even with the injury, his paycheck wouldn't bounce. But Henig looked like he was willing to play with one arm, so upset was he not to be on the field. You can't fake passion, and college kids have it in spades.

Auburn scores on the first drive of the second half to make the score 24–0. All around me, the ringing of the cowbells fades like crickets nearing dawn. The exodus of State fans begins. A few sporadic cheers begin to rise from the Auburn fans who are moving down from the upper deck closer to the field. Auburn scores again, just before the third quarter ends, to bring the score to 31–0. State fans begin to leave en masse. There is still a quarter remaining, but we decide to follow these fans outside and return to the Junction.

There are few downcast eyes or people who seem genuinely troubled by the result. The State fans are inured to the pain of

football loss. For over a half century, no State coach has left the
football job with a winning record. Now, Sylvester Croom is
attempting to do just that. The odds·are stacked against him,
no matter how many cowbells there are on his side. Indeed in
the entire history of the SEC, State has won just a single SEC
football title, sixty-five years ago, in 1941.

Already the strident ringing of cowbells has begun anew
outside Davis Wade Stadium. For sixty-four seasons, State fans
have watched other teams hoist SEC conference trophies, yet
still they cheer. On this day, Mississippi State has been beaten
but not vanquished. The cowbells will not stop ringing any-
time soon in Starkville.

THE SHAMING OF THE SOUTHLAND

Why do Southern men feel comfortable cheering with glorified pompons* at SEC football games? It makes no sense, especially considering most Southern men race in the opposite direction from anything remotely feminine, anything that might cause an onlooker to question their sexuality. For example, your average Southern man—let's call him Earl—would rather wrestle a syphilitic cougar than hug another man in public. Yet come Saturday, toss Earl a multicolored pompon and he'll gladly shake it in time to the music.

According to some diligent research I performed via phone calls to friends, men from the Big Ten, Big 12, Big East, and Pac-10 don't cheer with pompons. Yep, not even the Pac-10 guys, who wear turtlenecks and attend poetry slams for fun, shake pompons in the crowd. Only men from the SEC—land of the stoic upper lip, mandatory gun ownership, late night drunken trips to Krystal, and the wearing of camouflage gear at all times—wave the equivalent of colorful ribbons at football games.

Right now, several of you are in the process of drafting me angry letters that will begin something like, "Clay, you're an idiot. They aren't pompons, they are shakers. . . ." Please, before you send me this letter, pause and reread your sentence.

---

*For purposes of the DDT we have chosen to accept the term pompon as opposed to pompom or pom-pom. This is because we are not cheerleading idiots. And also because Wikipedia says: "The use of the similar-sounding but incorrect rendition 'pom-pom' is very common, especially among popular culture, including movies, entertainment sources and general laypeople, but most cheerleaders, coaches, cheer equipment suppliers and manufacturers and others involved in the sport will use the term 'pompon.'" We, diligent readers, are most assuredly not "general laypeople" but rather "cheer equipment suppliers." Ergo, pompon.

Look at the argument you're about to make. Can you really distinguish between shakers and pompons? By the same strained logic, if Barbie were called an action figure, this could make your Malibu Barbie Beach House the equivalent of Castle Grayskull. Nope, this homie don't play that game.

But, for the sake of fairness, let's take a moment to compare pompons and shakers. Pompons have multicolored threads and are used to cheer; shakers have multicolored threads and are used to cheer. Both make a readily discernible shaking sound when moved. The only real distinction between the two is that shakers have a longer handle to grip. This is not an argument you want to make. For all intents and purposes, pompons and shakers are the same.

Right now, I'm sure many of you are feeling shocked, defeated, maybe even a bit ashamed. Trust me, I've been there, too.

Until this past football season, I thought nothing of cheering with pompons. Absolutely nothing. In fact, it seemed perfectly normal. Then my law school friend Kelly, a University of Michigan grad, called from an Alabama house party where he was watching the Crimson Tide play and asked, "What's the deal with Southern guys cheering during football games with pompons?" The question floored me. I had no answer. For about a minute, I kept opening my mouth trying to verbalize a retort that would save me and my Southern brethren from ridicule. But I couldn't think of any excuse or justification at all. That's because there isn't one. Being a man and cheering with pompons is shameful. Period.

Things are about to get worse. Southern men ridicule male cheerleaders to no end. Pick any section of any SEC football stadium on a Saturday, and I guarantee you there are at least half a dozen fans making fun of the male cheerleaders down below, dressed in bright colors, doing high kicks, and flashing dimpled smiles. But, if you really think about it, Southern male cheerleaders are generally looking up hot women's skirts, while we stand in the crowd making fun of them and shaking pompons in time to band music. This is the rough equivalent of ridiculing Brad Pitt while he's making out with Angelina Jolie and you are in the process of rubbing lotion into Star Jones's stretch marks. It makes zero sense; hypocrisy abounds.

Right now, you're probably feeling like you want to blame someone. And that's okay; it's normal to feel betrayed and ashamed. You're probably wondering how your dad could have inaugurated you into pompon cheering as if there were nothing wrong with it at all, the blind leading the blind. You're confused as to how you've never thought it was odd that some guy behind you would gently caress your head with his pompon while shaking it in time to your school's fight song; why you've never questioned how a grown man could squeal and tussle with a sorority girl over the free pompons a cheerleader was distributing at a crowded stadium.

Trust me, we're all experiencing the same emotions. For me, my pompon epiphany was every bit as jarring as back in the first grade when I watched Roy Fokker die at the end of *Robotech*. Up until that time, Roy Fokker was the leader of the Skull Squadron and could do no wrong. I didn't think cartoon characters could ever die. Fokker was gallant, dashing, had an interracial relationship with a hottie named Claudia Grant, and he blew up alien spaceships. Then one day, he got shot and died. I cried and cried. But, with acceptance, I became a stronger man. So, too, with the demise of my own pompon. I treated my pompon the same way Old Yeller was treated. No one else could put it down. I owed the pompon that much.

So, here's what I want you to do. I want you to find your favorite pompon and I want you to carry it outside, where the two of you can be alone. I want you to caress its multicolored strings one last time. Give it a nice thread straightening for all the rhythmic shakes the two of you have shared. Then I want you to lift it above your head and give it a nice one-two shake. Pretend your school's fight song is playing. Shed a tear (if you must). Shake until your triceps begin to burn (if necessary). Then, I want you to gently lower the pompon to the ground and take out a bunch of matches. Light a match, hold it up to one of the strings, and watch that pompon burn. As the multicolored threads turn to smoke, repeat after me: "Pompon? What pompon?" It's only by way of denial that we can reclaim what we've already lost. Then go shoot something.

AUBURN

The last time I was involved in rolling a tree with toilet paper, I was riding in a car that took two bullets from a Vietnam veteran—one on the back rear panel just beneath the window, and the other in the wheel well that narrowly missed the tire. This was in 1997, when several friends and I decided to roll the high school cheerleading captain's house while she had the entire cheerleading team over for a sleepover. A neighbor who spotted us midprank decided that, despite the cheerleader's entire yard being covered in toilet paper, we were robbers deserving of death. So, he put two slugs into our car as we sped away.

Since that moment, I have not touched a toilet-paper roll outside of the bathroom. On September 16, in the immediate aftermath of Auburn's 7–3 win over LSU, I was just one of thousands of spectators who stood and watched as stream after stream of toilet paper rose into the coming darkness of an Alabama evening and nestled themselves in the branches of the trees overhanging Toomer's Corner. I suppose this was a legitimate case of toilet-paper redemption for me, but, before all that could happen I had to make my way to Auburn for the LSU game.

On the afternoon of Friday, September 15, I drive from Nashville to Birmingham, Alabama, where my aunt has arranged for me to meet her friend Sam Hutchison, an eighty-five-year-old Auburn alum with macular degeneration. He has distinguished himself over the years by, among other things, becoming physically ill whenever Auburn loses. I spend the better part of two hours talking with him about Auburn.

Hutchison initially arrived at Auburn in 1938 as a seventeen-year-old undergraduate. In 1938, according to Hutchison, Auburn only had three thousand students, two thousand seven

Sam Hutchison preparing to watch the Auburn game
on his big-screen television—the only way he can anymore.

hundred of whom were men. He said the school was a great place for those three hundred women. "One girl had never had a date in my high school and she got to Auburn and she didn't want to leave. All the boys were after her. I got home for Thanksgiving and her parents came over to me and said, 'Why is our daughter not coming home this year?' It was because she loved it. We all loved it."

Unfortunately for Hutchison, he had to leave college after a year because his family could no longer afford the tuition. In 1946, after serving in World War II, Hutchison returned to a vastly expanded Auburn and graduated on the G.I. Bill. He met his wife and was married in Auburn. "The fraternity across the street thought our wedding was a house party and they ended up coming over and having a great time," he says.

Hutchison has not missed an Auburn game on television in decades. Now, he has macular degeneration so severe that he can barely see. In order to combat the ravages of time, he has purchased a fifty-three-inch television and sits at an angle so that he can use his peripheral vision to watch the game. He sits on a stool within a foot of the screen. "If I don't sit as close as possible, I can't see what's going on." Then, "I take no calls during the game," Hutchison says. "If the house catches on fire, I tell people to call the fire department and leave me alone."

I ask Sam how he sees tomorrow's Auburn-LSU game coming out. "I hate to say it, but LSU will win," he admits quietly. Then Sam removes his Auburn cap from the top of the Bible, where it had been sitting, and places it on top of his head. As I drive away from Hutchison's home it's clear to me that no matter how old SEC fans are, the passion and intensity of Saturdays in the fall never fade.

• • •

Later that night, I go out with my friend Kelly in Birmingham's Lakeview district, where we are immediately overcome by the number of grown men who have short hair with long bangs. We're talking serious bangs. Bangs that hang down across the forehead and seem to be several inches thick. Long, waving bangs that appear to have been clipped and styled with infinite care and approximately fourteen different hair products. I've never seen this hairstyle anywhere else. It's as if Alabama men have really cold foreheads they have to protect. We wonder about the women who like men with bangs longer than their own.

Finally, Kelly and I decide that these forehead monstrosities need a name, so we christen them 'Bama Bangs. Later that night, Kelly says, "Whatever you call them, they have to go. These 'Bama Bangs are the kind of thing that will end up really cool in Eastern Europe in like ten years. Until then, if you see some guy with bangs like this, there is a 100 percent chance he is from Alabama."

Kelly and I met at Vanderbilt Law School where we both wore Adidas flip-flops for three years straight. He now lives in a high-rise condo in downtown Birmingham and, since he moved into the condo after we graduated from law school in 2004, he has not cleaned. There is a dull film of dirt and muck on everything. I tell him that I'd like to bring my wife to his place so she could see how comparatively clean I am. Kelly laughs. "My girlfriend won't even use the shower," he admits.

Kelly is from Michigan and, during law school, we considered him the most overextended man on earth. During our final year Kelly purchased a television, a couch, two chairs, a bed, and a piece of fancy artwork that cost over a thousand dollars all on the same day. All financed. On a credit card with a limit approaching five figures. Kelly claimed to have no idea how his credit rating had ever gotten so impeccable that he could finance all these things. Upon arriving in Birmingham he immediately purchased a condo with no money down. Despite being from Michigan, he completely fell in love with the South while living in Nashville. So much so that he was willing to move to Birmingham, a smaller Southern town than Nashville, to practice law even though he didn't know a single person in the state. Now, he has completely adapted to the rhythms of the South. Minus, that is, the 'Bama Bangs.

On Saturday morning, I take U.S. Route 280 from Birmingham on the advice of numerous Auburn grads. "Whatever you do, don't take the interstate toward Montgomery," says my law school friend and Auburn alum Rogers Rowder. Route 280 is the perfect choice. Not least because Alabama seems to suspend all restrictions on speeding on football game days. Everyone is going at least eighty miles per hour. At one point, I'm stopped at a red light alongside a menacing man with a tattoo and forearms the size of a pygmy. The man is driving a Ford F-150 with oversized wheels. If a death match suddenly erupted on 280, this man would be the favorite. As soon as the light changes, he floors it. As his truck fully passes me, I see an Auburn tiger tail attached to the rear of his truck bouncing in the wind. Yep, even the most fearsome men in Alabama are willing to pin Auburn Tiger tails to the rear of their trucks.

I arrive in Auburn and am immediately caught behind a train which is crossing through the center of town. Cars are stopped as far as I can see. This might be the most cursed train in Alabama history. But, once I am past the train, it is readily apparent that the entire town of Auburn is one gigantic tailgate. Several sorority girls are sitting in the open bed of a pickup truck with a sign that says: HONK AND MAKE US DRINK. Everyone is honking. I honk and the girls drink. These girls are one of approximately fourteen thousand individual tailgates currently proceeding in Auburn. The entire town is a roiling mass of pregame festivities.

Shortly thereafter, I meet my friend Rogers Rowder, who directs me to the Beta house, where we manage to squeeze my car onto their front lawn. Rowder then gives me a tour of the Beta house, which is gargantuan and filthy. Inside alums of the fraternity are splayed out on large couches in front of a big-screen television watching an SEC football game. All greet us as if we are lifelong friends. Outside the room, I ask Rowder who those guys were, "No idea," he replies. We pause in front of a hand-written poster board weather forecast. "They've got the pledges doing the weather forecast. Awesome," he says, nodding. As we cross the intramural fields in the direction of Rowder's tailgate, a current fraternity member in front of us is walking with his mother and father. "I gave this stupid pledge six bucks to bring me a chicken biscuit and instead he ended up puking on my door," the upperclassman says. The father nods his head remorsefully. The mother is unaffected. Welcome to Auburn, where even parents understand griping about pledges.

Rowder leads me to his tailgate, where he explains that he has decided he can't handle the karmic danger of allowing me to wear his Bo Jackson Auburn baseball throwback jersey. "I'm just not going to do it," he says. Instead, he hands me a vintage Auburn T-shirt with peeling letters that appears to have survived more seasons than I have. "This will be perfect," he says.

Rowder is the most quintessentially Southern of my friends. He has a deep accent and he's fond of employing Southern aphorisms like, "He's dumber than a bag of hammers" and "I'm happier than a dog with two peters." Rowder would break these out during law school classes and bring an entire room to dumbfounded silence. He's also a huge Auburn football fan. Basketball, not so much. As we're walking by the basketball arena Rowder points it out to me, "I wish they'd tear it down and put in more parking for football tailgating," he says.

I have a corn dog for the first time since second grade, when I got sick to my stomach in Mrs. Harper's second-grade class at Goodlettsville Elementary. I blamed the corn dog I'd eaten earlier that day for years and only now, when I'm starving and the options are slim, have I come to realize that it probably wasn't the corn dog's fault. After twenty years, I figure it's time to take a second chance. The corn dog burns the roof of my mouth on the first bite. Goddamn corn dogs.

Rowder informs me that one reason they are eating corn

The Bo Jackson throwback, my peeling T-shirt, and a half-eaten corn dog.

dogs at the tailgate is to make fun of LSU fans. It seems that somehow, some way, the rumor that LSU fans smell like corn dogs has swept through the Auburn faithful. Aside from being absolutely hilarious, this accusation makes LSU fans furious. "I'm telling you," Rowder says, "if you walk up to any LSU fan and you smell them and then step back and say, 'Yep, corn dogs,' they will get so mad." Which leads us to the ultimate metaphysical mystery, how can you prove that you don't smell like corn dogs? Exactly. That's why this corn-dog business is the funniest SEC insult I've heard yet.

Rowder aids me in finding a fifty dollar ticket through his friend, Bo Kerr, who is affiliated with the Birmingham Bowl game, and I head to the Auburn Alumni Tailgate to meet my law school friend Amy Jordan, the granddaughter of Shug Jordan of Jordan-Hare Stadium fame. As I walk, everywhere you go on Auburn's campus, people greet one another by saying, "War Eagle!" When someone shouts "War Eagle!" to you, you are obligated to respond "War Eagle!" in kind. Occasionally, while in my Auburn T-shirt, people I don't know see me, and scream, "War Eagle!" After a time, I feel like I've got the talismanic key to the kingdom. Which leads me to this realization, you can rape, pillage, maim, and kill, so long as when you're finished you smile and say "War Eagle" in Auburn on game day.

I become totally lost until Amy finds me and leads me to the tailgate, where I begin talking to her father, Ralph Jordan, who will be president of the Auburn Alumni Association beginning in October. Ralph moved to Auburn when he was three, in 1951, and did not leave until after he had received a master's degree in 1975. Before we really begin talking, he points to a bird that is among several being held inside the Auburn alumni tent. "That's a turkey vulture," he says. "Not a golden eagle. Just wanted to make sure you knew." Later, my wife will see me pictured with a turkey vulture and say, "Why in the world were there vultures in the Auburn alumni tent?" Now that she mentions it, I have no idea, but, somehow, it didn't strike me as odd at the time.

Jordan tells me, "My dad lettered in three sports at Auburn and basketball was his first love. He's still the only coach to have won an SEC championship in both basketball and football." Shug Jordan (so nicknamed because of his affinity for sugar cane as a child) was a 150-pound center on Auburn's football team. His son tells me this meant Jordan "didn't take too kindly to the 'too small' talk from anyone."

Shug Jordan lettered in baseball, football, and basketball before graduating in 1932. After graduating, Shug coached basketball at Auburn from 1934 to 1942 and, after returning from World War II, resumed coaching basketball for a final season in 1946. During the interlude in his basketball coaching career, Shug was awarded the Bronze Star and the Purple Heart after being wounded during the Normandy invasion.

Jordan ultimately took over the football coaching duties at Auburn and, six years later, won the 1957 national title. Ultimately, Jordan coached football for twenty-five years before retiring after the 1975 season. In 1973, Auburn renamed then Cliff Hare Stadium Jordan-Hare Stadium; it was the first time an SEC stadium had ever been named after a living coach.

I ask Jordan's son Ralph what the toughest thing about living in Auburn during those years was. "We loved it, but, I think, losing the games everyone expected you to win was the toughest. Here today, Auburn and LSU are playing and everyone knows we're playing a great team. If we lose, so be it, people can handle that. But losing to someone like Southern Miss," Ralph

Jordan pauses, "well, that's tough. Today, no matter what happens, the crowd is going to walk out with their heads held high."

Ralph's daughter Amy graduated from Vanderbilt Law School with me, and we discuss how Auburn's not having a law school was the only thing that made this acceptable. I tell Jordan about my father refusing to sign the tuition checks for my sister when she attended Vanderbilt undergrad. Jordan nods appreciatively. I ask him what would happen if Amy ended up marrying an Alabama graduate. He grimaces. "I tell her all the time, now that she's working in Birmingham, she's going to be meeting lots of Alabama grads and that she better not bring one of them home. I tell her Ole Miss, South Carolina, Tennessee, just please not Alabama. And I'd take it much better than my mother would. She's ninety-three and a South Carolina grad, so she likes other SEC schools. But she absolutely cannot stomach Alabama."

I ask Jordan about Auburn's future. "We'll probably expand to over one hundred thousand seats at the stadium in my lifetime," he tells me. (Jordan-Hare currently seats 87,451.) "But we want to be smart about it and make sure people don't end up sitting in their cars in traffic until Monday morning. Not just expansion for expansion's sake. We could sell that many seats now because we're a generational school. Personally, I'm a third-generation Auburn grad." Jordan pauses, "But, unlike our friends across the state, we don't bask in the past, we're focusing on the future."

Zinger for Mr. Jordan, Auburn alumni president-elect. "Be sure to get inside in time to see the eagle," he instructs me.

• • •

I take Jordan's advice, head over to the stadium and, as I walk up the aisle to enter, a drunken man behind me screams, "I think we're going to kill LSU. I've got that Tennessee feeling." I cringe. Auburn has destroyed my Vols the past several times they have played. This fan is the only person I hear all day who does not expect this game to come down to the final minutes.

I arrive in my seat in the south end zone. The seats are steel bleachers with no backs and the sun is fierce. It's got to be well above ninety. Everyone is sweating already. It is twenty-five minutes until kickoff and the stadium is full.

Everyone stands as Auburn's real, live war eagle begins the descent to the center of the stadium. As the bird circles the stadium, it swings out over different sections of the stadium and the crowd roars in accompaniment. It almost seems as if the eagle is floating on the full-throated roars of the Auburn fans. Then, the eagle swoops down and lands near midfield and the crowd is engulfed in cheers. Welcome to Alabama, where even the fowl are football fans.

I soon learn that 2006 is actually the first year for this particular golden eagle, whose name is War Eagle VII. Not surprisingly, he has replaced War Eagle VI in a stunning *coup d'etat*. I understand it was a bloodless coup, however. When I ask Rowder where the War Eagle tradition is derived from, he responds, "Scholars differ."

The most popular story as to how the War Eagle tradition began dates to 1892, when Auburn played their first-ever football game against hated rival Georgia. Supposedly there was a Civil War veteran in the crowd that day who had a pet eagle, which he had found injured on a battlefield. During the game the eagle spread his wings for the first time in weeks, broke free from his master's hold, and began to soar over the field. As the eagle soared above, the Auburn football players on the ground began to drive toward the Georgia end zone. The Auburn fans began to chant, "War Eagle!" as the eagle continued to soar. After Auburn won the game, the eagle crashed to the field and died, but according to the legend, his spirit lives on every time an Auburn man or woman yells "War Eagle!"

For the seventeen minutes leading up to kickoff, no one sits down. I notice through the cheers that hardly any Auburn fans pronounce the "r" in Auburn. When the crowd chants, you can actually hear, "Aw-buhn." This chant becomes magnified when former Auburn running back Bo Jackson is shown on the Jumbotron, causing the crowd to erupt. Among them, I'm sure, is my friend Rowder, who is clad in his Bo Jackson baseball jersey. Based on what I saw, no one is more popular at Auburn than Bo.

Jackson won the Heisman Trophy at Auburn in 1985, after a college career in which he averaged almost 6.6 yards a carry. After leaving Auburn, Jackson embarked upon professional baseball and football careers, becoming the first athlete in history to be both an NFL Pro Bowler and Major League Baseball All-Star. After a freak injury to his hip while being tackled in an NFL game, Jackson retired from football and saw his baseball abilities wane. Even still, in October 1992, Auburn retired his jersey number.

Personally, Jackson's "Bo Knows" television commercials, and his ability to break a bat over his knee when angered during a baseball game ensured that he was, and still is, one of my favorite athletes of all time. Jackson's Future Stars Topps baseball card was my most prized possession throughout my early childhood. And, as a third grader, I even had the iconic black-and-white poster, in which Bo wore shoulder pads with a base-ball bat balanced behind his head on top of the shoulder pads, on the wall above my bed. Right next to the Brutus the Barber Beefcake and Jake the Snake posters.

As if all this weren't enough, Bo Jackson is also the most dominant sports video-game athlete of all time. His feats on Nintendo's Tecmo Super Bowl are otherworldly, and have in-spired more broken controllers and outlandish taunts than any other video-game football player in the history of video games.

Combine all this and it's easy to see why Bo Jackson's image on a video-screen at Auburn is guaranteed to bring the faithful to their feet.

Back on the field, suddenly, through a billowing cloud of dry ice or manufactured fog or some other such unfortunate spectacle, the Auburn football team enters on the opposite sideline. LSU quarterback JaMarcus Russell takes the field, and I realize that he is roughly the size of a house. I'll say this for JaMarcus: The women wearing his LSU jersey in the stadium today are the hottest jersey wearers I've ever seen. It's like a Paris runway on Donahue Drive. Russell is a junior quarterback who can throw the ball farther than any quarterback I've ever seen in the SEC. He's also six-six and 250 pounds. When he stands under center he makes everyone else on the football field seem small by comparison. When he takes off running down the field, he looks like Godzilla loosed in the streets of Tokyo. At one point in the game Russell uncorks a sixty-five-yard bomb with touch, and I realize that JaMarcus's arm is so strong he just tried to finesse a sixty-five yard pass.

The LSU fans are to my left. Their entire front-row stands and rests their legs on the edge of the seating bowl. They look like purple-clad warriors about to storm the ramparts. At the end of the first quarter, there is no score, and Auburn has yet to get a first down. Hardly anyone around me is surprised. It is painfully obvious that whichever team's offense can manage to score one or, if they're lucky, perhaps two, touchdowns is going to win the game.

Auburn quarterback Brandon Cox goes down midway through the second quarter and, suddenly, the stadium is so quiet, you can almost hear the tremulous jingle of Mardi Gras beads shifting among the LSU faithful. Then, from the Auburn student section, a chant begins: "Brandon . . . Brandon . . . Brandon." Seconds later, Cox is up and sprinting off the field. The crowd erupts in one glorious exhale. Two plays later, Auburn's kicker hits the upright from thirty-two yards away on a field-goal attempt. I can hear the echo even in my seat. A man behind me says, "Awww, hell, it's like last year all over again." Last year, Auburn missed five field goals at LSU to lose the game. LSU kicks a field goal after Russell fumbles forward. It's 3–0 LSU at the half.

On the concourse outside, I watch an Auburn woman with a hot dog trying to work a broken mustard container. She turns to me and shrugs, "It's working about as well as our offense," she says.

In the second half, Auburn drives to the goal line, where Cox seeks to quiet the crowd. As his arms move up and down in an effort to bring on silence, he resembles nothing if not an eagle in flight. Moments later, he takes the snap and scores himself. Seven to three Auburn. All around me is bedlam.

My wife, the Michigan grad, texts me to say that Michigan

is leading Notre Dame 34–14. I text back, "Good for UM." Ten seconds later, she responds, "It's U of M." When the Notre Dame score is announced in Jordan-Hare, the crowd madly cheers. No one in Auburn has forgotten what the difference is between being ranked number three and number two.

That's because, in the 2004 season, the Auburn Tigers went 13-0 and finished undefeated after winning the Sugar Bowl. Only they never received an opportunity to play for the National Championship that season, because the Bowl Championship Series rankings favored two other undefeated teams, Southern California and Oklahoma. Southern Cal beat Oklahoma 55–19 and Auburn fans (and to a great extent SEC fans as well) have still not forgiven the BCS for this perceived travesty of football justice. So, Auburn fans around me are delirious at the possibility that, if they win, they could ascend to the coveted number two ranking in the country.

Neither team can clear space between the other on this nationally televised CBS game. On the field, the afternoon sun has sunken behind parts of the stadium. The Auburn sideline is now entirely in the shade, while the LSU team continues to bake in the sunshine. Sometimes, the home-field advantage is about more than the crowd's noise and support.

Late in the fourth quarter, with Auburn clinging to a 7–3 lead, Auburn coach Tommy Tuberville proves he has balls of steel by going for it from his own forty-two. All around me, fans are going crazy. "Punt the damn ball," one man yells. Here in Auburn, the crowd doesn't care how they win as long as they win. Style points are for other locales. Auburn converts the fourth down. The crowd sighs as one. Then, crazily, Tuberville channels Tecmo Super Bowl and runs the flea-flicker on third-

and-one. Yep, the flea-flicker. Even more amazingly, LSU has managed to double cover the receivers and does not bite on the fake. It's almost as if LSU expected the flea-flicker in this situation. (Later, at the postgame tailgate, I will mention the flea-flicker to Rowder. "The flea-flicker," he says, volume increasing as he speaks. "We didn't run the flea-flicker, we just went play action." So Tuberville faked me out.) Mercifully, Tuberville punts on fourth down. Auburn's fans are much more conservative than their coach, which is truly a football rarity.

Auburn fan O'Neal Shaw sits beside me for the entire game. He is a great seat companion who understands the game. At one point, he turns to me and says, "If these two teams played 100 times, one team would win fifty-one times and the other would win forty-nine." He is right. Rarely have I seen more evenly matched teams. I don't want to hear anything about these teams having bad offenses. Both would score forty or more on most teams (and have already done so this year). Each team's defense is really just that spectacular.

On the next-to-last fourth down of the game for LSU, the LSU pass falls incomplete near the goal line. Here is the crowd's emotional roller-coaster reaction during the minute that follows:

1. Absolute ecstasy. I can barely hear anything. My ears are literally ringing.
2. Someone notices a penalty flag in my section (that side of the field is farthest from us), the sound collapses upon itself. Indignant questions are raised. The entire section is one large interrogatory.
3. The pass interference penalty is waved off and once again the crowd explodes.

Together, these three stages represent the full expanse of football fan emotion in a single minute.

With the tension ratcheted up to an unbelievable level, the Auburn student section sings along to "Living on a Prayer." Unfortunately, the prayerful medley does not work and Auburn punts again with only a minute or so remaining in the game. Then, inexplicably, Auburn seems to forget that the east sideline is in play. Three times in a row, Russell throws darts to his receiver and LSU gobbles up huge chunks of yardage. Suddenly, this game between equals is somehow even more equal.

It's fourth down once again, this time with only two-and-a-half seconds left, and even though I don't particularly have a rooting interest, my own heart is in my throat. Russell completes a pass to his receiver, and Auburn makes the tackle inbounds at their own five. The LSU player is tackled in one of the last vestiges of sunlight on the field. All around me, the stadium becomes jubilation incarnate. Grown men hug other grown men, streamers from pompons cartwheel through the humid air, and a shouting that ends three hours of tension cascades through Jordan-Hare. Aw-buhn has won.

In a crushing tide of humanity, I'm off in the direction of Toomer's Corner. When I arrive, the trees are already covered in so much toilet paper it almost seems as if winter has arrived on the Plains. Already, the next generation of Auburn undergrads is painting the town white and, at long last, I've found my own toilet-paper redemption.

However, the Auburn victory has only completed half of my SEC football watching for the day. That's because Tennessee is playing Florida in an SEC showdown that same night. As I wade through the spiderwebs of toilet paper and rush back across Auburn's campus to meet Rowder, I pass Jordan-Hare stadium again. Some of the players are exiting the stadium and walking alone up a short hill to the athletic dorm. Several Auburn fans remain at their tailgates and cheer each of the players as they walk past into the Alabama night.

Suddenly, I realize that I am walking alongside Auburn's Kenny Irons. Irons is Auburn's star running back who has been much hyped as a potential Heisman Trophy candidate. As we walk up the hill side by side, it occurs to me again how small the Auburn universe truly is. Devoid of his shoulder pads, cleats, and uniform, Irons could pass for a regular guy. But not to Auburn fans, several of whom scream "War Eagle!" to Irons. He acknowledges them each in kind by nodding and responding "War Eagle!" Then, the two of us separate and he goes in his own direction and I go in mine.

When I locate Rowder, we realize that finding a place to watch the Tennessee game in time for kickoff might prove more challenging than we'd hoped. We rush back to the Beta house and get my car and head to Rowder's friend's tailgate, where the game is showing. After frantically driving around for a while, I spot their tailgate in downtown Auburn on a grass field. There's a satellite dish rigged up to a flat-screen television. From a distance, I can see the flickering images of my Volunteers.

By the time Rowder and I park ourselves in front of the tailgate television, the first quarter has almost ended and the score is 7–3 Florida. I'm literally shaking with excitement. Missing the first quarter of this Tennessee game is the worst thing to befall me thus far on the DDT. For a moment, I sit and try to remember the last time I missed even a single quarter of a UT-Florida game. Then, I realize that I haven't ever done it before. Not since 1985, when I was not yet watching football games on television by myself, have I missed a Florida-Tennessee quarter. I begin to feel that maybe my Vols are trailing because I've forsaken them by not getting to the game rapidly enough. While this thought may be ridiculous, in the past eight years, Tennessee and Florida have each won four games. If brushing a butterfly in the past can unleash a hurricane in the future, so, too, might my Volunteer betrayal unleash its own karmic whirlwind on the gridiron.

We are watching the game with a mother and father, several of their young children, and other ancillary figures I do not know. And I have been drinking. This is, all things considered, sort of a bad combination. This family has been tailgating now for over twelve hours and they have a brown jug of legitimate moonshine with them. The moonshine is in one of those old-school bulbous bottles with the cork stoppered in at the top. I try the moonshine. It tastes like fermented gasoline. "That'll put the hair on your balls," Rowder says, slapping me on the back.

Shortly after my swig of moonshine, Tennessee scores on a trick play to take a 10–7 lead. By God, maybe it's the moonshine that's causing the momentum to swing in my team's direction. I stand and scream to the high heavens. The mother looks over at me. Maybe karmic gridiron justice requires that I keep drinking moonshine in order for my team to play well. Somehow, this makes perfect sense. So I abandon my usual nondrinking policy during games featuring my teams and continue to consume the moonshine. If Phil Fulmer buzzes my cell phone seeking a play call suggestion on this night, I'm letting him go straight to voice mail. I have another swig of moonshine, followed by a handful of Fritos scoops to try and counteract the power of the moonshine. The Fritos taste like air.

Florida's quarterback Chris Leak throws an interception that Tennessee returns for a touchdown and a 17–7 lead. I stand and scream at the television, "Fuck, yeah, Chris Leak, you fucking pussy." The young son of the family stares wide-eyed at me. The interception return is called back for an entirely illegitimate illegal hands to the face penalty and I return once more to my moonshine. "That cussing in front of that little boy," Rowder says, "you don't feel one bit of bad about it, do you?" "No," I say. "Damn right," Rowder exclaims while giving me a five.

When halftime arrives, I'm able to pry my eyes away from the TV screen only to look around and realize that there is something akin to a cleanup going on at the tailgate. The family couldn't be leaving, right? I mean, they wouldn't start a game and then leave while others are relying on them. They couldn't. I drink more moonshine. The movement becomes less noticeable. I stand up to go pee in the bushes and almost trip over a bevy of young children sleeping in the grass.

Shortly after the third quarter starts, Tennessee scores again. This time it's 17–7 for real, and I am delirious with optimism. My team is leading by ten points against one of their most hated rivals. Unfortunately, I detect more movement in my surroundings. This time I see my hosts placing some chairs, a fold-up table, and a large cooler in the bed of their pickup truck. Of course, this is what I think I saw being loaded. In reality, with the moonshine-induced fuzziness, it could have been ten dead bodies and a Nordic Track. I refocus on the game.

I've consumed an awful lot of moonshine by this point, but it's clear, even to my bleary eyes, that there are less folding chairs around the tailgate than there were in the past. During another commercial break when I go to pee, I notice the children are gone. When I come back I lean over to Rowder.

"They're not going to leave before the game is over, are they?"
"Oh, no, you're fine," Rowder says. I sip my moonshine. Alarmingly, it's starting to taste like air, too.

Florida scores to bring the game closer. It's 17–14 Tennessee. I stand and curse and then decide to go for a small walk in the darkness. When I return I see the kickoff and then, without warning, the screen goes dark. "We're out of here now, y'all," say our hosts. I am shocked and then apoplectic. Sensing that I might lose my cool, Rowder stands rapidly, "All right, we got to move," he says. He shoots me an urgent look. "Now." I rush off for the car. Rowder and his friend Bucky and his wife join us in our race to relocate. Our destination is a sports bar in downtown Auburn.

We load into the car and I desperately search for the game on the radio. We're stuck in bumper-to-bumper traffic. Students and alums are walking by on the sidewalks screaming, "War Eagle!" and Rowder and friends are screaming, "War Eagle!" back at them. All I can see ahead of me is a shimmering convoy of red taillights. "Oh, man," I say, breaking out into a light sweat, "oh, man."

I manage to find the game on the radio. Although it is a faint signal that comes and goes as we idle in traffic, I can tell that Tennessee has the ball and that they are driving. Soon, I can hear that we are attempting a long field goal. I can make out that the ball is snapped and, then, I hear nothing. "War Eagle!" screams Rowder. Christ, what's going on here? I turn the radio up to ear-splitting levels. If a jet were taking off on a runway alongside our car, we wouldn't hear it. Do I hear the band playing "Rocky Top" or is it a moonshine-induced reverie? No, that's definitely the band. The radio returns, UT is now leading 20–14. "Got a field goal," I scream. My heart is pounding so hard I can feel it reverberating on the seat belt encasing me.

"Rowder," I say, "the traffic," gesturing madly at the road in front of me as if Rowder could wave a wand and make it all disappear. Rowder, sage and contemplative in the driver's seat, nods. "I think you're going to have to make a run for it." "How far is the bar?" I ask. "Awww, Bucky will run with you, it's not far," he tells me.

Bucky has been slumbering in the back seat on his wife's shoulder. At the mention of his name, he wakes. "Yeah, I'll go," he says. He's so delirious you get the idea Bucky would have agreed to a jog to Canada. I throw open my car door, and Bucky and I pour out of the car and start running down the street, my right shoe untied and the shirt around his waist flapping in the wind. Rowder bangs the side of the car and whoops, "Y'all ain't moving fast enough. War Eagle."

While I'm making a run for it, it occurs to me that moonshine sloshing violently in the stomach is probably not unlike what I would imagine being Tasered feels like. Sort of electric and nauseating at the same time. Bucky is breathing heavily behind me. Miraculously, the traffic has begun to move and Rowder and my car have caught up with us. We have stopped running and bend over to catch our breath. "Y'all ain't running now," Rowder says madly banging the side of the car.

Bucky and I straighten up and pick up our pace. We are training for the Moonshining Olympics. At long last we arrive in the sports bar and make a mad dash to a television in the corner. Florida is driving, still trailing by six. But, shortly after we arrive at the bar, they convert a fourth down with their freshman quarterback Tim Tebow. Tebow runs a draw out of the shotgun and is jumping around on the television like he just won the Royal Rumble. Shortly after this play Florida scores to take a 21–20 lead. I feel sick. Rowder hands me a beer. "We did a great job parking," he says, in a conciliatory tone.

I feel sicker still when UT is stopped on their next drive on fourth down. Rowder hands me another beer. "Don't worry," he says, "we'll get them when they come here to play in a few weeks." Taunting text messages arrive from my UF friends, Neville and Jeff. I read them, respond, then feel even sicker. To the bathroom I go, where let's just say the moonshine returns to the light of day.

Back out in the bar all around me is a whirl of celebration. Au-buhn has won but my team has lost. My emotions are those entirely rooted in defeat only everyone around me is celebrating. I feel like the only survivor of an Oregon Trail caravan who is watching the Indians dance around the fire, victorious scalps in hand. Rowder looks at me and shakes his head. "By God, you're hotter than a billy goat in a pepper patch about that game, aren't ya?" I just look at him. I've only been to three stadiums and I'm not sure my stomach can handle the entire SEC.

THE SPORTS GRIEF SCALE

As I make the long drive back to Nashville from Auburn, Alabama, I replay the Tennessee–Florida game over and over again in my mind. I analyze each play, I curse each error, and, on occasion, for mile after dark mile, I try to pretend the game hasn't even happened. My team has just lost to one of our most bitter rivals and once more I find myself contemplating the lonely stages of The Sports Grief Scale. It's a long and painful road we fans trod.

Every year, no matter which team you root for or which sport you favor, chances are you and those you root for are going to end up losers. Yet, for all the media focus on winning championships, very little attention is given to the much more common experience of dealing with defeat. While the media casually cover professional athletes' reactions to losing, much of their pain is tempered by their paychecks, which stanch the flow of their tears.

But what about the average fan whose team loses, and who does not gain any tangible compensation for his pain? I have no interest in considering the eternal question of why we care so much about sports we don't play, but would like, rather, to contemplate the nature of our loss. In the immortal words of Bill Clinton, I'm the writer who wants to feel your pain.

As I morosely drive through the Alabama night, the absurdity of my loyalty to the University of Tennessee is brought home by my wife, who asks via telephone, "How in the world is your life going to be remotely different tomorrow?"

When a sports fan is in a sports-related funk, there is nothing worse than the cold hard slap of logic. But she was right; my life was really not going to be any different.

As I wind my way across Alabama, I think about all the ways I could have spent the weekend that wouldn't have left me so disappointed. For instance, I could have gone camping, watched *Bring It On* for the 321st time, fished in a cool mountain stream, or even read nursery rhymes to orphaned children. I could have worked as a Candy Striper at a local hospital, given rides to hitchhikers, and taught neighborhood kids how to shoot bottle rockets at one another. Instead, I watched a football team (filled with players I don't personally know) lose and got upset. And now I'm in sports-loss recovery.

In order to cope with my loss, I decided to construct in my mind a road map for my own recovery, marking the stages I must go through in order to come out on the other side fully healed, and ready to stand behind my team once more. While I am certain that its stages will not be identical to the pain and misery felt by every sports fan, I think the overlap is significant enough that each of you will see echoes of your own emotions at least somewhere along my personal journey.

Of course, there are always skip-aheads—fans who are so optimistic and short-sighted that the moment their season ends, they've already sketched out the starting defense for next season, when, they are convinced, only better things will arrive. Chances are each of you know at least one of these infuriating types. They don't even have the decency to let you wallow in defeat at the end of a season. Well, those guys can skip the first eleven steps; they are far too healthy for you and me. Besides, this list is here primarily so fans everywhere can know they are not alone.

1. "If": These are the two letters that have tortured and will torture sports fans for all eternity. I can actually pinpoint the exact time

I realized that I was not alone in thinking obsessively about the what ifs. I was eight years old and riding home with my dad after watching Vanderbilt beat UT in basketball. Doug Roth, UT's blind-in-one-eye power forward, had missed some key free throws, and I had been sitting silently in the back seat of the car replaying the loss in my mind. Out of nowhere, my dad said something about every sports fan driving himself crazy if he played the what-if game for too long. I was absolutely flabbergasted that everyone else did the same thing I did in the wake of defeat: Replay the game over and over in search of a crucial moment that could have changed the outcome. I later grew up and became a lawyer, which means I only deal in ifs. Irony can be a cruel mistress.

2. "The refs, oh man, the refs": They hate your team and my team, they really do. At night, they sit on their hotel beds in their striped pajamas and laugh themselves silly thinking that fans of Team X really believe they have a chance at winning in the morning. "Oh, if they only knew what was planned for the next day," these referees will say, while gleefully rubbing their palms together. It's just so obvious to the clear-eyed fan that this cabal of umpires, linesmen, referees, and timekeepers has been formed for the very purpose of snatching victory from your team at the very moment when victory should be theirs. How could those pantywaists with whistles be so biased and unfair? Blaming the officials and convincing yourself that it is as a result of their robbery that your team has lost is completely irrational and stupid. But, even still, a necessary stage of your road to recovery.

3. Boastful hyperbole: "I'm never going to watch them again," you'll say. Or, "See if I care . . . we're through and I'll even burn all of my jerseys." You are a fan, damn it, and this loss cannot be stood for! The most dramatic gesture I've ever heard of was when a

long-time Vanderbilt season-ticket holder stood up and tore his season tickets to shreds . . . after the first football game . . . while still standing in the stadium. That ticket tearer always impressed me because he truly managed to shock with his fandom divorce. These days, fans will do or say almost anything after losses. It has gotten to the point where fan hyperbole almost doesn't exist, because every exaggerated statement seems to have been already made by another fan. Regardless, the temptation will always be there to do or say something outlandish to draw attention to your plight and how forsaken your lot is. If you doubt me, go on to any sports message board. The doom and gloom there will boggle the mind.

4. The silent rage: This phase arrives when those around you persist in wanting to talk about the game and you want to strangle the next person who says anything at all because you have absolutely nothing left to say. Personally, at this point, I want to go to a dark room and be left alone. I've known others who want to approach the head coach/starting running back/quarterback/point guard/third baseman, and slap them until they admit they are fools and have personally wronged you with their errors. I've always loved the image of some bespectacled forty-five-year-old slapping a starting running back for his perceived transgressions. Is there any way more certain to court death?

5. Sick to your stomach and can't even bear the thought of the sport: For most of the drive back from Auburn, I couldn't bear to hear, think, or say anything about football. In the immediate aftermath of a crushing defeat, it is always wise to impose upon oneself a rigorous avoidance of sports scores and highlights lest you be forced to relive the searing pain.

6. Read the paper or watch television for confirmation: After a night of tossing and turning, the next morning I always read the

paper because this brings the loss home. It's sort of like going out to the bar and seeing your ex-girlfriend with a new guy. In order to confirm that no, it wasn't just a nightmare, I have to read every word plus review the box score. The worst part of the newspaper after a loss is the annoyingly catchy headlines. For instance, immediately after Wichita State beat UT in the 2006 NCAA Basketball Tournament, I was inwardly cringing at all of the Shocker puns that I knew the media would plaster all over the newspapers and Internet. It's like even newspapers are talking trash about your team, making witty remarks at your expense. Don't they know your pain?

7. "The media are out to get me": Paranoia is a natural reaction to reading the newspapers. You'll get sick pleasure out of accusing the media of unequal treatment. For instance, you'll convince yourself that another team's loss is being reported infinitely less extensively, and in a more sympathetic manner, than your team's. Believe it or not, this is a positive move. It means you are starting to circle the wagons and cope with your defeat.

8. "Whichever team beat mine sucks and so do their fans": Comforting yourself with juvenile thoughts is a great way to move forward in your recovery. When I was about ten and UT had just lost to Auburn, my dad said, "Clay, right now there is a boy the same age as you in Alabama who is really happy that his team beat Tennessee. Sometimes you'll be happy and sometimes he'll be happy, but you really aren't that different." After seventeen years, I have a much better perspective about things like this. For instance, now that little boy from Auburn is also twenty-seven and, right now, I am still sure he sucks and so does his team.

9. "Fire the coach!": I'm sure that every one of you has a friend who wants to fire the coach after every loss. "It's time to clean house," he'll say even though he has not cleaned his own house since

1988. Maybe you are this guy. Just about every one of us has been this guy at some point during our respective fandoms. Something that's enjoyable about this stage is when you drag completely un-interested people, like your wife or the street vendor, into your misery. Particularly your wife, because your previous silence on the loss will have given her the feeling that you are a grown man and have gotten over it. In reality, you've just been silently boil-ing over the loss. This phase will really disappoint her.

10. "Why does my team always lose?": Now you've reached the phil-osophical wasteland of fandom contemplation. I wonder, do New York Yankees fans ruminate upon this eternal question? Some-how, I bet they do, even though they've won more champion-ships than any other team I can think of. In my life as a sports fan, exactly once, in 1998 with the Tennessee Vols, did one of my teams win a championship. Every other year of my life, I've ended up a loser. Yet, I come back every season for more helpings of defeat. And it doesn't matter how many games my team wins during the regular season; I always feel like sitting in a corner and pouting when they lose to finish their seasons. But the truth of the matter is, yes, your team almost always loses. It isn't your imagination. Fans have much more experience with losing than winning, yet somehow, season-ending losses always come as such a shock.

11. Perspective: Honest to God, this is the image I always go with: I could be living in a Third World country without a mosquito net. For some reason, the thought of infectious little insects bit-ing me brings home how insignificant my teams' losses are better than anything else I could say, think, or do. That and the fact that I have the freedom, time, and health to actually get worked up about a sports team, but this is almost getting too logical. Re-member, for the most part, logic is the enemy of fandom.

12. A reminder that redemption is only a season away: For me, this comes from the weather. In the middle of summer, out of nowhere, there will be a cool night that feels just like fall and you'll find yourself thinking about footballs soaring through the air amid falling leaves. Or, in late summer, you'll step into a gym and hear the squeak of a sneaker on a hardwood floor. Or, in the midst of winter, some idiot from your office will go find someone to throw a baseball with him, even while there's still snow on the ground.

For a few days, you'll stand at the window looking outside at these fools tossing a baseball in their jackets and wondering what in the world they're thinking trying to fashion baseball season in the midst of winter's grasp. And then, one day, hardly thinking about it, you will pack your glove and find yourself blowing into your palm to keep your fingers warm while you toss alongside them. You won't have forgotten the season just past, but you'll realize yet again that there is no loss so bad that keeps the season from beginning anew. In popular parlance, hope springs eternal, but I've always thought hope was the wrong word. Because those of us whose lives move to the rhythm of athletic fandom know that, in the end, sports spring eternal.

Yeah, this realization is pretty mature of me. But I still hate Florida.

ARKANSAS

Ask any person not from Arkansas to name the first person or thing from Arkansas that comes to their mind, and 95 percent will say Bill Clinton or Wal-Mart. Of course, I have no actual evidence that this is true, but it seems like it probably would be. (For the record, my wife said "Bill Clinton." When pressed for a second word association, she admitted, "I can't think of anything else.")

So, based on this highly technical reporting sample, Wal-Mart and Bill Clinton pretty much sum up Arkansas for the rest of America, or at least for me and my wife. Other than driving across the bridge from Memphis with my dad when I was very young ("Okay, you've seen Arkansas now," said my dad as we got off at the first exit and headed back to Tennessee), I had never been to Arkansas.

My knowledge of Fayetteville, the sixty-thousand person town in the foothills of the Ozark mountains where the University of Arkansas is located, boiled down to memories of Arkansas basketball and football teams and also a vague recollection that Kelly from *Real World: New Orleans* might have gone to school there.

Arkansas and South Carolina are the two newest additions to the Southeastern Conference. Beginning conference competition in 1993, to bring the number of schools to twelve, both Arkansas and South Carolina spent the first sixty years of SEC existence playing other schools and setting up their own rivalries apart from the SEC. This means that most current fans in the SEC don't have memories of sleepless nights brought on by losses to either South Carolina or Arkansas. These are new gridiron combatants without decades of animus and hate.

So, I set out for Fayetteville with less of an idea of what to expect than I had for any of the other schools I had visited or would visit on the DDT. Fayetteville was a complete mystery to me; a far-off land, quite literally. Located in the northwestern tip of Arkansas, Fayetteville is a long way from every other SEC school. Arkansas's closest geographic rival is Ole Miss, which is 402 miles away. Of course, 402 miles away seems downright neighborly when compared to the 1,040 miles that separate Arkansas from Florida. In the SEC, where the fiercest rivals are often the closest of geographic foes (think of the 100 miles separating Ole Miss and Mississippi State, or the 180 miles separating Auburn and Alabama), Fayetteville is a displaced and enigmatic distant cousin, the Puerto Rico of the SEC. A distinctly foreign place with its own rules, rhythms, and way of life. As former Arkansas coach Lou Holtz once said of Fayetteville, "It's not the end of the world, but you can see it from there."

• • •

On the afternoon of Thursday, September 21, I begin the 1,060 mile roundtrip drive from Nashville to Fayetteville. On Thursday night, I'll stay with Junaid in Memphis and, once I arrive in Fayetteville on Friday night, I'm to meet my law school friend Hinton, a lifelong Arkansas Razorback fan. This means that for the entirety of my drive to and from Fayetteville I will be alone in my car. My mom is concerned about me driving over 1,000 miles by myself in a single weekend so, before I leave, she gives me a jar of peanuts and a pocket flashlight. Yep, peanuts and a pocket flashlight. If I get lost on an elephant farm at night, I'm golden.

As soon as I leave Nashville on Thursday evening, I get a call from my law school friend Kumar. "I just bought twenty-five Tickle Me Elmos," he says. "I'm going to sell them on eBay when it gets closer to Christmas." Then, he sends me a cell-phone picture of his front room filled with Tickle Me Elmo packages. "You have to be the only prosecutor in America with twenty-five Tickle Me Elmos," I say. There's a pause while Kumar thinks. "I'd say that's probably an accurate statement," he replies.

Later on Thursday night, I arrive in Memphis to stay with Junaid, who accompanied me on the first stop of the DDT in Knoxville. The two of us stay up until one-thirty watching replays of the Tennessee-Florida game on Phil Fulmer's coaching show. Fulmer looks like he just ate glass. Junaid says, "I'm a firm believer that if you watch a game enough times, eventually the result might change." Even though we watch every important play approximately five times in super slow motion, the result does not change.

The next morning, on my way to Fayetteville, I stop in Little Rock and tour the Bill Clinton Presidential Library. As I'm eating lunch in Café 42 (oh, the presidential humor) a group of Alabama fans already clad in full Alabama regalia, and en route to Arkansas, do a "Roll Tide" cheer. Even without the accompanying band music, the fans manage to make a lot of noise. There may not be a place on earth Alabama fans are uncomfortable doing a "Roll Tide" cheer.

The Clinton Museum is definitely worth touring. For an SEC fan, there are two particularly interesting letters that the former president received on display in the main hall: One from former Razorback basketball coach Nolan Richardson, dated March 10, 1994, wishing Clinton luck in dealing with the complexities and challenges of his job. The ever-erudite Richardson has spelled tough "though" "Though times don't last, though people do," he informed the president, who, I would imagine, was delighted to receive such sage advice. The entire team signed the letter (apparently, nobody noticed the misspelling). Clinton responded on March 18 with "Win the NCAA."

Then, a few cases later, there is another letter dated November 18, 1998, from Southern writer Willie Morris. At the end of his note, Morris wrote: "P.S. Now if we could just take that Razorback fumble back with 1:49 left. I was yelling for the Hogs and it damn near killed me." Clinton responded to Morris on Nov. 24, "I used to think every Arkansas game was a metaphor for life—I don't anymore—and hope (indecipherable words here) in my old age."

I ask four people standing beside me to try and figure out what Clinton's writing says. I get four different guesses and no one is certain. (If someone from the Clinton Library or Clinton himself can provide some clarity, it will be much appreciated.) Regardless, every Arkansas fan on earth knows that Clinton and Morris were referring to quarterback Clint Stoerner's infamous fumble in Knoxville that led to the Vols' miraculous 28–24 victory in 1998 and helped preserve UT's perfect National Championship season. It was a heartbreaking loss for the Razorbacks but, curiously, in a bit of football symmetry, Arkansas upset UT by the same score, 28–24, the next year in Fayetteville.

In addition to browsing letters that came in and out of Clinton's mailroom, you can also review Clinton's official schedule via computer screen for every day he was in office. I choose to review Clinton's official schedule for April 6, 2000, which happened to be my twenty-first birthday. One of the few things I distinctly remember is hearing the presidential motorcade roaring through town late that night as we stumbled down the Washington streets. Yep, there it is. Clinton was on his way back from a dinner. I was on my way to waking up with drink tally marks from my hand rubbed onto my forehead. So, all in all, pretty similar days.

On the third floor of the library, Bill Clinton is pictured in Arkansas warmups, holding a basketball on the cover of *Sports Illustrated*. Later, I'll learn there was a firestorm of controversy in the state of Arkansas over the incorrect spelling of *sooie*, the final syllable of Arkansas's trademark athletic cheer (known as *calling the Hogs*), with a y on the magazine cover. People haven't been that angry in Arkansas since cockfighting was banned. Regardless, this is an absolutely classic photo. Any middle-aged white guy in warmups is hysterical, but the president? Say what you will about Clinton as a president but, as a sports fan, the guy had no fear. Somehow, to me, Clinton always seemed the most believable when he gave himself over to his inner fan. I still remember him slapping his leg and cursing while he watched Arkansas play basketball in person. There didn't seem to be any political calculus or deeper meaning behind his reactions. He was, quite simply, a fan.

On the third floor, I learn that Clinton liked to have friends over to watch sports in the White House. "There was only one catch; he always had complete authority over the remote control," says a placard. Which makes perfect sense. If you can bomb a small country you shouldn't be required to get caught on Cialis commercials during halftime.

After leaving the Clinton Library and heading farther west, eventually I turn off I-40 west and begin to drive north on 540. All around me are the verdant hills of the Ozarks. In a few weeks, when late summer runs into autumn, these hills will have burst into thousands of colors but, now, I am surrounded by green. There are no towns, few people, and, at one point, there are clouds resting gently in between the valleys of the hills. As I drive through the clouds, I feel as if I am flying in a plane. It's like driving into the Emerald City.

I drive through a long mountain tunnel on 540 and, shortly after, I come out on the other side where farmers wear hog hats and call hogs by standing and twirling their fingers in the pig sooie chant. I've entered a strange and beautiful land where tornado threats can suddenly materialize out of placid fall evenings. At least, that's what I learn when I turn on the radio and hear that there are huge clouds racing across the western horizon and tornados will arrive in the area shortly. We're not in Nashville anymore, Toto.*

---

* In the interests of preserving my own heterosexuality, I apologize for the *Wizard of Oz* reference generally and, in particular, for the reference to a small dog named Toto. To cleanse the palate here are two words that have never before been linked in the merry old land of Oz: Munchkin *bukkake*. Enjoy the image.

I arrive in Fayetteville after a drive that seems like it should have deposited me in the suburbs of San Francisco. It's a long way to northwest Arkansas. Last week, I discovered that it was cheaper for me to fly to London than to fly to Fayetteville. Now that I've completed the drive, I think it might be faster to drive to London, too.

My friend Hinton and I will be staying in Rogers, which is about twenty miles north of Fayetteville. The cities of Rogers and Bentonville (Wal-Mart's home base) merge together in a glorious suburban medley of riches that seems particularly incongruous given the isolation of these towns from any large pocket of civilization. Hinton grew up an Arkansas fan, and his parents as well as both sisters attended the university. Eschewing family loyalty to the Hogs, Hinton attended Dartmouth prior to meeting me in law school. For three years, Hinton constantly lamented the Hogs' uncanny ability to lose close games, and we also filled our spare time coming up with one inventive sports bet after another to wager upon.

One bet in particular stands out of the three-year haze that was law school. It was late one night, after a long period of drinking during our first year of school, that I informed a crowded room I could throw a football fifty yards. Immediately, Hinton challenged this statement. "There's no way," he said, "absolutely no way you can throw a football fifty yards in the air." Another friend piped up, "Dan fucking Marino can only throw a football fifty-five yards; there's no way you can throw it fifty." I still have no idea whether this Marino fact is true, but it prompted an immediate call out from Hinton, "Right now," he said, "we're going to the Vandy practice football field and you're proving it. Twenty bucks." We shook hands to confirm the bet. In those days, I always had a football, basketball, or Frisbee in my car, just in case a game should break out.

So, about a half-dozen of us would-be learned legal scholars caravanned over to the practice field some time after two in the morning. Of course, the fields were locked, so we managed to drunkenly pile over the iron fence, screaming, yelping, and taunting each other at the tops of our voices. After a few tosses to get loose, I stood at midfield and stared at Hinton standing alongside the goal line far in the distance. Fifty yards was a long way, I suddenly realized; in the darkness I couldn't even see the goal line. I took a deep breath, stepped back and uncorked the football with all my might.

It came to rest forty yards away, just short of the ten-yard line. Derisive taunts followed me. Someone informed me that I might win the NFL's punt, pass, and kick contest . . . for ten-year-old girls. Again and again, I tried as my shoulder began to ache. Again and again, the football came up short of the goal line. After about twenty tosses, my shoulder was almost done for. But I persevered. Eventually, I managed to get one to the five-yard line. But no closer. Glumly, I paid Hinton his money. The drunken catcalls at my failure echoed across the Nashville night and when morning arrived I could barely move my arm. Fortunately, only my ego suffered permanent damage.

On Friday evening, Hinton is scheduled to arrive at the Northwest Arkansas Airport, but it seems possible the apocalypse has arrived and will prevent him from doing so. There is lightning striking in several different directions at once. In fact, some of the strikes seem to defy my rudimentary knowledge of physics by going entirely sideways across the night sky. Rain is pouring and the tornado watches remain in effect, which makes it virtually impossible for me to be certain his flight will even land.

Worse, when I leave the hotel to drive to the Northwest Arkansas Airport, I rapidly find myself on a forlorn and winding road where the only light comes from the near-incessant lighting. After fifteen minutes of driving, I am in the middle of nowhere. In fact, these are the rough directions to the Northwest Arkansas Airport: "Drive six miles on a road with no lights where you see no other cars. Come to an abrupt stop at a large tree with two dead limbs and wait for a dog with one eye to bark at you, then drive a circle around the tree while playing a harmonica, and drive two more miles on a dirt road that is bordered by a raging river on one side and a rapid descent to Hell on the other. When you reach the old clapboard house with AIRPORT spray-painted on the side alongside an arrow, you are close. Then, you only have to drive two more miles where it appears no one has lived in 100 years, knock on a chain-link fence and ask for Jed, then turn left. Welcome to the airport."

Hinton is ashen when he gets into the car. "We had this pilot who thought he was a funny guy, and he kept making jokes about the lightning." He takes a long gulp of fresh air. "I thought I was going to die." Around us, the sky is continuing to erupt. We miss the exit from the airport because although the Northwest Arkansas Regional Airport has more signs per capita than any airport I have ever seen, none of them offer any help on actually exiting. Finally, after another pass by the main terminal, we leave and do what any smart person would do on the eve of humanity's death—we drive to the bars in Fayetteville.

As we travel in the lightning flashes, we pass by the enormous Wal-Mart distribution center, and the mansions of the Wal-Mart elite reveal themselves alongside large, downtrodden farms. Later, we'll pass sushi restaurants and expensive and trendy retailers like Coach, Sephora, and Fossil (At least I'm told by my wife these places are expensive and trendy retailers. I really have no idea.) If there is a place in America that has changed more in the past twenty years than Rogers, Arkansas, I'd be surprised.

Hinton has been to all fifty states (thanks to a Greyhound bus tour after college) and he says, "I'm telling you, Fayetteville is a great town. I loved it here. I even interviewed for a job here. But people here don't let in other people very easily. Everyone knows everyone."

Dickson Street, the main strip of bars and restaurants in downtown Fayetteville, is not very crowded. This might be because we are in the midst of a torrential downpour. Still, Hinton and I manage to visit at least five bars. Every bar in Fayetteville has one single name, most of them of one syllable. My favorite is Stir. Is there any less appropriate place than Fayetteville, Arkansas, for a bar named *Stir*? It's like naming a bar in Tehran *Jesus*.

At one of the bars, several drunken Arkansas fans climb onto picnic tables and call the Hogs. Bar patrons grudgingly oblige. It appears that being the drunk guy who decides to call the Hogs at the bar is sort of frowned upon. This is despite the fact that the hog call has defined Arkansas athletics since the 1920s when, legend has it, a group of Arkansas farmers attempted to encourage the Arkansas football club by "calling the Hogs." In order to call the Hogs, fans extend both hands into the air and begin the cheer with the trademark "Woooo." Then they put their hands down for the "pig" part of the cheer before raising only the right hand (crucial detail) once more for the final syllable, the "sooie." After three calls, the Arkansas faithful then scream "Razorbacks!" in unison. The complete cheer goes something like this:

> "WOOOOOOOOOO, PIG ! SOOIE!
> WOOOOOOOOOO, PIG ! SOOIE!
> WOOOOOOOOOO, PIG ! SOOIE!
> RAZORBACKS!!"

And I'm not kidding when I tell you that there is a debate among Arkansas fans about how long the "Woooooooo" part of the cheer should last. Traditionalists hew to eight seconds while nontraditionalists, in the midst of a Hog Calling rebellion, want to break off the Woooooooo far too early.

Departing the bars, we make a late-night stop at a pizzeria, where we hear a table full of sorority girls wishing their friend luck in getting admitted to Vanderbilt Law School. Hinton and I consider telling them that Vanderbilt is great, but the problem with law school is that when you finish you're a lawyer. Then we decide that we will seem like really lame liars, because none of the girls will believe that we actually went to Vanderbilt, much less that we're lawyers.

After a night out on Dickson Street, Hinton and I head back to the hotel, stopping at the Super Wal-Mart in Springdale on the way. Springdale is the home of Arkansas's freshman starting quarterback, Mitch Mustain. It is two-thirty in the morning, yet Hinton and I are moderately surprised that Mitch Mustain is not hanging out in his hometown Wal-Mart. Hardly anyone is, actually. The entire gleaming expanse of the store seems ready and available for our drunken convenience. We buy two T-shirts, a set of Razorback cupcakes, and a Hog hat. At the checkout line, a young Indian girl named Chitra is upset because I have managed to select the only Hog hat without a price tag. "Price check on the Hog hat," she says. Another young guy rolls his eyes. "You're going to make me work," he says, then goes in search of the price. Later, he will tell Hinton and me that he graduated with Mitch Mustain at Springdale High School. See, Arkansas is a small place. Chitra and I discuss what the Hog hat will cost. "No way it's more than ten dollars," she says. Mustain's classmate returns, "Hog hat's sixteen dollars and ninety-five cents," he says. Everyone is shocked. Hog hats might be the highest margin item in the Wal-Mart.

Yeah, I bought Razorback cupcakes. In the morning, this made less sense, but late at night, wasted in the Wal-Mart, I was dazzled by the fact that each of the ten cupcakes had RAZORBACK written on it in individual icing letters. I still have no idea how Wal-Mart can make money charging forty cents apiece for ten cupcakes. If you put me in charge of writing RAZORBACK in icing on the cupcakes, they would end up costing about four hundred dollars, and all the icing would be as illegible as Bill Clinton's handwritten notes. Of course, if you put Bill Clinton in charge of the cupcakes, they would never make it to the floor, and a Wal-Mart store manager would end up censured. I guess we all have our flaws.

The next morning, I take a picture of the Razorback cupcake on the air conditioner in our room.

Hinton cuts the Starter insignia off his new T-shirt while I take the cupcake photo. "I didn't even know Starter still existed," he says. Then, by way of explaining himself, he says,

"I'm still bitter about all those kids with the puffy Los Angeles Raiders jackets." It's completely amazing to me how a company like Starter just collapsed. When I was in fifth grade most of the kids I knew would have taken a bullet for a chance to get an unlimited supply of Starter's puffy jackets, even

I'm like the Andy Warhol of Razorback cupcake photos.

though we didn't have much need for them in Nashville. And then the company just died. Still baffles me.

Hinton and I arrive in Fayetteville around eleven-thirty on Saturday morning and immediately discover the ticket market is pretty weak. About an hour before the two-thirty central kickoff, we buy two tickets in the south end zone for thirty dollars each. Face value is forty dollars. The DDT is now four for four on buying tickets on the day of the game.

I am disappointed to discover that no hogs are being called. I thought the area around Arkansas' football stadium would be one large cacophony of hog calls, not unlike the "War Eagle!" chants of Auburn. As is, Hinton and I walk around outside for over an hour and don't hear a single person utter Arkansas's signature cheer. Despite the absence of hog calling Hinton and I do find the Webhogs Razorback Club where a dozen or so members are in the process of doing their Victory Circle. They stand in a circle and pass a whiskey bottle around. When the whiskey bottle reaches you, you say something football-related and then take a swig. One man says, "I hope we get a turnover today." So far, Arkansas has yet to get a turnover this season. Everyone in the circle nods his head and the man drinks. The process continues until the bottle of whiskey is finished. Then they sing an Arkansas fight song. The Webhogs are of varying ages and of both sexes. They also have the best tailgate that Hinton and I see at Arkansas, replete with three flat-screen televisions, two satellites, tents that take an hour and a half to set up, and enough food and drink to sustain a small army.

As we walk around outside the stadium, Arkansas and Alabama fans are almost impossible to tell apart. Each fan base is clad in red, and the difference between the two A's on their caps is fairly subtle. If it weren't for Alabama fans and their pompons (for a case study, please close the book momentarily, turn to the cover, and check out the man in the lower-left corner), the fan bases would be almost indistinguishable.

The south section of the Arkansas football stadium is new. As such, it is remarkably nice. So nice, it even has Starbucks coffee. Yep, Starbucks . . . in an SEC stadium.

The concession stand also sells something called pulled pork nachos, which are also called *The Widow-makers*. Hinton gets an order and pronounces them tasty. Then I try some as well. They're excellent, although I can feel my arteries clogging as I swallow.

• • •

What's next? A Sephora store?

We're on the third row in the end zone, and our seats have backs. These are the first backed seats in an SEC stadium that I've ever seen. And a cup holder, too. I lean back and test out the seat. Then, I put my cup into the cup holder. It doesn't take much to impress me.

Arkansas appears to have approximately 543 cheerleaders. There are tons of them. I think each player must get a personal team of ten to follow him around wherever he goes.

I discover that no fans wear their Hog hats during the game. This is because it's almost impossible for the people behind you to see. Arkansas fans are courteous about this, though; they actually take off their hats willingly, without being asked. Whereas, when I'm at professional games, it always seems like I end up sitting behind some clown with one of those fake afros on. Aside from the fact that you have to have an I.Q. of twenty-one or less to actually find this funny, those things absolutely ruin everyone's view. Not so with the Razorback hats, which are gently placed at their wearers' feet during games.

By kickoff, the weather is perfect. Hardly any clouds and sunny skies. Nice call by the weathermen who had been predicting a second batch of apocalyptic showers. Presumably, this aided us in procuring such great seats.

Despite the pleasant weather, the crowd is not particularly loud early in the game. Hinton tells me that Arkansas hasn't had many big wins lately in Fayetteville, and the trepidation of the crowd seems to back that fact up. When Arkansas kicks a field goal to take a 3–0 lead, the crowd perks up. But then Alabama scores on a seventy-eight-yard touchdown pass, and the crowd immediately deflates and turns visibly pessimistic. The first audible Roll Tide cheer reaches us from the Alabama section near the other end zone. Several rows behind me, a

man is screaming insults at Arkansas head coach Houston
Nutt.

Nutt has been Arkansas's head coach since 1998. Often,
other teams' fans will deride him by using his full, and quintessentially Southern, name, Houston Dale Nutt, Jr. After decent
initial success, Nutt's last two seasons have been 5–6 and 4–7
campaigns. Consequently, there is much restlessness in Arkansas over his performance as head coach, and a not insubstantial
group of fans are calling for his ouster. "It could," says Hinton,
"get ugly if this is a bad year."

As the Arkansas fan behind me berates Nutt by screaming,
"You can go to hell, Houston Dale Nutt, and take your damn
contract with you," I take notice of my surroundings and consider the existential question: Does every SEC stadium have
hedges along the outer rim of the field now? All four I've visited
thus far do. Is there any trend that can't be copied in the SEC?
What if Georgia added a drawbridge and moat surrounding
their hedges? Would everyone else follow?

Just as quickly as my attention veers away from the game in
front of me, it zooms right back in as the Arkansas crowd cheers
wildly for freshman quarterback Mitch Mustain. Mustain was
Arkansas's top recruit last year, and is also the young man who
disappointed me and Hinton by not hanging out at the Super
Wal-Mart in Springdale, where we made our drunken pur-
chases the night before. After Mustain completes a pass for a
first down, the man in front of me asks, "How many weeks do
you think it will take for his jersey to be for sale?" "It's already
for sale," says the man sitting beside him.

Alabama boots a field goal to end the half with a 10–3 lead.
The grumbling around us increases. Hinton reports "There's a
rumor that everyone who wanted to see Nutt gone was going to

wear black shirts today." There don't appear to be very many black shirts, so, even though Nutt is losing at home yet again, the *coup d'etat* appears stifled.

Arkansas scores to begin the second half, but misses the extra point, a crucial mistake, bringing the score to 10–9 Alabama. The crowd continues its alternate bouts of exhilaration and despair. Right now, they are exhilarated.

Alabama's John Parker Wilson throws an illegal forward pass. This is Wilson's first year as the starting quarterback for Alabama. Currently, his younger brother, Ross, is the starting quarterback on MTV's television show *Two-A-Days*, a reality show in which the Hoover, Alabama high school team's pursuit of a state title is being chronicled in typical high drama. Hinton and I watch the ref make the call, and agree that the illegal forward-pass signal is the most ridiculous one in college football. The elbow bent and touching the small of the back. It almost requires the referee to have a double-jointed elbow. How did this signal ever make it this long?

Arkansas decks Wilson a few plays later, and picks up a fumble return for a touchdown. But when the play is reviewed, the jubilation in the crowd disappears instantaneously. This is the most bipolar football crowd I've ever been a part of. The instant replay guy on the sideline wears a large neon bib that says IR on it. Couldn't they give the guy an actual shirt, rather than reducing him to children's wear?

After a tense few minutes, we learn that the call stands and watch as Houston Nutt does a fist pump that begins somewhere near the top of his shoes. I actually thought he might tip over.

Then Arkansas scores on the two-point conversion and once again the crowd is euphoric. Seventeen–ten Arkansas.

I'm sure the Webhogs Razorback circle whiskey drinker who had requested a turnover is particularly happy. For the first time this year, Arkansas has their turnover.

The Holler Meter comes on the high-tech scoreboard. I love this, because I can't imagine the word *holler* being used anywhere outside the South. I'm picturing the Holler Meter coming on in Ann Arbor, Michigan, and people being like, "What the hell's a holler?" But, in Arkansas, everyone knows. Screaming cheers cascade down from all directions.

Alabama finally decides to throw the ball. They score a touchdown shortly thereafter to tie the score at seventeen. Hinton rolls his eyes and seats himself dejectedly. "If Alabama would just throw the ball every down, they'd have thirty points," he says. Thankfully for Arkansas, Alabama's head coach Mike Shula continues to pound the run to no avail.

With 3:11 to play, Alabama has a thirty-yard field goal to take a 20–17 lead. Hinton refuses to stand. "There are only two teams that miss this field goal in the SEC," he says glumly, "Vanderbilt and Arkansas." And yet, Alabama misses wide right. Hinton stands and cheers. Maybe Alabama isn't Alabama anymore.

Just before overtime arrives, Alabama's quarterback, Wilson, completes a pass to himself, then tries to throw the ball again. This maneuver sort of serves as a metaphor for the game itself. Not spectacular, but weirdly and crazily compelling. Later a friend will describe this game as the equivalent of watching two fat women have sex. You don't really want to watch, but once it starts you can't look away. As I'm sure you've figured out on your own, this is one of my wiser and more profound friends.

Overtime arrives, and the zeroes are centered on the scoreboard. We're tied at seventeen, and this game is no longer con-strained by the clock. The bipolar Arkansas crowd is eerily silent.

College football's overtime is significantly different from, and better than, the NFL's. In the NFL, the first team to score wins. In college football, each team takes possession at the twenty-five-yard line and attempts to score. The clock is turned off. The regular rules remain in effect and teams can score a touchdown, a field goal, or neither. In each overtime period each team will play both offense and defense. If the teams re-main tied after the first overtime then a second period is played. This continues until one team defeats the other one, a system that ensures college football's overtime is outrageously exciting and laced with tension.

Arkansas takes possession first in overtime, and Mustain throws an interception. Electing to play it conservative with his team, Alabama coach Mike Shula runs three times in the center of the field and sets Alabama up for a thirty-seven-yard field goal to win the game. Only Alabama's kicker, Leigh Tiffin, misses wide right again. We're going to a second overtime. I've never seen a game before where neither team scored in the first overtime period. Yet, somehow, this fits the tone of this game perfectly. We're still tied at seventeen and the Arkansas fan sit-ting in front of us says, "Maybe it's just in the cards for us to win this game."

The teams switch ends for the second overtime period, and the photographers and cameramen are caught in a mad scram-ble rushing to the other end of the field. Now, those of us in the south end zone will primarily watch the game on the score-board. It's an odd thing to watch a game you're attending in person on the scoreboard.

In the second overtime, the teams alternate the order of possession and Alabama scores a touchdown on the opening drive, but Tiffin misses the extra point wide right, a predictable mistake at this point, given his kicking failings thus far. It's like Tiffin is suddenly Kevin Costner in *Tin Cup*. Every kick is the exact same miss. Alabama leads 23–17 but with this missed extra point Arkansas needs a touchdown and the ensuing point after and they will win. Suddenly, victory for the Razorback faithful seems tantalizingly close.

Hardly anyone around me is speaking as Arkansas takes possession. Even the cheerleaders have stopped cheering. It is the quietest I have ever heard seventy-five thousand football fans in the midst of a game.

Then, on third-and-eight, Arkansas's Mustain throws a pass to his former high school teammate, Ben Cleveland. While the ball is in the air, Mustain and Cleveland are just two young kids with the hopes of a fan base riding on their shoulders. By the time Cleveland lands in the end zone with the ball clutched to his chest, they are Razorback legends in the making. The cheers crest for a minute or two, then silence descends as Arkansas lines up to attempt the winning extra point. Hinton leans over and whispers, "If they block this . . ." He doesn't finish the thought. The extra point is good and the Arkansas fans flood the field with their own particular brand of red.

The Arkansas faithful raise their twirling fingers in unison and call the Hogs in one long redemptive cheer as Alabama's players sulk their way off the field. Houston Nutt sprints across the field, leaps the dividing wall, and climbs into the student section, where he then climbs the ladder and leads the band in song. In the other corner of the same end zone, Alabama's Mike Shula has just exited the field. It is a subtle difference—this color of red that distinguishes the teams of Alabama and Arkansas. But on a fall afternoon when hardly anything separates the two teams, ultimately it is a very large difference indeed.

After the game, Hinton and I drive through Fayetteville to a local cemetery. While I wait in the car Hinton walks down to the grave site of one of his older sisters, Kimberly Suzanne Johnson. She died in a car accident after being a student at Arkansas. He stands beside her grave for some time as night advances on the hills of Fayetteville. By the time he returns, it's clear to me, the mystic chords of football life intertwine themselves around every moment, every family, and every life in the South. When cheers rise into the air on football Saturdays in the South, sometimes we're cheering loudest for those who can make no sound at all.

Hinton returns to my car. "What a game," he says, almost to himself.

THE BYE WEEK

Typically, the bye week is a time when teams assess their strengths and weaknesses, heal their injuries, and gather their fortitude for the final stretch of games. Now that college football has gone to twelve games, there is only one bye week. Since the DDT is nothing if not a rigorous, precise, and scientifically exhaustive analysis of the Southeastern Conference, I thought it would be ridiculous not to have a bye week myself. And so I did.

I spent my bye weekend watching college football for twelve and a half consecutive hours. I began with UT-Memphis at eleven central, followed that up with Florida-Alabama at two-thirty, left in the fourth quarter to watch Vanderbilt-Temple in person (the lowest cost for a scalped ticket on record at six dollars), and finally returned home to watch the end of Michigan-Minnesota, Kansas-Nebraska, and most of Georgia-Mississippi. It was a thoroughly unproductive day that felt, paradoxically, extremely productive. And, by the end of the weekend, I felt rejuvenated and ready to embark on the DDT the following week.

After four weeks on the road and stops at Tennessee, Mississippi State, Auburn, and Arkansas, I was feeling pretty good about the status of the DDT. So far, no one had taken a swing at me, I hadn't been arrested, and I hadn't even gotten a speeding ticket. Also, I hadn't had to pay more than fifty dollars for a ticket to any game.

Now that the bye week had come and the DDT was officially one-third complete, I figured it was time to take a breather and do a bit of self-assessment, examining some of what I'd learned thus far. Naturally, the best way to do this was to com-

pile a top eight list. I am choosing to include eight pieces of information, because this will be exactly two for each game I've
attended, and also the maximum amount of hard-hitting journalistic analysis I can force myself to summon up on my restful
bye week. So, without further ado, allow me to share some of
my hard-won wisdom:

1. Cymbal players can, in fact, get scholarships. Some of you will
   probably recall that I ruminated upon this with Krishna, Shekhar, Shaw, and Cliff while we were in Starkville. Now, we have
   the answer, thanks to cymbal player Andrew Barnes of Mississippi State, who wrote to me after reading one of my CBS Sports-
   Line columns, in which I mentioned my curiosity about this and
   other band-related matters.

   Andrew wrote: "I read your interesting article about your
   trip here and the exciting time you had . . . I also agree that we
   should have ordered the khaki shorts along with the polo and
   the band T-shirt, etc. (It does look pretty tacky.) But of course,
   you had to bash the cymbals."

   Was this pun intended? If so, well done, Andrew Barnes.

   The potential pun-ster continued.

   "This is the first time I actually played cymbals for any
   marching band, and it's harder than it looks. They do get heavy,
   and it's hard to memorize scores of random crashes and chokes (if
   you don't know, chokes are when we crash the cymbals and immediately bring it to our chest to muffle the sound, which re-
   sulted in numerous bruises). And yes, we do get scholarships. We
   deserve it, and it IS possible to be a better cymbal player than
   someone else. If you ever joined a drumline, you would understand things a little better."

   Clearly, I have struck a nerve in poor Mr. Barnes's cymbal-bruised chest. Bottom line: Playing the cymbals is the easiest way to get a scholarship on campus. You don't have to get a particular score on a standardized test, be particularly athletic, be any smarter than average, taller than average, fatter than average, or dumber than average. You really don't have to be anything except willing to bang two metal objects together, something I think even I, who could only throw a football forty-five yards and was once instructed by my high school chorus teacher not to sing because I was tone deaf, could handle.

2. LSU fans are really sensitive about the allegation by Auburn fans that they smell like corn dogs. I even received nasty e-mails from various LSU fans blaming me for reporting this little known, yet absolutely priceless, fact in one of my online columns. All I can say is, did you blame Bob Woodward or Carl Bernstein when they brought down the Nixon administration? Of course not. So, why would you blame me? Woodward, Bernstein, and I are all just steadfast journalists pursuing truth, justice, and equality for all (even for people who smell like corn dogs). I'm going to keep looking into this. I might even go ahead and buy the polish for my Pulitzer.

3. If you show up at an SEC stadium on game day and wait until kickoff, the ticket prices are very affordable. So far, I've paid face value at three stadiums and less than face value at Arkansas. I suspect this occurs because most people panic and buy tickets online before they arrive at the stadiums, which are so big there will undoubtedly still be tickets available, even seconds before kickoff.

4. Conversely, the Tickle Me Elmo resale market is really strong. My friend Kumar, who, as you may recall, purchased twenty-five Tickle Me Elmo dolls to resell, reports, "I only have 20 now. I sold five for between ninety and one hundred dollars (they retail

for thirty-five dollars at Wal-Mart). Now, I'm not selling the other twenty until December because the market is liked stuffed-animal gold bullion. The other day, my fiancée said she wanted to go shopping and asked me how much she could spend on clothes, 'I told her about two Elmo's worth.' " You've been warned.

5. Every team's traditional walk is exactly the same. Each week, when I return from a game, somebody will ask me, "How in the world could you go all the way to (insert city or stadium here) and not see the (insert team mascot, name, or other identifier) Walk?" Auburn fans, in particular, were disappointed (bordering on enraged) that I missed their beloved Tiger Walk. In response to them, I say: "Look, how many different ways can a team walk into the stadium?" Every team does a walk, and they all look exactly the same: Young guys with police protection walk inside a cordoned off area while old people scream and yell for them. It's like the Christians being led into the lions in ancient Rome, except people aren't rooting for the lions. Until bulls start chasing the team into the stadium or Coach Shula mandates that the Alabama offense crawl on their hands and knees so they don't risk injuring themselves, I will stand by my claim that once you've seen one team walk into its stadium, you've seen 'em all.

6. The most ridiculed coach in the SEC is Ole Miss's Ed Orgeron. Everywhere I go, I have conversations with fans who, seemingly out of nowhere, blurt out, "Oh, and Coach Orgeron is an idiot." Orgeron doesn't do himself any favors by sounding like the Incredible Hulk if the Incredible Hulk spoke with a small ferret attempting to escape from his esophagus. During my bye week, I think about how much I am looking forward to seeing the man in person. For some reason I expect to see him enter the field at Ole Miss while wrestling a cougar.

7. Former Arkansas basketball coach Nolan Richardson can't spell. He has a particularly *though* time spelling the word *tough*. And Nolan's mispelling makes him sound very philosophical in the way that someone can sound philosophical if they write something that makes no sense. "Though times don't last, though people do." Basically, Nolan Richardson is like Thoreau if Thoreau wore snakeskin boots and espoused a philosophy rooted in forty minutes of hell.

8. Auburn coach Tommy Tuberville wears transition lenses that adjust based on the sunlight. One reader of my online column, who goes by the name "Rocky Top Frog," has written in to share this fact. Quoth the Frog, "Surely he can afford two pairs of glasses? One regular pair for indoors and one dark pair for outside." Yes, Rocky Top Frog, financial constraints should not be an issue. Of course, today's SEC football coaches are not known for their stylistic traits. The same quirky ridicule could be foisted upon Kentucky's Rich Brooks for wearing a shirt that appears to be constructed of space-age fibers, LSU's Les Miles for his inability to wear a baseball cap without looking like the Pontiff, Georgia's Mark Richt for his obsession with fondling his mouthpiece, Arkansas' Houston Nutt for tucking his khaki pants into his socks, Mississippi State's Sylvester Croom for wearing wristbands, and Ole Miss's Ed Orgeron for, quite simply, being Ed Orgeron.

GEORGIA

I've been to Athens, Georgia, more times as an adult than I have any other SEC town outside the state of Tennessee. Primarily, this is because one of my best friends from high school, Doug, ended up in graduate school at the University of Georgia. I distinctly recall asking Doug why he decided on grad school in Athens. He didn't skip a beat in responding. "Wait until you see the girls in the bars." He had gone down there for a visit and had seen the girls dancing on top of the bars at last call. And he was sold.

"Wait until you see the girls in the bars," might be the best collegiate recruiting slogan I've ever heard. The appeal is universal (excepting, of course, Georgia's astute President Michael "No Cocktail Party" Adams who refuses to recognize the fact that there are actual bars in Athens or that students and alums might ever drink in such establishments). I have yet to meet any guy who visits Athens and doesn't mention the women and, judging from my experiences there, I can vouch for the fact that they ain't kiddin'. Everywhere you turn there is a girl in a black or red dress with a plunging neckline and red heels. The women probably account for at least half of Georgia's recruiting prowess. I can just picture Georgia football coach Mark Richt concluding letters to top football recruits, "P.S. Wait until you see the girls in the bars."

One man I meet attributes some of the attractiveness of the women to the Hope Scholarship (state-lottery-funded college scholarships). "Once the Hope came and everybody started getting scholarships there were a lot more SUVs and a lot more fake breasts." I think the economic term for this is a *free ride*.

Athens was also the first stop on the DDT where I would be experiencing things as a visiting fan as opposed to a home fan. Going to a road game in the SEC is a bit like being the guy in the leather jacket at the PETA convention. You're pelted with insults, told you're inhumane, and accused of liking jean shorts. But if you win on the road, all the home fans slink back whence they came and curse the referees while you sing your school's fight song on foreign soil. Basically, there's a high level of risk and a high level of reward.

On Friday, October 6, my friend Junaid, who accompanied me to Knoxville a few weeks before for the University of Tennessee's home opener against California and hosted me for a night when I was en route to Arkansas, drives in from Memphis. He arrives earlier than planned because the building next to his burned down and his law firm was flooded. This is the equivalent of a legal snow day. "I was planning on going into work and I started getting all these e-mails about how I should turn on the television. I could see flames, huge flames. It was great."

We take off that afternoon and, despite our early start, I manage to set us back by getting on the wrong interstate leaving Nashville to drive to Atlanta. This is rather inexcusable. It's made even more so because the interstate I choose, I-65 South, is a complete parking lot. Junaid doesn't say anything at the time, "I thought you were making a tactical decision to avoid going east and were planning on cutting across on 840." Junaid gives me way too much credit, as I have no idea what 840 even is. I inform him that he should exercise the same diligence in questioning my decision-making as driver as he would apply if Randy Sanders were still calling offensive plays for the Vols.

After a 250 mile, traffic-ridden drive, we arrive at our friend Kumar's house in Atlanta at eleven-forty that night. Kumar graduated from Vanderbilt Law School with us, and has spent the past two years changing jobs, hurling fantasy football insults with reckless imprecision, and embracing one harebrained money-making scheme after another. During law school Kumar loved to talk about how he wanted to put a laser inside every football to make certain the ball was adequately spotted on the field. "There's billions in it," he would say, while gleefully rubbing his hands together.

Kumar's newest scheme, as you may recall, is to scalp Tickle Me Elmo dolls on e-Bay this Christmas season. As soon as we arrive, he points to the twenty Tickle Me Elmo dolls stacked in his living room. Then, he pulls out the badge that he gets as a prosecutor for the state of Georgia. "People with badges get fifty percent off at Chick-fil-A," Kumar says proudly. I am impressed by the Chick-fil-A deal, and pepper him with questions about it. His fiancée rolls her eyes, "Kumar knew you were going to be so impressed by the Chick-fil-A thing," she says. In my opinion Chick-fil-A is the best thing to ever come out of Georgia. To

put it in Georgia Bulldog terms, Chick-fil-A is to fast-food restaurants what Herschel Walker was to college running backs.

We go out in Virginia Highlands, a popular going-out destination in Atlanta, to a bar called Hand in Hand where, ironically, there's barely enough space to hold even a beer in your
own hand, much less that of another human being. I would
have thought having hallways that are too narrow for two fat
women to pass each other would be a readily apparent design
flaw for a bar, but then, what do I know? At one point, a bouncer
comes up to us and asks to see our identification. Kumar shows
him the badge. The bouncer steps back and raises his hand.
"It's nice to have you here tonight, officer. You aren't armed,
are you?"

"No," Kumar says, "not tonight."

As soon as the bouncer leaves Kumar, who doesn't even own
a gun, giggles as he practices flashing us the badge. First, he does
it in an understated manner, "How about if I just open my wallet
like this, you can still see it, right?" Then, he does it more blatantly, flipping open his wallet and holding up the badge to
shoulder level so that the badges' metallic face captures the
flickering lights of the bar. "It's so cool," he says intently gazing
at the badge. Junaid and I pretend we are not jealous.

We come back at three in the morning, whereupon Kumar
asks us to take a picture of him amidst his twenty Tickle Me
Elmo dolls.

Just before bed, Kumar informs me, oh, by the way, that
he has blamed me for pornography his fiancée found on his
computer. "I told her you sent me the links. See, her sister
was visiting from out of town and using our computer. Usually
my fiancée only uses Internet Explorer, but I always use Firefox,

so I didn't worry about it. But her sister uses Firefox. So, I came back home the other day and they were sitting looking at all these pictures of naked women. My fiancée was like, 'What is this, Kumar?'

Every soccer mom's fantasy. At least the Elmo dolls are.

And without skipping a beat, I said, 'Oh, Clay sent me those. He loves pornography.'"

Then, his fiancée turned to her sister and said, "That's true. Clay does love pornography."

So, now, I'm the sicko sleeping on the couch who loves pornography. The truth of the matter was that I did send the initial link to Kumar. But only once. And only because he and I share an—how shall I put this delicately?—appreciation for amateur porn. Real women, real pictures. No money changing hands. To me, it's the love of the game factor. Like the difference between college and pro athletes.

Junaid and I arrive in Athens the next afternoon at around twelve thirty. We listen to the radio during the entire drive, and every single sportscaster picks Tennessee to win—even the Georgia fans. Junaid refuses to accept the fact that we are favorites. "I refuse to accept the fact that we are favorites," he says.

In order to fully experience the fine culinary delicacies of Athens, we eat at Zaxby's. As soon as Doug arrived in Athens, Zaxby's chicken-finger dipping sauce became his second favorite thing in the city. His first remained, not surprisingly, girls dancing on bars. I'd guess there are at least eighty-seven Zaxby's restaurants in the Athens area. Predictably, the place is packed.

Of all the cities in the SEC, Athens is my favorite to go out in so far. The main campus easily connects to the strip of bars and restaurants in the center of old Athens, and there are people everywhere and tons of places to eat and drink. A man spills his cooler in front of us, and his beers roll ominously into the street. "Oh, God," says his friend, as if he has just witnessed his wife being struck by a car. The beer is rescued and crisis is averted.

On campus, we meet up with Terry Mosteller, a UGA law student, and hang out at his tailgate, where we meet the man with the coolest hat in Athens: Kevin Davis. Kevin's hat is a 2002 replica of a Herschel-for-Heisman hat from 1982. (This will be the first mention of Herschel Walker by Georgia faithful.) Kevin has also managed to find some 1970's era red-and-black pants that he purchased at a place called Thread Zeppelin. He wears a sports jacket with a T-shirt underneath, and has sunglasses that look exactly like my ninety-nine cent Mapco Express shades.

As we are leaving, we receive our first taunt of the day, "That shirt's way too orange," says a large man dressed entirely in red to Junaid. "The only person to ever look good in orange was Charlie Brown and he was bald." Neither Junaid nor I have any idea what this taunt means. When I tell my wife, she says, "Charlie Brown wore yellow." So, I still don't have any idea. Georgia fans are not on their trash-talking game yet.

We see several UGA students playing beer pong on the quad. But, wait, that's not beer in their pyramids of plastic cups; it's Smirnoff Ice. "We don't really like beer," Juleah Pierzchala says by way of explanation. Amazingly, she is not immediately struck down by light-ning . . . or appointed new president of the student body by Presi-dent Adams. We watch them play a round, then move on. Smir-noff Ice Pong just doesn't have the same ring to it.

Smirnoff Ice Pong.

There are more men in red pants than there ever should be. I expected this, but what gets me the most is how many different varia-tions of red pants there are for men. I can understand maybe one company producing red pants, but a hundred? Is there some Isaac Mizrahi of red pants who keeps jumping from fashion house to fashion house convincing people that red pants are the new blue jeans? Hon-estly, what would happen if some guy wore red pants to your office? If the answer isn't "He'd receive so much ridicule he would spend the rest of the day working in his gym shorts," you need to find a new job.

We arrive at our law school friend Kevin Glidewell's tailgate. Glidewell is a graduate of Georgia who distinguished himself during law school by stating before every Tennessee-Georgia game for three years, "We don't even consider y'all rivals." To my eternal dismay, Georgia won all three years, proving him right. Glidewell is wearing a black polo shirt, because he assures me that there is a movement afoot to black out the stadium. And yet, Glidewell is the only person at his own tailgate in a black shirt. "I'm telling you," he says, "Erik Ainge is going to be over center and then he's going to look up into the stands and see me in this black shirt and just be terrified."

Another friend from law school, Mark Reeves, arrives with his wife. Neither is wearing black. Glidewell rolls his eyes. Like almost every Georgia fan we talk to, Reeves expects to lose. "Twenty to ten Vols," he predicts. I am now officially as disconcerted as Junaid is. It's like every Georgia fan has entered into a secret agreement designed to instill overconfidence in us.

Doug, my friend from high school who chose Athens for the girls, arrives. Doug and I met in seventh grade when he was one of the few white men with an Afro, and I was one of the few men on earth who spiked his hair in only the part. At that time, Doug also wore a large retainer, and was attempting to prove that a person could live only by drinking Coke. He refused to drink water. Literally refused.

Doug lived with his Mom in a converted flower shop. Fortunately for us, this meant that he was given the house's huge upstairs area, where all the flowers had been stored. This also meant that we could play the following sports games upstairs:

two-on-two six-foot basketball (you had to be barefoot and there was no dunking), Ping-Pong, sock basketball (on your knees beneath the six-foot basketball hoop but wearing socks wrapped around your knees to prevent rug burn), Wiffle Ball home-run contests over his mother's fancy Japanese screens (eventually we tore lots of holes through the screens, which we blamed on the dogs), wrestling competitions, goal line football challenge on our knees where you had to tackle the ball carrier, indoor soccer with small goals and small soccer balls, and one game where we took rolled up socks, stood completely still at a distance of about thirty feet, framed our cock and balls with both of our hands (we were clothed), and stood absolutely still while the other person wound up and tried to hit you in the crotch throwing the rolled up socks as hard as he could. And these were only the indoor games.

I vividly recall coming downstairs once to get a drink of water from the drinking fountain his mom had left installed from the days when their home was a flower shop and seeing his mom, Pam, sitting on the couch looking up at the ceiling that was warbling and bouncing above her as we played six-foot basketball upstairs. "What are you doing?" I asked.

"Waiting for the ceiling to collapse," she said.

But the ceiling never collapsed, which meant Doug and I survived, flourished into grown men, and are now able to hang around a tailgate in Athens, discussing the subject that has haunted man since the dawn of time: Georgia quarterback Joe Tereshinski III's arm length. "He has alligator arms," says one man. Five minutes of discussion ensue, during which time more than a couple of people attempt to demonstrate how short Tereshinski's arms are by folding back their own arms. Apparently, if Joe T. had arms a little longer he'd be able to throw the football over the mountains like Napoleon Dynamite's Uncle Rico.

Alligator arms aside, Tereshinski III personifies the generational unity of SEC fandom. That's because Tereshinski is a third-generation Georgia Bulldog football player. His grandfather played for Georgia in the early to mid-1940s and his father played in the 1970s. After Tereshinski III won an SEC Championship with Georgia in 2005, each of the three generations of Georgia Tereshinskis had won an SEC Championship during his career. Now, Joe T. will be trying to lead Georgia to his first SEC Championship as a starting quarterback. In addition to his short arms, Tereshinski is attempting to overcome a high-ankle-sprain injury that he suffered at South Carolina in September.

The alligator arms conversation is interrupted by the appearance of a small child, who is learning to walk. Ominously, said ambulation training is occurring directly alongside the satellite dish. The satellite dish is precariously balanced on a folded-over napkin that has somehow been necessary for us to get reception and watch the fourth quarter of the Arkansas-Auburn game. Glidewell and I turn and look at the kid. Neither of us is comfortable saying anything to him because he is so young. Then, it happens. The kid falls into the satellite dish, and uses it to balance himself. The television screen goes dark. Cursing ensues. Out of nowhere, a mother materializes. Walking practice will continue in the grass far from the satellite.

A Georgia fan has painted "Vol's Suck" on his back. Excessive apostrophe use by fans really entertains me. Especially when it's so flagrantly incorrect. Glidewell is unaffected by the error. "I think he's just saying that the Vols literally possess the word suck," he says.

We leave Glidewell's tailgate to visit the Clinch County Bulldog Club. They set up their tailgate at seven in the morning for each home game. While we are there, we watch on television as Florida's wunderkind Tim Tebow throws a jump touchdown pass to give Florida a 14–7 lead over LSU. If there is one thing that I've learned on the DDT, it is that every SEC fan base hates Florida. "Last time I went to Gainesville, they threw cups of urine on us," says Shannon Lanier. The only common bond between Georgia and UT fans all day long is a shared hate for Florida. At tailgate after tailgate across Athens, Vols and Dawgs unite to root against Florida. Junaid shakes his head, "Tim Tebow is well on his way to becoming the next Shane Battier," he says.

We head to the public bathroom across the street and, upon our appearance in orange, the Georgia fans begin to chant Bulldog cheers. This is a bit disconcerting while one is standing at the urinal. I'm all for taunting, but not when it makes the bathroom lines longer due to urinal stage fright. You try peeing while a grown man is barking behind you.

A Georgia fan comes up to Junaid and me outside the bathroom, "Don't worry," he says, "I had your back. I went into a bathroom in Gainesville once, and didn't think I was coming out alive." It's two hours until kickoff, and the alcohol is turning Athens into a buzzing mass of growling humanity.

We start to price tickets. One hundred dollars is the cheapest we see offered. Ominously, there are many more people seeking tickets than there are selling tickets. And, with my friend Doug in tow, we need three seats. Buying three seats is tough because usually scalpers sell in pairs or groups of four—except for Kumar, of course, who is happy to sell one Tickle Me Elmo at a time, if the price is right. While we're pricing tickets, a group of Georgia fans walk past us and one screams, "Go back to Rocky Top or wherever the hell you came from."

On the flip side, as we cross the campus a Georgia fan approaches me and says, "I just want to go ahead and congratulate you on kicking our ass." Then he shakes my hand. The Georgia Bulldogs are the defending SEC Champions yet, based on their fans, you'd think they were Vanderbilt about to kickoff against the Chicago Bears. You definitely wouldn't think Georgia had the nation's best defense in terms of points allowed.

For the next half hour, the three of us walk around with our hands raised in the universal sign of ticket need. We rotate the responsibility for holding up the hands and negotiate over and over again with different scalpers. We almost make a deal with a hickish white guy with four teeth. He has three seats together and is asking one hundred dollars apiece. His sales pitch? "The black guys are asking one hundred twenty-five dollars." Classy.

But, attend any SEC game and the ticket sales on the street will almost entirely be done by black men. Which is all the more surprising because, once you get inside the stadiums, the crowd is almost entirely white. This is changing some (witness Junaid and several of my other nonwhite friends with me on the DDT), but the vast majority of the crowds in SEC stadiums are still white. Of course, the majority of the SEC football players are black. Which is a seismic change from just thirty-five years ago, when many SEC schools fielded almost entirely white teams. I expect that as the years continue to pass the SEC crowds will come to reflect greater diversity.

Free of sociological ruminations, we continue to price tickets up and down the raised walkway alongside Sanford Stadium. Part of our problem, we learn, is that Tennessee is by far the best home opponent for the Bulldogs this year. Georgia's SEC home games this year are Vanderbilt, Mississippi State, and Tennessee. So, Tennessee holds the most interest. Plus, Georgia is currently undefeated and ranked in the top ten.

So, with forty-five minutes left till kickoff, we pull the trigger and pony up one hundred dollars each for three seats together in the lower level. Face value is thirty-five dollars. Doug makes us promise not to tell his wife what we paid. I promise him that my lips are sealed.

We enter the stadium, and are immediately confronted by a drunk girl jumping up and down exclaiming, "I just met John Rocker." She repeats herself several times. This is probably the most excited anyone has ever been to meet the former Atlanta Braves closer, who is one of the most famous racists in America.

Our seats are in section 102, row 56, around the ten-yard line in the lower level. Junaid and I are landlocked by Georgia fans, but on the positive side we are not very far from the UT cheering section. The stadium is rapidly filling and already it is loud. I head to the bathroom where I stand behind several members of the Tennessee band. Unfortunately, none of them play the cymbals. Yep, the band members have to use the regular bathrooms at opposing stadiums. For my money, that's much tougher than actually playing in the game.

Georgia elects to go with an understated pregame opening by having three men parachute into the stadium trailing the American flag, a University of Georgia flag, and a state of Georgia flag, respectively, as well as huge clouds of red smoke. This spectacle provokes an absolute frenzy among the Georgia faithful.

I am unimpressed by the exhibition, and turn my attention to more interesting matters by asking Doug whether he thinks the spiky black dog collar on Uga, Georgia's bulldog mascot, makes him look better or worse, "Oh, it definitely makes him look tougher," Doug says. There are lots of grown men barking around me. Evidently, they agree.

Uga the bulldog (his name derived from the University of Georgia) is literally on ice. Says Doug, "I still don't understand why Uga always has to sit on a bag of ice. And his doghouse is air-conditioned on top of that. It can be like thirty degrees and Uga's still got a bag of ice. Why is this?" His query is interrupted . . . Herschel Walker is on the Jumbotron for the first time and the crowd has erupted in cheers.

Eventually, I learn that, because Uga is an English bulldog, he is extremely susceptible to the heat and humidity of the American South. Apparently it's not uncommon for English bulldogs to fall victim to heat stroke, which, as you can imagine, would be tough on kids (not to mention grown male fans) were this to happen during a game. This particular Uga, Uga VI, has been the Georgia mascot since 1999. His five forefathers, and I am not making this up, are buried in a mausoleum outside Sanford Stadium. This is a family crypt of sorts, since each Uga is the son of the prior mascot. Uga I began to roam the sideline in 1956. Georgia has been known as the Bulldogs, however, since 1920 which provides clear evidence that the Georgians from 1920 to 1956 were extremely lazy in procuring an actual bulldog. There is no doubt, however, how proud Uga I would be if he could see his great-great-great-grandson, Uga VI, sitting atop his bag of ice today.

"Glory, glory to old Georgia and to hell with Tennessee," sings the entire stadium. I find Georgia's creative modification of "The Battle Hymn of the Republic"—the song, after all, that celebrates the triumph of the North in the Civil War—particularly amusing, in light of the many Confederate flags I saw earlier in the day. Somehow, I bet the loudest singers in the crowd are flying Confederate flags, unaware of the irony of their actions.

Herschel Walker makes his second appearance on the Jumbotron. The crowd explodes in cheers again. Earlier I saw Herschel's likeness on ads for both a bank and a condo project in Athens. The man is everywhere, and Georgia fans cheer him deliriously each time his image appears.

Walker won the 1982 Heisman Trophy, and led the Bulldogs to the national championship in 1980, his freshman year. Among other things, he is famous for the strenuous workout routine he started doing on his own accord in high school: two thousand five hundred sit-ups and one thousand five hundred push-ups each morning. Since he turned pro early after a junior year in which he won the Heisman Trophy, Walker's mystique here in Georgia has only continued to grow. His number thirty-four jersey was retired not only for football, but for every single sport in which Georgia fields a varsity team. It's altogether possible he is the most beloved player of the past thirty years by any fan base. My favorite quote of Walker's? When asked if he ever got tired of carrying the ball thirty times in a game, he replied, "The ball ain't heavy."

It's five minutes until kickoff and exceedingly loud. The blackout appears to have won over at best five percent of the stadium. Junaid and I try to pick out Glidewell in the crowd. Everyone else is in their regular red.

I realize the term is overused but, in this case, the stadium really is electric. After hours and hours of tailgating, the seven-forty-five kickoff for an ESPN telecast has finally arrived, and there is a collective intensity and tension among the 92,748 in attendance. Our section stands. We will remain standing for every play of the entire game.

By kickoff, both Junaid and I are trembling with anticipation. "You know," Junaid screams over the din of the crowd, "if we can find a way to win this game we'll have won two out of three over the damn Bulldogs." I nod. After the early season loss to Florida that still makes Junaid and me sick, if UT is to have any kind of season at all, we absolutely have to win this game. Unfortunately, Georgia strikes first with a field goal that sends the Bulldog fans into a cacophony of barks.

But, before the barking can become completely overwhelming, UT scores a touchdown to take a 7–3 lead. For a moment, the bedlam is quieted. And, then, an onslaught of cheering begins. First Georgia converts a third and fifteen followed by a third and twelve en route to a touchdown to take a 10–7 lead. Then, in typical Georgia versus Vols fashion, Mikey Henderson, a play-making junior punt returner for Georgia, strikes a blow for grown men still called Mikey everywhere by going eighty-six yards for a punt return touchdown. It's 17–7 Georgia and the entire stadium is one surging tide of red ecstasy. In fact, it's so crazy, Herschel Walker is on the Jumbotron again. I'm sick to my stomach. Before I've even had time to comprehend my team being down 10–7 we're already down 17–7. Doug taps me on the shoulder, "Mikey Henderson," he says simply, then he laughs at me.

Here is what being a fan of UT's special teams against Georgia is like: As soon as Georgia's player hits the seam you turn from the actual play and start looking for flags. I didn't even see the Georgia touchdown because I was too busy imploring the refs to throw a flag. Junaid says, "All day long, we knew they were going to get a punt return for a touchdown on us." This is true; we had been telling every Georgia fan that they were starting plus seven thanks to the inevitable punt return for a touchdown. And then, of course, it happened. UT special teams motto: Punt the ball, wave at air, hope for flags.

Then, Georgia scores again and, with a few minutes left in the second quarter, UT is down 24–7. Joe T. appears to have borrowed Dominique Wilkins' arms (the Human Highlight Reel, a former Bulldog basketball player, is introduced on the field at one point during the first half). Suddenly, the man with alligator arms can do no wrong. Junaid turns to me and says simply, "This is not good." It seems like every player on the Georgia sideline is jumping in celebration while, on my own team's sideline, no one is moving at all.

I've seen my team lose lots of time, but rarely has it been accompanied by an avalanche of grown men barking. This is the rough equivalent of bombing the SAT while someone consistently rakes her hands across the chalkboard. I'm beginning to think this is the worst one hundred dollars I've spent since losing my math textbook in college and having to buy another one.

Just as I'm about to accept a long night of derision from Doug, UT drives and scores a minute or so before the half ends to make the score 24–14. Junaid and I exchange a fairly covert high five. After all, we're still losing by ten. Included in the drive was one fourth-down conversion during which Junaid and I both screamed for an attempted field goal. The score serves notice that the game will not be a complete rout . . . at least not yet. It also features a first and goal at the Georgia one that terrifies every Vol fan who remembers the game in 2003. In that game, Georgia returned a fumbled snap the length of the field just before the end of the first half to take a 20–7 lead. This disastrous play caused more dogs to be kicked in Tennessee than any other single play in the twenty-first century.

During halftime, I realize it's getting cool in Athens. The temperature dips below sixty for the first time on the DDT. Junaid turns to me and says, "Our chances of winning are twenty percent at best." We both stare glumly at the bands as they move across the field. When your team is losing, halftime seems as if it lasts for several hours.

UT opens the second half with a brilliant directional kick that pins Georgia at their five. A couple of plays later the Vols intercept a tipped pass that seems to hang forever in the air before a UT player cradles it to the ground. Several plays later, the Vols take the ball in for a touchdown. On this interception, Junaid and I both scream louder than we have all night. Suddenly it's 24–21 with 11:47 remaining in the third quarter. As Junaid and I rejoice, we can actually feel the uncomfortable stirring in the crowd. Several Georgia fans in our section give us angry glares as we celebrate among them. "Fucking UT," screams one Georgia fan two rows behind us.

Perhaps to help ease the discomfort of Bulldog fans, the man in charge of the Jumbotron plasters only hot girls on the screen during a commercial break, for which he deserves credit. Of course, this is tantamount to shooting fish in a barrel, but still, I've never seen such steamy Jumbotron scenes at any stadium before. Usually you get babies and guys with painted letters on their chest. At Georgia, you get only knockouts.

Doug comes back from trying to buy something at the concession stand and says the UT band was making the line too long. Yep, the band stands in the concession line, too. He notices the scoreboard and sees that UT has already scored. "Uh oh," he says.

On the Jumbotron we watch a video tribute to Uga III, who served as mascot from 1972 to 1981. According to the tribute, Uga III presided over the most victories over ranked opponents (twelve) and was mascot when Georgia won their last National Championship in 1980. The best part is that the announcer continuously attributes the team's victories to Uga III himself ("He went . . ."). After this tribute, I keep picturing Uga III lining up in shoulder pads at defensive tackle.

Back down on the field the teams trade field goals. It's 27–24 Georgia. Despite making a run, UT has been unable to catch the Bulldogs yet. Then, UT intercepts another Tereshinski pass and Junaid and I engage in unrestrained jubilation. Multiple fives and a couple of shoves, definite screaming. Perhaps an alligator arms reference as well. As solidly as Joe T. played in the first half, when he could do no wrong, Joe T. has played that poorly in the second half.

The third quarter ends with the Vols at the Georgia fifteen and no barking from the Georgia faithful. Junaid and I are jumping up and down in the stands. We're close, oh so tantalizingly close, to storming back from a seventeen-point deficit and reclaiming the lead. On the field below, the Vol offense is also jumping around with enthusiasm while the entire Georgia crowd is standing, holding up four fingers to signify the start of the fourth quarter.

At the start of the fourth quarter, Erik Ainge passes fifteen yards to Robert Meachem in the left corner of the end zone and the Vols reclaim the lead, 31–27. Around me, there is nary a bark. Like Lazarus, the Vols have risen. Junaid and I explode in uproarious yells. I attempt to send Glidewell, clad in his black shirt, a taunting text message on the other side of the stadium, but can't receive a signal.

Herschel Walker is on the Jumbotron again. Doug leans over and says, "I keep waiting to hear, 'Hi, I'm Herschel Walker and I just finished fucking your wife.' Wild cheers. 'Go Dawgs.' "

Five plays later, UT blocks a kick in the end zone and recovers for a touchdown. It's 38–27 Vols, and Junaid and I come undone. I don't ever remember cheering so loudly in person. Certainly not on the road. Our fortunes have completely reversed themselves. We've outscored Georgia 31–3 since going down by seventeen. Below us the UT crowd is a roaring orange mosh pit in an otherwise silent stadium. UT's special teams have scored something other than a field goal for the first time since 1947. Georgia has now given up more points in this game alone than their defense had given up all season. Beside me, Doug is in shock. As if he just called his wife at home and Herschel Walker answered the phone.

Just as the first despondent Georgia fans begin to file out, UT's special teams strike again. Georgia goes ninety-nine yards for a touchdown on the kickoff return. The Georgia fans reclaim their barks. It's 38–33 after a missed two-point conversion. Like many in the stadium, Junaid and I are speechless. "Just kick the damn ball out of bounds and give them the ball at the thirty-five," I yell.

UT takes the ball and scores on the ensuing possession before missing the extra point. It's 44–33 Vols, and the entire stadium is quiet, almost as if fans on both sides are trying to catch their breath. Junaid and I can barely speak because our voices are so hoarse from cheering. UT begins kicking the ball short in an effort to actually tackle someone on kick returns. I silently thank the heavens for this coaching decision.

Joe T. is sacked, and UT recovers his fumble. Junaid and I debate in the stands whether it was a fumble. Being UT fans, we are inclined to believe that it was, in fact, a fumble. There is a long review of the play before the referee comes on the field and confirms that my Vols have possession of the football. Junaid and I exult. "Two out of three," I scream. The Vols march down the field where they finally put the game away by scoring on an Arian Foster run. It's 51–33 and the Georgia fans are all leaving. In thirty-three glorious minutes, my Volunteers have scored forty-four points on the road against one of their archrivals. Rarely has victory been so sweet.

Junaid and I make our way down to the UT cheering section along with other Vol fans arriving from all corners of the stadium. The game is not yet over but, already, the celebration has begun. No Vol fan can fathom the wonderful offensive plays that have somehow conspired to put that many points on our side of the scoreboard. It is, quite simply, unbelievable. A second half where UT could literally do no wrong.

All around us, UT fans are taking pictures of the scoreboard, as if they might later need photographic evidence of the rout. Several UT fans reach out and snatch pieces of the hedges that surround the field as souvenirs. Hedge warfare has begun.

The game ends, and Georgia immediately cuts off the scoreboard. The Vol players join the Vol fans in the corner of the end zone in a raucous celebration. The visitor has conquered. A man beside me begins screaming, "Which way to the sorority houses?"

Amidst the bedlam, I meet another Vol fan, Peggy Lewis, a middle-aged blonde woman from Nashville who is clad entirely in orange and is holding up a faux newspaper headline that already bears the final score of the game. As soon as the game ends, there are tons of people hawking five dollar final score printouts. Peggy Lewis holds hers up proudly, "I lost a finger changing a tire before the California game this year," she says, "but I still traveled." She is rocking ever so gently to the rhythm of an almost empty stadium filled with the sounds of Rocky Top.

Yep, a finger. "Our husbands don't travel to away games," she tells me. "We're the real fans." Peggy is one of several thousand Vol fans who are left in an otherwise empty stadium. Even after the band stops playing, several fans don't want to leave

For SEC fans, losing a finger is no obstacle to attending games.

their seats near the field, "If I leave here," says one man, "the score might change." We know exactly how he feels.

The next afternoon on the drive back I tell Junaid, "Last night I dreamed we scored fifty-one points." Junaid nods, "Dreamed the same thing myself," he says.

'BAMA BANGS

The day after the 'Bama Bangs Wikipedia entry* went up, my wife confronted me at home. "I think you had 'Bama Bangs at our wedding," she said.

My wife has still not gotten over the haircut that I got three days before our wedding. Which is understandable, because my hair was shaped in an awkward bowl cut for all of our photos. Come to think of it, my life could probably be described as a series of awkward bowl cuts. I show up, turn over my ten dollars to the fine craftsmen at Supercuts and leave looking like I am seven years old. Since marriage (and this is completely true), when I go to Supercuts, my wife sends me with a photograph of myself to present to the haircutter so I don't come back looking like I just danced a duet with a weed wacker.

Not content to merely allege that I had 'Bama Bangs, my wife pulled a picture off our dresser and confronted me. "These are 'Bama Bangs," she said, wielding the picture before me like a sword and pointing to the bangs in the photo. You can imagine my horror at the allegation. Having 'Bama Bangs myself would make me the most hypocritical person on earth. I'd be like the follicular version of Reverend Pat Robertson. Plainly, this would not do.

After convincing my wife that my wedding hairstyle, while horrible, was not 'Bama Bangs, I headed to the computer where I found an e-mail from Auburn grad Zach Peagler inquiring, "Clay, do I have 'Bama Bangs? Do you? What other options do

* If you look on Wikipedia now, you will not see this entry. I believe that dual Alabama and Auburn grad and Wikipedia founder Jimmy Wales pulled it down in a killer coup and dastardly move to protect the state of Alabama's honor.

we have? I've gotten my hair cut roughly the same way since I was six and have never thought that I have bangs, but now I'm convinced that I do."

Rather than explain and delineate 'Bama Bangs to the world at large, as was my intent, I had managed to confuse many who hadn't previously experienced 'Bama Bangs as to what exactly BBs are. Clearly, the world could not rest until I took a shot at explaining 'Bama Bangs with the detached scientific precision for which I have attained a measure of renown (honorable mention in the seventh grade science fair at Martin Luther King Magnet).

I ask you to come along on a journey into the Southern male bang psyche. Ideally, this inquiry will become collaborative (the human genome wasn't decoded by only one person) with everyone contributing his or her knowledge. I believe it was Sir Isaac Newton who said, "If I have seen far, it is because I have stood on the shoulders of giants." What Newton didn't say was that he also saw far because he did not have to worry about 'Bama Bangs blocking his vision.

All legitimate scientific inquiries begin with a definition. So here is mine: 'Bama Bangs is a hairstyle popular among Southern men between the ages of twelve and twenty-six. It is characterized by an overabundance of bangs that lie upon each other like feathers from a mallard's flank and completely cover the forehead. While appearing to be extremely thick, the bangs are often lifted by wisps of air, giving the appearance that the hair might actually be attempting to fly away.

'Bama Bangs are particularly prevalent among Southern male athletes and adolescents. They are rumored to account for approximately 38 percent of all teenage male traffic accidents in the southern United States, and Geico has recently begun requiring a 'Bama Bangs rider on all car insurance policies. It's rumored that former Alabama quarterback Brodie Croyle has recently been elected high priest of the 'Bama Bangs cabal and now presides over secret meetings. But this has not been confirmed.

Now that we've got the definition covered, it's important to acknowledge that 'Bama Bangs are slowly infiltrating the country.

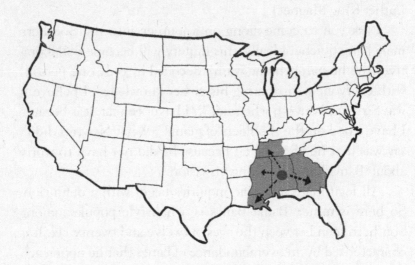

While I initially rooted 'Bama Bangs in the state of Alabama, I have since learned that they may have actually been born elsewhere. I took a poll among the readers of my column and shall now defer to their wisdom.

Wes Brister stated: "'Bama Bangs, while most prevalent in Alabama, have their roots in Mississippi. The hairstyle is referred to as *the Delta Boy Swoop* and is one of two hairstyles available in the area between the Mississippi River, I-55, Memphis and Jackson (the other is bald). As for the hairstyle's migration to central Alabama, I cannot opine, but as an insurance agent working in Birmingham, it's as important to doing business as a country club membership."

Rich Varner offered an echo of this opinion: "'Bama Bangs (aka *the Southern Swoop*, aka the *Jackson Swoosh*) . . . is not just an Alabama thing but it's definitely a characteristic of the region. It takes no hair product, which is exactly the point because that's gay . . . and for Yankees. By the way, in your pictures you appear to be wearing Adidas sandals, so I'm not sure if you can make fashion statements."

According to several e-mails I received, 'Bama Bangs have also crossed over from Alabama into southwestern Tennessee. Most people traced this migration via Jackson or Memphis.

Reader Shane Roberts wrote: "Clay, I just thought you might find it interesting that the 'do you christened 'Bama Bangs has been alive and well for over a decade in your own backyard. I myself sported the look while in high school back in the early '90s in Jackson. I picked it up from older athletes when I noticed it was perfect for athletic endeavors for guys who still wanted hair but as much breathability as one could muster. It showed nicely poking out from football helmets and ball caps and gave a free-throw shooter something to casually toss from his eyes as he toed the line and did that backspin dribble thing with the ball.

"All the teams I faced in high school from around west Tennessee also sported the look. . . . I also have two younger cousins, the eldest of which, true to form, played ball and pimped the backwards Tennessee Tophat while in high school. The youngest cousin is just now a freshman and while he doesn't quite have it yet (more like a ducktail up front), give him time. I know when he makes varsity, the bangs will happen."

Readers also informed me that 'Bama Bangs could be found in Georgia, Louisiana, and, alarmingly, North Carolina, signaling northern migration. Thankfully, the hairstyle has not yet leapt across the Atlantic into Europe. We know this thanks to Auburn grad Joseph Walker, who reported on 'Bama Bangs from Budapest, where he lives and follows the SEC by listening to the games online: "About the 'Bama Bangs becoming trendy in Central Europe—we have suffered through terrible shades of dyed red hair, and enormous high platform shoes. But now the girls (and guys) seem to have the fashion thing moving in the right direction. So, don't off load bad fashion on us. We'll stick with the short skirts and tall boots, thank you very much." Several readers also offered their own names for this hairstyle.

C. Jones of Birmingham said: "They are not 'Bama Bangs, they are 'tellums'—'mullet' spelled backwards. This time, the party's in front." After diligent research, I have determined that the name "tellum" has already been appropriated by hipsters.

Joshua Pruitt wrote: "I am from Atlanta and used to go to Auburn (around the turn of the millennium) and ended up great friends with one of these folks. Only we call him Unibang since his bang sweeps all the way from one side of his head to the other while still being as thick and long as you described. As for the name, it was kind of a play on Frau's lesbian lover Unibrow from *Austin Powers*. He still gets mad to this day when we call him that but he keeps on rockin' the unibang." I also heard from Southerners now living in California, New York, Michigan, and Montana who had spotted the hairstyle infringing upon their borders. Two of the readers said they were

so emboldened by recognizing the hairstyle that they each approached a complete stranger and engaged him in conversation. Yep, both men were from Alabama.

However, all great theories of science ultimately require a
hypothesis. Best I recall from ninth-grade science class, a hypothesis is basically an educated guess. So, here are eight hypotheses to explain why 'Bama Bangs exist and how they have
come to steep the region in follicular pride.

1. Women sleep with men more often who have 'Bama Bangs and
   thus more children are born with a genetic predisposition to believe the forehead should be covered, particularly during the
   time of optimum fertility (sixteen-to-thirty-five).
2. Alabama, with more hilly terrain than Mississippi, is more palatable for 'Bama Bangs because the bangs provide warmth in the
   colder winters. Hence, like kudzu in Georgia, they have flourished here.
3. In the event of an accident (car, tractor, loss to Big 10 school,
   etc.), 'Bama Bangs
   cushion the forehead
   allowing more men
   with 'Bama Bangs to
   survive. Thus, sur-
   vival of the fittest is
   tilted in favor of men
   with BBs.
4. The bangs are a re-
   pudiation of North-
   ern hairstyles which
   seem to focus on
   spiking the front of

One 'Bama Bangs.

the hair and always leaving the forehead uncovered.

5. Abraham Lincoln had a large and prominent forehead and 'Bama Bangs were initially a repudiation of Lincoln.

Two 'Bama Bangs.

6. Southern men were jealous of Southern women's poofy bangs in the 1980s and sought their own bangerific creations.

7. Southern men are more likely to suffer from receding hairlines and BB's allow the receding hair

Three 'Bama Bangs.

battle to last up to forty-three years.

8. Women sleep less often with men who have 'Bama Bangs. (In seventh-grade science class at Martin Luther King Magnet in Nashville, we were instructed to craft antihypotheses. I have no idea why. In honor of that assignment, I have continued it here.)

Since we are engaged in a scientific experiment here, I would welcome further hypotheses, sightings, and 'Bama Bangs analysis. Feel free to use footnotes, but remember to cite only reputable scientific journals in your work. Remember, this is not a fly-by-the-seat-of-your-pants investigation; this is serious stuff.

7

LSU

About the time I started drinking a daiquiri called the TKO (short for the boxing term "technical knockout"), and chasing it with beer because the daiquiri was so strong, a girl walked by our tailgate with a yellow boa constrictor named Jasmine draped over her shoulders. At any other time and place, the appearance of a yellow boa constrictor would signify the end times. At LSU, it's simply another excuse to have a drink. Pour one out for the snake. Yep, it was at this point that I realized people in the state of Louisiana take their drinking and their partying very seriously. After all, it was four in the afternoon on a Saturday, the LSU football game was still three hours away, and we'd already been tailgating for several hours. But, wait, before I can get my picture taken with a yellow snake that would make Jake "The Snake" Roberts jealous, I have to tell you how we got down to Baton Rouge for stop six of the DDT.

• • •

On the previous Wednesday, my law school friend Tardio e-mailed his college friend and current roommate Keven and me to inform us that we had mistakenly booked a room at the Baton Rouge La Quinta for two weeks later than when we are actually going to be in Baton Rouge. This error was made all the more glaring by the fact that this was a collaborative mistake; Tardio had booked the room while we were all three present. So, we scrambled, and somehow managed to find a room at some place called the University Inn and Conference Center.

Tardio and I met the first week in law school and proceeded to spend the next three years drinking together at least three nights a week. He and his college friend Keven now live together just off Vanderbilt's campus, where Tardio laments the fact that he is no longer either an undergrad or a law student. He is the only man I've ever known who started lying about his age when he was only twenty-three. He said he was twenty-two then. After he had been practicing law for a year, he met a girl on a dance floor and in the silence following a song from the live band, she asked, "What do you do?" For once, Tardio was completely honest. "I'm a lawyer," he said. "Nun-uh," said the girl, "you look like the kind of guy who works in those cell-phone kiosks." Somewhere, the admissions officer for Vanderbilt Law School just shot himself.

On Thursday, I talk to John Purdy, who was an athletic trainer for twenty years at LSU (from 1978 to 1998) but now lives in Nashville. Recently, Purdy had been rehabbing my wife from a foot injury and, fortunately for me, this led to him offering to help show me around LSU via his friends.

John tells me that in the mid-1980s, he and a friend went for a late-night walk in Tiger Stadium on the night before a game. During their walk, the police suddenly arrived and set up floodlights that pierced the night sky and interrupted the walk. "We were really upset. Saying, 'What are these yahoos doing with all these lights?'" They continued strolling until they were informed that Tulane's students were playing a prank and had managed to free Mike the Tiger from his cage. Yep, a real live tiger . . . loose in the stadium. Later, Mike the Tiger (named after a former athletic trainer) was tranquilized in the bleachers. "Those were fun times," John said, clapping his hands together. "Another time, a trainer locked himself in Mike's cage because he didn't want to get deported."

John Purdy also tells me that Tiger Stadium was originally built as a dorm on the outside because Governor Huey Long didn't have approval to build a stadium. Instead, Purdy said, Long hoodwinked everyone by building a football stadium inside the dormitory. This story isn't true (although there were dorm rooms in the stadium) but the story retains such appeal to LSU fans that I'm told you'll hear it everywhere. "It's a crazy, crazy place," he says.

Back in Nashville, John introduces me to his wife, Elaine Bird Purdy. Elaine had season tickets to LSU that she shared with her first husband, now deceased. "When he died, I went to the stadium to change the season tickets to my name and they asked me for a copy of my husband's death certificate," she said. Luckily, Elaine knew the season ticket manager and was able to talk to him. He switched the tickets to her name and explained that LSU's season ticket ownership had dragged them into the courts tons of times. After they switched Elaine's tickets, the ticket manager pulled her aside. "Could you maybe fax us that death certificate?" he asked, slightly embarrassed by the request. "And he was at the funeral!" she exclaimed.

The final thing John Purdy shares with me is his favorite quote from former Louisiana governor Edwin Edwards: "Some people like to kiss babies, I like to kiss the babies' mommas." I smile and think to myself: If Edwin Edwards had twenty-inch rims and gold grills, he could have founded Southern rap in the 1970s. But, back then, lines like these got Edwards elected to four terms as governor. His most famous quote is, "The only way I can lose this election is if I'm caught in bed with either a dead girl or a live boy."

Tardio, Keven, and I are flying to Baton Rouge to watch the Kentucky-LSU game. We leave Nashville on the same plane as the crew of SEC refs who will be calling the game. We recognize them from television and also because they are carrying a variety of SEC apparel. Tardio points to one of them, "ten to one black jeans is the crew chief," he says. "You don't wear black jeans unless you're the boss."

Keven works for Sprint, though none of us has any idea what he does for them. This is roughly his title, "The assistant to the regionalized undersecretary for phonetic impressions utilizing capabilities inherent in mass communications to defecate." Not surprisingly, Keven is a cell-phone wizard. Really, the coolest thing he can do is leave voice messages for people without their phones ever ringing. He's like the Voldemort of Sprint. Outside of work, he does dumb things like purchase jeans that already have holes in them. I ask him why he did this. "Preripped jeans are just cool," he says. Also, and this is key, within five minutes of arriving in any bar, Keven orders a round of Jager bombs.

We have a layover in Memphis's 1950s-era airport and sit around waiting two hours for our flight to Baton Rouge. Tardio attempts to aid me in surfing the Internet on his BlackBerry until he gives up on me for accidentally signing out about fourteen times. "Just tell me where you want to go," he says. "You suck at technology." While Tardio pulls up my e-mail, Keven counters Tardio's technological expertise by pointing out that his and Tardio's power was shut off for lack of payment earlier in the week. Tardio shrugs. "It wasn't that big of a deal, we just had to pull a lever and turn the power back on." I'm pretty confident this makes Tardio the first Vanderbilt lawyer of the twenty-first century to have his power turned off. "They usually give you a couple of warnings," he says. "Who knew?"

Incidentally, when she heard that his power had been shut off, Tardio's mom palmed him sixty dollars the next time they went out to dinner. "For the power," she mouthed. For the record, Tardio's salary as a practicing attorney is not insubstantial. Just barely enough to cover electricity. And running water in really good months.

On our flight to Baton Rouge, Northwest Airlines gives me a choice of orange juice or water in those tiny plastic cups that look like they've previously served as urine-testing repositories. My orange juice is completely frozen. I try to bang the congealed mass of orange ice against my tray table to dislodge a piece and wake up three people. I tilt up the cup and the slightly melted orange goo falls into my lap. Perfect.

We arrive at our hotel in Baton Rouge after a cab ride with an eighty-three-year-old driver. Our hotel, the University Inn and Conference Center, vaguely resembles Angola Prison. "Oh, man," Tardio says, "this is the only place on earth that makes the La Quinta Inn look like the Ritz-Carlton."

Comfort Inn has actually gone so far as to pull its name off our hotel because it wasn't up to their standards. There is one elevator and the doors have curse words scratched into them, alongside what looks like fingernail scratches. Upon arrival in our room, we discuss whether the hotel staff would give out shivs with the room key if you slipped them twenty dollars and Keven ridicules Tardio for wearing boat shoes. The boat shoes ridicule has been going on for several months now. Thankfully, the boat shoes offer me an opportunity to break out our newest insult. "They're pretty bicurious," I say.

Everything that used to be gay is bicurious. In these politically correct times it's a much more socially palatable insult. Plus, and this is key, how much worse does it make you feel if you have a new shirt and your buddy says, "Nice shirt. Very bicurious." Much worse, right? See, calling something gay is played out. No power there anymore. But bicurious? I'm telling you, it's the sexually derogatory gold bullion of the twenty-first century.

We take a cab ride to the riverboat casinos in downtown Baton Rouge after drinking in the room for about forty-five minutes. On the plus side, for the first time since he bought them, Tardio will actually be on a boat with his boat shoes. On the negative side, it's a boat that never moves. At six on Friday afternoon we arrive. "Boat shoes going on the boat," Tardio announces.

The place is jammed. If you're a gambling woman who weighs less than two hundred pounds and has at least one eye to see with, you could be considered hot at this place. Somehow every dealer is an Asian woman. Evidently Louisiana borders Cambodia. We start gambling.

You know how in Vegas they do a decent job getting smoke eradicated from the casino? Yeah, not so much here. The casino could easily double as the smokestack of a factory. I can barely open my eyes. Keven, a former smoker, takes a deep breath, "It smells great," he says, with a satisfied smile on his face. We're getting killed at the tables, so we head back across the riverboat walkway to the so-called best restaurant in the place.

It's called Shuck's and there is hardly anyone there. Tardio sits down and orders a massive seafood plate while Keven and I opt for hamburgers, which seem safer. We're all drunk and, by the time the seafood plate arrives, we all realize we've made a bad decision. "God," Tardio says after one bite of a shrimp that looks like it was plucked out of the sea at least a year ago, "this place is awful." Somehow, Tardio's meal ends up costing over fifty dollars. "Fifty fucking dollars at Shuck's," Tardio says and just shakes his head. When we return to the blackjack tables, our Asian dealer is puzzled. "You didn't like Shuck's? Everyone likes Shuck's," she informs us. Everyone is a damn fool.

Our law school friend Kelly (previously my host in Birmingham before the second stop on the DDT) has arrived in Baton Rouge and is wondering as to our whereabouts. "I've been looking for your hotel for an hour," he says. "I'm giving up." Turns out, Kelly was very close. He stopped next door at a restaurant called Mestizo. Yep, the restaurant is actually called *mestizo*. Isn't this the rough equivalent of naming a place Mulatto? I guess it beats the previous restaurant name idea: "Mexican guy bangs white woman."

We all meet up at a bar called JL's in Tigerland, which is, in a word, fantastic. Kelly arrives with several Tri-Delts from LSU. "I told them to look for the old guys in the bar," he says. Keven taps me, "It's like Shane's World invaded here," he says.

For most of law school, we made fun of Kelly, because he's a decent looking guy, and yet, sometimes when he looks in the mirror he sees the equivalent of an extremely obese woman covered in acne. So intent was Kelly's dissatisfaction that somehow we ended up calling him KWo (his first initial and the first two letters of his last name) because we wanted to instill in him the confidence that if he were a girl he'd be as attractive as JLo. As you can imagine, this nickname was and is a favorite of his. Other times, however, Kelly is amazingly confident, bordering on the cockiest person you've ever met. At these times he is known as Cocky KWo. The best time of all is when these personalities reveal themselves at the same time. Tonight he is Cocky KWo because, thanks to his girlfriend's younger sister attending LSU, he has arrived in the bar with a gaggle of sorority girls. He leans over to me, "Keep me away from this girl," he says blatantly pointing to the hottest in the group, "she wants to have sex with me."

The twenty-seven-year-old Tardio immediately approaches one of the Tri-Delts. "How old do you think I am?" he asks. "Twenty-five," she replies. He takes a step back and raises his arms, "Twenty-five, good God. Hell no, I'm twenty-four." They exchange high-fives and Tardio rubs her head. By the time I turn around Keven has ordered a round of Jager bombs. "Drink up, ladies," he says. Kelly looks at his drink. It's his birthday and he has just turned twenty-eight. Of course, none of us knew until he told me. This calls for many more rounds of shots, and then my notes get too sketchy for me to read. . . .

At ten the next morning, we are awakened by Baton Rouge-born Kerry Guidry pounding on the door of our hotel room. Kerry attended Kentucky undergrad with Tardio and Keven, but his family lives in Louisiana. None of us have been answering our cell phones, and the front desk has told Kerry what room we are in. "I told them you wouldn't mind," he says. This same logic has probably led to fifteen murders at our hotel in the past five years.

When I come out of the shower written in steam on the mirror is, "Clay's sunglasses are bicurious." Nice. Shortly thereafter, we're en route to the tailgate.

As we traverse LSU's campus, we can't help but be impressed by the best of European and Southern architecture and style surrounding us. There are huge oak trees everywhere, and the ground is almost completely flat. The buildings make you think you've suddenly run into Europe in the middle of southern Louisiana. And everyone, and I mean everyone, is having a great time.

The DKEs have a banner hanging outside their house that says, "Hey, girls, Kim Jong Il stole your sunglasses." Nothing kills a fashion craze better than associating it with a North Korean dictator who is testing nuclear weap-

LSU's DKE wages a noble battle against oversized sunglasses on women.

ons. This is just what the DKEs are hoping to do, and they are not alone. Just last week in Athens, my friend Doug was lamenting that attractive girls now choose to cover their faces with sunglasses that are roughly the size of Liechtenstein.

. . .

I've been set up via John Purdy to take a tour of the LSU locker room. This is, of course, fantastic. Lifelong LSU fan Kerry Guidry is accompanying me. While we're standing outside the Jeff Boss Locker Room entrance, who should walk by but LSU All-American basketball player Glen "Big Baby" Davis?

I ask Big Baby if I can take a picture with him. When he puts his arm around me for the photograph it occurs to me that if he wanted to, he could break me by squeezing hard. This also confirms for me that Big Baby is the largest person ever to have braces. He has made orthodontic history. All of a sudden, LSU seems like the smallest gathering of 92,400 people you've ever seen. I'm half expecting LSU's head football coach Les Miles to walk by and let me try on his baseball cap.

Ferrell Shillings, who has been working at LSU since 1981, arrives to give us our tour. We spend twenty minutes or so walking around the locker room, which is covered in carpet and features oak lockers with Tiger heads engraved on them. Ferrell hands each of us a helmet, and explains that each player has two helmets that he rotates between games. Every image or letter on the helmet is also a sticker. Nothing is painted on the helmets. Somehow, I should have known this, but I didn't.

The LSU jerseys are all laid out along with the cleats, gloves, pads, and assorted other game necessities. Each player also receives a program for the day's game. Most of the linemen already have their jerseys taped to their pads so they can simply slip them over their shoulders. "They don't want to give the other guys anything to grab," says Shillings.

Today, LSU will be dressing ninety-five players, which Shillings tells us is the limit for home conference games. For road conference games, LSU can dress only seventy. "Next week against Fresno State, we'll probably dress one hundred fifteen," Shillings says.

It's roughly one in the afternoon, the game is still six hours away, and the jerseys are already prepared. The team will not arrive until two hours before kickoff.

We walk outside the locker room where players-of-the-week photos and blurbs are affixed to the wall. Here, there is room for the offensive, defensive, and special teams players of the week for each game LSU wins. For games LSU loses, no players have been selected. So, for the Auburn and Florida games, LSU losses so far this season, there are three blank picture frames.

We exit the locker room and enter the field through the eye of a Tiger. Literally. Just above the doors is a piece of the crossbar that was used at LSU from 1955 to 1984. Each player slaps the crossbar where the word WIN is written. I give it a shot.

We walk to the edge of the field, where the sprinklers are

Slapping the crossbar at LSU as I enter the field.

running. Evidently LSU has a sand-based field that requires watering even on game days. There is a strong breeze and, above us, the flags are snapping wildly in the wind. The stands are completely empty and, around us, the expansive emptiness rises to the heavens. Sometimes the scope of an empty stadium can convey immensity as well as, if not better than, a full one does.

Back inside, we come across a sign inside the LSU equipment room: "We issue everything except guts." Perfect.

Across the street from the stadium is the $3 million, fifteen thousand-square-foot home of Mike the Tiger. The tiger habitat features a waterfall, lush vegetation, a meandering stream, and outcroppings of rock for climbing if the tiger so desires.

If I were playing in the SEC, unfortunately, I'd need guts.

LSU fans of all ages crowd the outer rim of the habitat looking for Mike the Tiger, but Mike is nowhere to be found. I'd give up my condo to live inside Mike's cage.

Currently, Mike V (1990 to present) is residing in the Tiger cage. LSU has featured a live tiger as a mascot since 1936, when the original Mike the Tiger was purchased from the Little Rock Zoo with money raised by collecting twenty-five cents from each LSU student. After satisfying myself that Mike V is nowhere to be seen, I bid farewell to Shillings and head back to the tailgate, where Kelly and Julie Walker, two forty-something rabid LSU fans who are husband and wife, are putting on quite a tailgating party. Kelly, an investigator for the district attorney's office, is carrying around a microphone that he occasionally uses to speak when his blasting music is turned down. He keeps the microphone in his jeans pocket and regularly announces the arrival of guests, "The Guidry family (Kerry Guidry's parents and siblings) has just arrived at the tailgate," Walker says. He and his wife have been tailgating underneath a large oak tree on the west side of the stadium since 1986. They have a trailer for tailgating that was painted by inmates at Angola Prison. "They did a pretty good job," admits Julie. GEAUX TIGERS is painted on the back. Something I've picked up on here in Louisiana is that locals will never miss an opportunity to turn a word ending in *o* into *eaux*. Must be a Cajun thing.

Julie shows me a hat she is selling on behalf of a high school girl who wants to take a trip to Europe for a choir tour. The trip will cost $5,000. The best way to raise $5,000 in Baton Rouge? Paint a tiger's face on a cowboy hat and sell them for thirty dollars each. The fund-raiser is well under way. Eighty-five have already been sold, and the student is more than half way to earning her trip.

Back at the tailgate, we are putting away lots of Coors Light. For some reason, Coors Light now has camouflage beer cans. I suppose this makes hunting easier. Even still, it's the first time silver aluminum has ever been considered a concealing color.

At this point, I feel comfortable reporting that no LSU fans actually smell like corn dogs. This doesn't mean they are without flaws, however. Kerry Guidry pulls me aside, "I've got to be honest, there's way too many dudes at LSU who shave their arms and legs," he says.

While we are drinking at the tailgate, Vanderbilt upsets Georgia and the LSU fans cheer madly. It's about two-thirty,

the sun is beating down, and I have never seen alcohol consumed in such quantities. Everywhere, girls are in Mardi Gras
beads. Evidently I found this observation so compelling at the
time that I repeated it on my notepad one page later. My powers of perception are dulling.

At the tailgate, we eat boudin, jambalaya, and assorted
other Cajun delicacies. All the food is excellent, however it
also is beginning to taste the same. Like alcohol with bread.

Kerry Guidry's sister, Stephanie, arrives with daiquiris for
everyone. The daiquiris are sold at a drive-through stand, and
there are two ways you can avoid an open container violation:
Don't put the straws inside the drink or have the lid taped shut.
My drink is called the TKO, and it's well named. It tastes like
rum via straw.

Jasmine the yellow boa constrictor arrives, and I have my
picture taken alongside holder Sarah Hilburn. The most amazing thing about the presence of the enormous yellow boa constrictor is that no one even bats an eye. In response to my
surprise, Kerry Guidry merely comments. "That snake is native
to South America and Baton Rouge."

It's three-thirty in the afternoon, and I think to myself that
it's entirely possible that there is not a single adult in Baton
Rouge who is not the equivalent of ten beers deep. LSU fans
don't come for a football game. They come for a party. All
around me a carnival in the sunshine is breaking out.

"Ice Ice Baby" comes on the sound-system at the tailgate.
I'm embarrassed to report that everyone I'm with can still
flawlessly repeat every word to the song. Kerry leans over to
me, "LSU games have the hottest collection of women over
thirty on earth," he reports. This seems like it might be true.
Of course, if I were at a nursing home right now I'd probably

think it was the hottest gathering of women over thirty on earth, too.

I meet eighty-seven-year-old Bill Dupré who has been attending LSU games since 1940, when he played in a band in the end zone. "It was before the stadium was enclosed," he says. I ask him how to spell his name and have trouble understanding that he is telling me his name ends with an accent. He takes my notebook and writes down the acute accent himself. Then, he hands me the first praline of my life.

Several Kentucky fans get wind that I am writing a book about the SEC and are now regaling me with stories about how Kentucky is going to win. "Andre' Woodson is going to throw for 700 yards," slurs one man. "Write that down," he demands. So I do.

A rumor spreads through the tailgate like wild fire: My friend Tardio has discarded his Bellini daiquiri without being able to finish it. Fellow tailgaters Brandie and Brooke react with disgust. Tardio mumbles an insubstantial defense. In between the day's third rendition of "Brick House," Kelly Walker takes the mic and announces to the entire tailgate, "Chris Tardio did not finish his daiquiri." Boos cascade forth.

Tardio reclaims his daiquiri from the trashcan and attempts to finish it. Simultane-

Tardio with a pair of ladies, as well as the Bellini daiquiri that he reclaimed from the garbage.

ously, he is regaled by a drunken chorus of modified "Hey Baby": "I wanna know-o-o . . . if you'll finish your daiquiri." Tardio finishes his drink but not before everyone begins calling him "Daq."

Everyone at LSU loves Michael Jackson. "Beat It" is playing from at least eleven tailgates nearby. It's like 1984 never ended in Baton Rouge. The guys we gambled with at the casino the night before wander by our tailgate. "Yo, dudes," they say. "Fred's, come to Fred's after the game." In addition to inviting us to an afterparty, they officially confirm for me that LSU is the smallest gathering of 92,000 people in the history of the world.

Finally, it's time to head to the game. We buy lower level tickets in section 101 for twenty-five dollars (face value is thirty-six dollars) and head to the Porta Potties beside the stadium. As Kelly and I stand in line, the people around us suddenly scatter. "Somebody's pissing from the upper deck," yells one guy near me as we all race away from open air. It's like a mortar round landed. Everyone ducks and covers. I'm still praying that what came off the upper deck and splashed my neck wasn't actually urine.

Night has come to Baton Rouge. The weather is perfect and the field seems to shimmer in the lights. LSU fans have always said a night game in Baton Rouge is the best possible football experience. For months, I worried that the Kentucky game was going to be moved to daytime. Thankfully, it wasn't. LSU fans have good reason to cheer for night games. Since 1960, LSU is 196-59-3 (.759) at night in Tiger Stadium compared to a 18-22-3 (.453) during the day. Tiger Pride is rising as the night advances and, at this moment, I completely understand why they wanted me to be there for a night game.

KWo and I enter the stadium and find that our seats are in the fourteenth row behind the LSU bench. As we're walking along the side of the field, the LSU Golden Girls are stretching and doing sundry other things in preparation for their role as the hottest women in Tiger Stadium. Golden Girl Lindsay Wynn poses for a photo with me. Cocky KWo is ascendant, "If I went to LSU, I think I could date a Golden Girl," he says.

We're really close to the field. So close, in fact, that I'm a bit concerned that LSU's head coach Les Miles's baseball cap, which he wears as high on his head as he possibly can, is going to block my view. Also, for some reason, our double seat folds up and down. It's like a metal love seat.

LSU's field is unique in that they actually paint out the numbers ending in five as opposed to just the numbers ending in zero. So, you know, file that nugget of brilliant observational note away somewhere until you're on *Jeopardy!* and the category is "Numbering of American College Football Fields."

The crowd around us is fairly indifferent. Maybe they're sort of upset that the party had to stop for this particular game against an overmatched opponent. Kelly taps me, "JaMarcus Russell really is as big as a house," he says. Russell has been a man among boys since his days as a high school quarterback in Alabama. During his high school career in Mobile, Russell passed for 10,744 yards and eighty-four touchdowns. So far this season, he has specialized in destroying the mere mortals on the football field who are trying to stop him. As if this weren't enough, after Hurricane Katrina in 2005, Russell hosted twenty displaced residents in his own apartment, including, in the most overtold sports anecdote of the 2005 football season, Fats Domino. It's a little over six months until Russell will become the overall number one pick in the NFL Draft. But tonight he's still an amateur. A giant amateur, but an amateur nonetheless.

The game has zero suspense. LSU stops Kentucky, then scores on their first possession. By halftime, it's 28–0 LSU and the game has all the excitement of watching a cobra kill a mouse. Only a couple of times does the crowd rouse itself to cheer with anything approaching intensity.

The highlights of the first half are (1) when I decide to order cotton candy and provoke a mild storm of cotton-candy fever among the kids sitting around us, and (2) when I drop my pen into my nacho cheese. Honestly, these two events were probably more exciting than any offensive play by Kentucky that day. It's possible no one has ever had a better view of LSU's punter Chris Jackson punting on the sideline into a net than we do. Jackson seems as uninterested in the game as most of the fans are. A couple of times he fakes as if he is going to punt into the net for laughs. I don't know about you, but fake punts on the sideline always kill me.

LSU begins the second half by scoring to make it 35–0, and pulling their starting quarterback JaMarcus Russell. Then, LSU scores again with their reserves and it's 42–0 with about twenty-three minutes remaining in the game. LSU is the best team in America at stomping bad football teams. All around us, people are streaming toward the exits to recommence their partying. I start to get text messages encouraging me to return to the tailgate. So, Kelly and I follow the LSU fans who have seen enough and head back to the parties outside. From there we hit bars, named Walk-On's, Fred's, and JL's, where we had been the previous evening.

The highlight at Walk-On's is two white guys with frosted blond tips rapping along to Lil John's "Get Low," and watching these same two white guys try to avoid using the word *nigger* in the song. Everyone in the crowd is really uncomfortable when this word comes up in the song, too. I know I am. I can be having the best time, screaming along with a song, and then all of a sudden that damn racial slur arrives. A whole crowd of white people just sort of dies over the racial slur and then everyone starts singing again. The best is when you're with a black guy or girl and they get to keep singing and you sort of nod at them while they utter the racial slur and you stay quiet. Then, for like a verse or two, no white person really looks at any other white person. This is pretty classic. And it's everywhere we go at LSU tonight.

Tardio gets his boat shoes' revenge in Fred's, where many of the LSU players arrive late that night. None other than LSU tailback Justin Vincent is wearing boat shoes out at the bar. "Boat shoes . . . bang," says Tardio, gesturing excitedly at Vincent's shoes. "That's what I'm talking about. Justin Vincent and I are getting it done." Justin Vincent is the Rosa Parks of boat shoes.

Shortly after this, a hot blond girl taps me on the shoulder, "This is going to sound weird but aren't you Clay Travis, the guy going around to all twelve SEC football stadiums on the DDT?" For one moment, I

Tardio's boat shoes.

LSU tailback Justin Vincent's boat shoes.
Whose look cooler?

believe she's a reader. Then, I see Keven over her shoulder ordering drinks. "He put you up to it, didn't he?" I ask. She lowers her eyes. "He bought me a Jager bomb," she says, shrugging her shoulders. The bastard, a setup. I'm the Johnny Drama of SEC football.

Sometime early Sunday morning, everyone at JL's steadies themselves and focuses. "Geaux Tigers" blares over the speakers and there is one final delirious party-infused, beer-soaked rendition of LSU spirit. And then the cheer is over and the party rolls on and on and on until eventually you realize that life in Baton Rouge is a never-ending party itself.

Even at six years old the expression on my face suggests
I was skeptical Coach Majors would ever beat Alabama.

The 1933 Tennessee football team. My grandfather, Richard K. Fox, is in the back row (third going right to left).

The University of Tennessee band at the team's home opener
against California on September 2, 2006.

The Auburn band, overcome by the pregame heat, rests in the shade.

Me, Shaw, Krishna, Shekhar, and Cliff at Mississippi State on September 9.
Two Indians and a Jew vacation in Starkville for the first time in Mississippi history.

Young Auburn fans train for college by rolling Toomer's Corner
in the wake of the victory on September 16.

Hinton and I are in Arkansas on September 23. Hinton was very jealous not to be wearing a Hog hat.

Junaid and I supporting our beloved Vols at Georgia on October 7. This is what it looks like in the wake of your team hanging half a hundred (plus one) in another team's stadium.

Golden Girl Lindsay Wynn begged to have her photo taken with me at LSU on October 14 . . . or not.

Alongside Kerry Guidry, I contemplate whether LSU's LaRon Landry will kill us for not kneeling before his locker.

Welcome to LSU, where even boa constrictors tailgate.

With Chancellor Gee and his wife Constance at Vanderbilt on October 21. Gee opened up his suit coat to prove he wasn't packing heat . . . and also to show off its Vandy-colored lining.

With my parents in the upper deck at South Carolina on October 28. (I accept full responsibility for my dad's backward hat. For the last time, Dad, no one is going to give you a record deal for the rap album.)

My wife, Lara, and I at Ole Miss on November 25. (Ottoman not pictured.)

Kentucky fans celebrate their surprise victory on November 4.

UK grads Keven, Tardio, and Dave relax on the UK sideline after storming the field.

The man, the myth, the Tebow, sandwiched between me and Neville on the night of November 11.
(Note: This most definitely is *not* the wallpaper on both Neville's and my computers . . .
uh uh, no way. And no, you may not see my computer.)

Florida Fan Beth Justice is planning her marriage
to Tim Tebow. They haven't actually met, but that
doesn't stop her.

The Houndstooth Twins, Alabama fans Meagen and
Ashley Bailey, cozy up to the late, great coach Bear
Bryant before a Bama home game.

MY GRANDFATHER'S FOOTBALL CAREER

In the fall of 1931, my grandfather Richard K. Fox arrived in Knoxville, Tennessee. He was a freshman who had never played football in his life. Instead, he played in the high school band because his mother was convinced that he would be injured playing football. This was despite the fact that my grandfather had spent the better part of his teenage years delivering fifty-pound blocks of ice to help pay the family bills and, at six feet and two inches and 185 pounds, was a giant for that time. He was indisputably *country strong*, a term I often heard my grandfather use to describe someone who had come by their muscles and strength as a result of manual labor, not athletic training.

When he arrived in Knoxville in 1931, the Depression was in great force and my grandfather was poor. And hungry. Partly to fill this hunger, my grandfather joined the freshman football team at the University of Tennessee. As a football player he received one free meal a day, a meal that was spectacular for its excess. Ham, turkey, steak, fruits and vegetables all piled on the training table as high as he could see. And he ate as much of that meal as he could, often because he was subsisting on just one meal a day. The rest of the time he ate dry cereal in his dorm room. As a football player, my grandfather also got free lodging in the dorms beneath Neyland Stadium. The only catch was that each year, once football season ended, he was forced to move out of the dorm to make room for basketball players, and find another place to live.

For these benefits of food and lodging, my grandfather gave himself over to the game of football. Grandpa told me about lying on the grass field after having his legs cut out from under him and how long it seemed to take to have someone reach him. My dad recalls a spring football game at Neyland Stadium when my grandfather walked to a corner of the field, looked around, and said, "Right here, I was knocked out cold." Later that same day, my grandfather had his picture taken with another Chattanooga native who played football for the Vols, Reggie White.

The version of football that my grandfather played in the early 1930s was nasty and brutish. Injuries were common. Diving at a player's knees was encouraged and taught. Limping was endemic to the game. My grandfather told me about having the wind knocked out of him and how, at times, it seemed possible that he would never breathe again. How he stared at the sky, and all the sounds around him faded to nothing. He told me about some of the best players on his team choosing not to play professional football because they could make more money doing other jobs. And he told me about the roar a cheering crowd made that roused him when it seemed he had no energy left to play. And, finally, my grandfather told me about how close everything that had ever happened to him in his life had come to not being.

When I was very young, my grandfather pulled me aside and handed me an old newspaper clipping from his freshman year of college, December 1931. Before I could read the paper, he said, "Sonny boy, I almost died three times before your mom was even thought of. Here was the second." During his freshman year my grandfather had foiled a bank robbery in Knoxville. Two police officers had already been shot by a bank robber, and one of the officers was calling for help. My grandfather, an unarmed freshman football player, rushed to the officer's aid. He came face to face with a pistol-carrying robber who had already shot several people. The robber pointed the gun at my grandfather from point-blank range and pulled the trigger. "Nothing happened," my grandfather said, eyes twinkling, "the gun was out of bullets and I knocked the snot plum out of him." The foiled robbery was front-page news in Knoxville.

Then, he told me about the other two times. The first time my grandfather almost died occurred while he was crossing a railroad bridge in Chattanooga. A train came while my grandfather and a friend were too far along the tracks to run for safety, so they both dropped down and hung to the track's supports while the train passed above them. Away down below his feet a river roared beneath them.

After these two near-death experiences, my grandfather survived to play on the 1933 Tennessee football team under General Robert Neyland. Before that, he played on the freshmen team, but 1933 was to be the only year he played on the varsity. After this year he dropped out of school and never graduated from Tennessee.

Nineteen thirty-three was the first year of the newly formed Southeastern Conference. The Tennessee football season began on September 30, with a 27–0 win over Virginia Tech. And it ended on December 9 with a 7–0 loss to LSU. In between, my grandfather played SEC games against Mississippi State, Florida, Ole Miss, Vandy, and Kentucky. Oh, and on the third Saturday in October against a team named Alabama. My grandfather lined up that day against a guy named Bear Bryant in a game the Vols ultimately lost 12–6. The 1933 Vols would finish the season 7-3 overall and 5-2 in the SEC. With the football season over, my grandfather moved out of the Neyland Stadium dorms and relinquished his room to a member of the Vol basketball team.

Shortly after this season, my grandfather and several friends decided on the spur of the moment to hop a train and ride to the Kentucky Derby in Louisville. This was the third time he almost died. They had no tickets, no money, and no way to reach the event otherwise. And it was during the Depression. So, they simply hopped onto a moving train en route to Louisville. Only my grandfather hadn't jumped well enough and he fell back out into the night and dangled from an open train car, his legs close to being pulled under the belly of the train. At the last moment, just as he lost his grip, a friend dragged him inside. When he finished his story he said, "It was so crowded on the infield we couldn't even see the horses. Go to the Derby sometime, Sonny boy." Then he smiled at me. "Three times you came pretty close to never being," he said, and then he rubbed my head.

After the 1933 season, my grandfather never suited up for the Tennessee Vols again. He returned to Chattanooga, married my grandmother, moved to Buffalo, New York, moved to Tampa, Florida, moved to Birmingham, Alabama, and eventually returned home to Chattanooga. For her entire childhood, my mom remembered my grandfather would listen to three or more college football games on the radio at the same time. "He would be sitting there fiddling with the radio and my mom would walk in and say, 'I don't understand how in the world you can keep up with what's going on in all of those games at the same time.' But he did. He never missed games."

My grandfather loved Southeastern Conference football more than any other sport. Probably because he was there at the inception.

VANDERBILT

8

NASHVILLE, TENNESSEE
THE UNIVERSITY OF SOUTH CAROLINA VS. VANDERBILT UNIVERSITY
OCTOBER 21, 2006

For most of my, life I hated Vanderbilt. Rooted against them in every sport with a fervent passion and went to bed at night smiling if they lost. Growing up in Nashville as a Tennessee fan, there was nothing more annoying than hearing about Vanderbilt's new coach and how the road to Commodore rebuilding was paved with promise. Time after time, the cycle repeated itself, a bright-eyed coach spoke of winning, discipline, and execution, and, several years later, the same coach with bags under his eyes quietly sunk into the recesses of his profession after being fired. Vanderbilt was a football coach's cemetery. The place where promising careers curled up and died. And, with each failure, I found myself more and more pleased.

During this period, while my hate flourished, I was accompanied in my anti-Vanderbilt fervor by my dad. The two of us cheered when Vanderbilt missed a field goal that would have won the game, exchanged high fives when they fumbled on the goal line in the fourth quarter, and celebrated with glee each defeat snagged from the jaws of victory by the hapless Commodores. Unless you have followed Vanderbilt closely for a couple of decades you cannot imagine the variety of ways Vanderbilt has managed to lose football games. The litany of failures and inexplicable results legitimately boggles the mind. It's as if the biblical Job were placed upon a football field. For twenty years of my life, failure after failure reigned forth upon the star-crossed Commodores, and neither my dad nor I could have been happier. And then my sister chose to go to undergrad at Vanderbilt.

My dad accepted the decision with great maturity. He insisted that my mom sign the tuition checks because he could not bear to sign them himself. Then, just as my dad gained a measure of peace about my sister's decision, he learned that I would be going to Vanderbilt Law School. Prior to enrolling, I received a call from my dad while my mom was also on the line. After small talk, my mom spoke up: "Well, tell him, Norm." There was a pause, then my dad sheepishly said, "If you go to Vanderbilt Law School, I'd be proud." His words were so precise I pictured him sitting at home reading language that my mom had already dictated to him off a tablet.

So, I went to Vanderbilt Law School. Now my dad finds himself surrounded by Vanderbilt graduates. He has a son who graduated from the law school, a son-in-law who graduated from the medical school, a daughter with both her undergraduate and master's degrees from the school, and a daughter-in-law who will shortly graduate with a master's in education from Peabody. It's possible my dad has more immediate familial connections to more different schools within Vanderbilt University than anyone else currently living in Nashville. I believe this is the definition of irony. It is also the reason why, somewhere along the way, the Travis family learned to stop hating Vanderbilt.

Stop seven of the Dixieland Delight Tour arrived with Vanderbilt's homecoming game against South Carolina and, at a little over a mile of travel distance, just about all I needed to do was open my front door. The day's festivities began at ten in the morning when I walked up the steps of Kirkland Hall to meet Vanderbilt's chancellor, E. Gordon Gee. Yep, the actual chancellor.

Actually, it would probably be more accurate to say that stop seven began the night before the meeting during a conversation about what to wear for my meeting with the chancellor. During this conversation, I promise my wife, Lara, that I will not stay out late and that I will dress decently and in no way embarrass her with my attire. Then I stay out until almost two and decide upon a Vanderbilt Law T-shirt and jeans. For impression's sake I drop my flip-flops and wear actual shoes.

I walk inside Kirkland Hall four hours before kickoff, and almost stride directly into the chancellor's address to the board of trusts from South Carolina. As I stand awkwardly within eyesight of everyone, several people from Vanderbilt arrive and suggest that I might be more comfortable out of sight in the foyer. Then they offer me orange juice. This is a bit of an inauspicious start.

The South Carolina Board of Trustees leaves, but not before several people ask me if there are paper cups so they can carry their coffee out. Evidently, everyone believes that I am the waiter. I pull out my notepad and jot down a few notes. "Do you take orders?" asks one woman with silver hair.

The rich South Carolinians leave and, suddenly, Kirkland Hall on the center of Vanderbilt's campus is very quiet. I proceed into the chancellor's office where I meet his staff and take a picture of the chancellor's Homecoming Day schedule. Near the front of the office Commodore Cornelius Vanderbilt's

white bust is covered in black and gold beads, and the commodore is wearing a rakish Vanderbilt cap tilted at an odd angle. The commodore, dead for one-hundred-and-twenty-nine years, looks vaguely as if he is prepared to enter a hip-hop dance contest.

In life, Commodore Vanderbilt made few friends. In fact, the tightfisted native New Yorker disowned his $100 million estate

A beaded Commodore Vanderbilt was not pleased with the crass "show your tits" chants.

from all but one of his children, a son named William, whom he felt was an equally rapacious businessman and would continue the family's torrid pursuit of money. Despite this avarice, Commodore Vanderbilt, perhaps in a fit of philanthropy or overcome by a sudden and misbegotten desire to be remembered as something more than a robber baron, endowed the as-yet-unnamed Vanderbilt University with a one million dollar bequest. Never having visited the South in his life, the commodore nevertheless stipulated that the bequest was to be used to found a university which he hoped would assist in healing the sectional rifts of the recently passed Civil War. Named after its benefactor, Vanderbilt University began teaching students in 1875, and in the school's history has had only seven Chancellors. Chancellor E. Gordon Gee is the seventh. I begin to wonder if my T-shirt decision was the wrong one.

Just before ten in the morning, I meet Chancellor Gee. I have met the chancellor several times before during law school, but at no time did any of our conversations last longer than three sentences. Gee would show up at law school events and introduce himself as if nobody had any idea who he was. "I'm Gordon Gee," he would say, as though he had just walked in off the street. Then, and this is where he would prove himself even more exceptional, Gee would actually listen to your own name in response.

Gee, a Mormon born in Utah, became president of his first university, West Virginia, at the age of thirty-seven. Since that time he has been president of the University of Colorado, Ohio State, Brown, and, now, Vanderbilt. He is sixty-two years old and, with his unlined face and smooth skin, appears much younger. Gee is the only living person in America to have been head of five different universities. In contrast, I am the only living Vanderbilt Law Student to have received a D in First Amendment and gone on a pudding strike. So, we make quite an august pair about to head across the Vanderbilt campus.

As if being the only living president of five universities isn't impressive enough, Gee is also a lawyer with a doctorate in education who clerked for Supreme Court Chief Justice Warren Burger. As a youth Gee also, predictably, became an Eagle Scout and ushered the Marshall Plan through Congress. In his spare time, Chancellor Gee enjoys solving world hunger, pretending that his first name is not Elwood (hence E. Gordon Gee), and eradicating malaria. Shortly after our meeting, Gee's wife, Constance, arrives.

Constance Gee is a character in her own right. In the past few years, she has made national news for flying the flag at the chancellor's residence at half-mast in the wake of George W. Bush's 2004 presidential victory and, in the early fall of 2006 the *Wall Street Journal* ran a front-page exposé intimating that she had been smoking marijuana in the chancellor's residence. This marijuana smoking was alleged to have violated the Vanderbilt residential standards, which forbids drug use in university housing. Chancellor Gee and his wife declined to comment on the marijuana allegation, and the story only minimally touched his status as one of the most popular university presidents in the country.

Indeed, in 2005, Gee's approval rating among Vanderbilt students was an astonishing 88.4 percent. This approval rating was aided in no small part by Gee's ability, despite his high stature and many accomplishments, not to take himself too seriously. During the spring of my second year of law school, in March 2003, a newspaper hoax was perpetrated by several Vanderbilt students. These students distributed a mock edition of the *Vanderbilt Hustler* student newspaper emblazoned with the headline, GEE DEAD. Upon the distribution of these newspapers, the campus came undone.

Professors insisted on moments of silence in class. Students cried. Phone lines lit up in the chancellor's office and condolence flowers arrived. There was only one problem: Gee wasn't dead. The chancellor responded with alacrity and good humor to reports of his death, even posing with a huge smile alongside the offending newspaper headline. The chancellor even broke out the old Mark Twain line. "Reports of my death have been greatly exaggerated," Gee said. Perhaps made aware of what they had almost lost, Gee's popularity surged even higher among the students.

Miraculously risen from the dead three-and-a-half years later, the chancellor and I leave his office and walk across the campus to where the Vanderbilt Homecoming Parade will begin. Vanderbilt's campus is the most easily walked of any I've visited thus far in the SEC. From the center of campus, it's possible to believe you are truly removed from downtown Nashville, even though you are only a mile and a half away. The sounds of the city completely fade in the center of campus where you walk amidst the arboretum featuring each tree native to Tennessee. Magnolias, oaks, hackberries, and tulip poplar trees climb into the sky, and now their colored leaves are falling on the quiet brick walkways of the campus. Student groups have to tie up posters and signs (rather than use nails) to protect the trees here from damage. It's not uncommon to see tall banners stretched tautly from one large tree to another advertising various events. In fact, the rapper Ludacris performed the previous night at the Commodore Quake as part of homecoming and there is a sign to this effect. I ask Chancellor Gee if he managed to make the concert. "No," he says. This interview is going great.

En route to the parade, our conversation centers on the chancellor's pants which have V's embroidered on them. I ask his wife whether the pants were her idea, "Oh, no," she says, "I am not responsible for that." Then, she continues, "But he used to have pants with O's (while at Ohio State) so I can't claim I didn't know what I was getting into."

Midway through the campus Gee stops for the first time to greet others. He introduces himself to alums as if they have no idea who he is. Then he poses for photos with the children of the alums. Associate Vice Chancellor Jennifer Howe looks down at her watch. This is a common move for the staff charged with assisting the chancellor around the campus. As Gee himself says, "I am constitutionally unable not to shake hands."

The Vanderbilt Homecoming Parade has recently been moved to the day of the game, instead of the Friday night before the game. When we arrive at Vanderbilt's fraternity row there is a trolley replete with a large bow tie on the front (Gee has over nine hundred bow ties and always wears one).

The bow-tied trolley is 12,364 percent cooler than a non-bow-tied trolley.

Already, there are approximately eight Vanderbilt students on board who will be charged with throwing candy and beads out the windows of the trolley. Gee takes the trolley floor and announces to the students, "Okay, the deal is this: We have fun." The students cheer, and Gee throws himself into their midst, shaking hands and asking where they are from and what they are studying. And whether they enjoyed the Ludacris concert the night before. Then, he takes the floor again, "All you have to do is throw candy out the window and say bad things about South Carolina" he says. The students cheer again and, shortly after that, the trolley is off at the head of the parade. This is the first time I have ever been on a trolley outside San Francisco, and certainly the first time I have been on a trolley with tires.

It's possible there has never been a larger collection of people on a parade route who cannot catch. Time after time, I see black-and-gold beads smack people in the face or M&Ms glance off hands, then chests, then upraised knees before finally coming to rest on the ground. It's not so much the dropped candy or beads that's entertaining, but the reaction of the people on the street, as if the very concept of catching itself is an alien and foreign idea.

Quickly, instructions pass back through the trolley, "Try and make eye contact with the person before you throw," says someone who presumably has experience throwing candy from a moving trolley. An older man takes a candy bar directly in the temple. Clearly, nothing is working.

Constance Gee accuses her husband of eating the candy before she can throw it off the trolley. "I keep throwing empty wrappers," she yells. The chancellor offers up a soft laugh in his own defense.

We finish the parade and the chancellor climbs off his trolley and sprints up the stairs at the Phi Kappa Psi house and begins shaking hands with the fraternity members and their dates. Many of them pose for photos alongside him as music pours out of their house. Constance Gee and I follow him. Shortly, Constance is standing beside me singing along to the Rolling Stones. She begins to sway and dance to "You can't always get what you want," and then I sort of awkwardly begin to dance and sway beside her. This is definitely an unexpected part of the DDT. I would have put the odds at my dancing on a fraternity patio with a university president's wife at practically zero.

As we leave the house, Constance says, "I loved the music there." The music failed to register, however, with the chancellor who was unaware what song was playing. Constance turns to me, "We met George Harrison once and Gordon comes up to him and says, 'And what do you do?' He had never heard of him. I was like, he's a Beatle, Gordon!"

En route to a buffet lunch across the school grounds, Gee constantly stops and greets students, parents, and alumni. The chancellor seems to know everyone on campus. At one point he welcomes a gentleman dressed in a South Carolina hat to campus. Of course, he also introduces himself. It turns out the man is from South Carolina and has a son at Vanderbilt. "Now, who is your son?" Gee asks. The man gives his son's name. Without pausing Gee says, "Oh, yes, Jay is a sophomore and doing quite well. Now, how about your hat?" The shocked man stammers a response about being a Gamecock fan. Gee nods, "I guess of the two we'd prefer you wear the USC hat and send us your money," he says, with a twinkle in his eye.

As we approach the luncheon, I ask Gee about the conversation. He nods. "I'd guess I probably know about 75 percent of the students' names on campus here. We're small enough to do that. At Ohio State we had fifteen thousand freshmen and you couldn't do that, but here . . ." Gee shrugs and waves his hands at the mention of yet another familiar face. Each year, Vanderbilt enrolls roughly one thousand six hundred new freshmen. To the chancellor this is an inconsequential number of students to meet.

Confession time: Several years ago my parents met the chancellor at a Vanderbilt event and my dad said he had two children at Vanderbilt. On the mention of my name, Gee responded promptly, "Oh yes, I know Clay. Nice young man."

Since then, my parents, like virtually everyone I know associated with the university, love Chancellor Gee. How much? If he were Vanderbilt's quarterback, I think my dad would buy season tickets.

Inside the student life center, Chancellor Gee remarks that all five of the universities he has presided over won their football games last weekend. "That doesn't happen too often," he says. Gee then recalls that he recently flew from Chicago to Nashville and a student from each of the five universities of which he had been president came up and talked to him during the course of the flight. "That was amazing," Gee says. "Graduates of all five on the same flight." He shakes his head. What's even more amazing is that they all recognized Gee as having been at the helm of their university. And that they wanted to talk to him.

During the buffet I ask Associate Vice Chancellor Jennifer Howe how Gee manages to remember everyone's name. "It's just natural. He's amazing like that. Most people you work for you have to be constantly reminding them about details but he just consumes and retains it all. He remembers everything." Then she acknowledges the chancellor's greatest flaw, "We have Gee-walk time on the schedule," she says. "He stops and talks to people everywhere." For our trip to the Vanderbilt Alumni Tailgate, Howe has just reserved a golf cart, "We definitely need a cart because otherwise we'll never get him through Vandyville," she says.

Having met everyone at the Outstanding Seniors Luncheon, the chancellor has a moment to himself. Standing alongside the buffet, he looks around, then reaches in and snags a single potato from the serving tray. He pops it into his mouth, sees me watching him, and flashes me a guilty smile. Gee is like this, a sixty-two-year-old man who somehow retains an ability to seem downright boyish at times, but he's also moving so fast and talking so much on this day that he hasn't had a chance to eat.

During Gee's speech I talk to Charles Epps, who has been a food server at Vanderbilt for seven years. Eventually I ask him what he thinks about the chancellor, "He's a good guy. One of the best," Epps says.

In his talk to the outstanding seniors (Vanderbilt's recent replacement for the homecoming king and queen) Gee says he is tired because they hosted the fifty-year class reunion at their home last night. The classmates stayed until three in the morning and according to the staff, "drank more alcohol than any group in the past six years."

As we climb into the golf cart for our ride across the campus to the huge alumni tent, I engage the chancellor and Constance Gee in a discussion about the relative distinctions between pompons and shakers. Constance Gee is certain that a pompon is entirely different from a shaker, "Shakers have long handles," she says with confidence. The chancellor is more philosophical, "Hmm," he says. Then I discuss with him how Vanderbilt Law School helped me to finely hew my antipompon arguments. In the ensuing silence the chancellor seems to be contemplating whether or not he can retroactively rescind my law degree.

Upon our arrival at the Vanderbilt Homecoming tent, Chancellor Gee climbs out of the golf cart, and, just for a moment, pauses and takes a deep breath. No one has recognized him yet and we are blissfully ignored in the midafternoon sunshine. I tell the chancellor that my day is taking me other places now and that I appreciate his allowing me to join him for two hours. The chancellor nods, smiles, and shakes my hand. From under the tent, he has been recognized. "Hey, Chancellor Gee," calls a figure waving his hand in the shade of the tent. Chancellor Gee raises his own hand. For a moment, I

Action shot of the golf-cart ride, with Gee at my side.

look away at the Vanderbilt band in the street, and when I turn again, the chancellor has already been swallowed by the crowd of beaming alumni.

"Not bad for a man who doesn't know the Beatles," says Constance Gee.

I leave them both to a huge crowd at the Vanderbilt Alumni Tent. I have a new appreciation for the complexities of the role of a chancellor or president at homecoming. And even more of an understanding that I would be extremely bad at it. I head across the street to "Daq" Tardio's where I will begin my pre-gaming with several members of the Vanderbilt Law School class of 2004.

Since our trip to Baton Rouge the weekend before, Tardio has not been able to live down the fact that he didn't finish a daiquiri. Earlier this week, I logged on to my computer to find his roommate Keven had sent everyone a detailed recipe for the Bellini drink that Tardio was unable to finish. The powerful Bellini is composed of peach nectar, lemon juice, peach schnapps, champagne, and ice. Just reading all those powerful ingredients makes me shiver.

Outside of Daq Tardio's apartment I buy a ticket for thirty dollars. Face value is forty dollars but the scalping market doesn't appear to be as weak as when I entered Dudley Field for the Temple game for six dollars on my bye week. I'll be tailgating at Tardio's apartment. (And, yes, I realize this is a very expansive definition of tailgating. But his apartment is a long pass from Vandyville, a collection of tents outside Vanderbilt Stadium, and only a quarter mile from the stadium.)

I arrive in the midst of a scintillating debate about the relative merits of the Northeast versus the South. My law school classmate Andrew, from Massachusetts, says, "I went on an apple-picking date the other day." Much derision ensues about his date but Andrew perseveres. "I can tell you more about Fuji apples than you'd ever want to know." Then, he closes off his argument with a powerful truth, "You can't go apple-picking in Atlanta." The northeast is vindicated.

My friend Demko mentions that he liked the new Martin Scorcese film *The Departed*. This means *The Departed* must be among the greatest movies ever filmed. That's because Demko is a consummate critic who generally likes nothing. At least every other week I get an e-mail from him ridiculing something that appeared in one of my columns. At no point has he ever given me a compliment. Also, Demko has never made a joke without a deadpan face. During at least half of all my conversations with Demko, I'm not sure whether we are being ironically funny, sarcastic, or absolutely serious. In ten years, if Demko walked up to me and said, "My first-born child was eaten by a ravenous monkey after getting lost on a zoo field trip," I'd have no idea how to react. Demko said more things that afternoon but shortly after his movie review he went off the record.

We are all eating and drinking. There are two dips, thanks

to our law school classmate, Heather, who recently married our fellow classmate John. Heather went to South Carolina for her undergraduate degree and has come back to Vandy for the homecoming game. She's wearing a garnet shirt, which clearly demonstrates that her allegiance in this particular game rests with South Carolina. When she e-mailed Tardio to ask what she could bring to the tailgate he responded, "Thin females between the ages of twenty-two and twenty-seven; pleading in the alternative, bring dip." Yep, legal humor . . . it's hard to beat. So, Heather brought dip.

Three guys are dressed in yellow polos for the Vandy game, which leads to a discussion about Andrew's Ralph Lauren Polo shirt that he self-designed on a Web site. With a bright green collar and neon pink and white stripes throughout, the shirt is especially heinous . . . not to mention pretty damn bicurious, as more than one person remarks. Once, while Andrew slept, we took pictures with his camera of each other wearing his shirt without telling him. He got home to find photos on his digital camera of eight different guys sporting his trademark shirt. "I'm not going to lie," Andrew says, "the shirt started a few fights in Destin." Demko goes back on the record and informs us that you can no longer design your own shirts on Polo's Web site. "A friend of mine works at Ralph Lauren and he said that people were destroying the brand with their color selections." Andrew bows his head.

Keven made Jell-O shots because "Girls love Jell-O shots." There is currently one married woman at the apartment and sixty Jell-O shots. All the guys start pounding the Jell-O shots with reckless abandon. Amidst the Jell-O shot pounding it occurs to us that it is after two and the game has already started. So, in typical Vandy fashion, we head for the game late.

We arrive just as Vandy kicks a field goal to take a 3-0 lead. En route to the game, we pass a large collection of people still tailgating. It's hard to be too tough on Vandy fans. They come for the game, but have learned to be entertained by things other than the final result. This happens when you haven't had a winning football season since 1982. Plus, Vanderbilt occupies a unique spot in the SEC as a private, academically elite school surrounded by eleven other state schools; their student athletes hold the distinction of actually, you know, being students. Vanderbilt isn't big enough to hide people with limited academic interest. For instance, when we started law school in 2001, Vanderbilt's starting safety had scored a perfect 1600 on the SAT. So, he got beat deep a lot. But he was great with analogies.

We are seated in the student section. Gazing around him, Keven says, "On a per-capita basis Vanderbilt has the hottest girls." This is a controversial statement, but one that has been endorsed by most Vanderbilt Law School grads who attended other SEC schools for undergrad. There's a reason why men from the law school sprint up the hillside to eat lunch in the campus cafeteria. For those inclined to disagree about the per-capita argument, Keven is wearing his trademark pre-ripped jeans, which provide the perfect way to challenge any of his contentions, particularly those relating to style and/or taste.

The weather is perfect. There is not a single cloud in the sky and it's approaching seventy degrees. Perhaps this explains how South Carolina was able to drill a fifty-five-yard field goal to tie the game at three. Then again, they are playing Vandy.

Vanderbilt has only a single hedge running through the north end zone. So, they have a hedge but they don't technically play between the hedges. I believe this makes it the only school in the SEC that I have visited so far without a full square of hedges. Slackers. The north end zone does feature several large magnolia trees and a looming Marriott hotel with rooms that overlook the field. Currently, Vanderbilt Stadium seats 41,000 people and is the smallest in the SEC. Today, South Carolina has at least ten thousand fans in attendance.

Back on the field, in the end zone in front of the magnolia trees, sophomore receiver Sidney Rice catches a touchdown for South Carolina and Vanderbilt is down 10–3. Rice should name his first-born son after South Carolina's second-year coach and SEC legend, Steve Spurrier. Spurrier's made Rice millions by finding new ways to get his talented wide receiver the ball on offense. Speaking of Spurrier, he's on the sideline in white, long sleeves, despite the warm weather. It's amazing how much Spurrier hates the cold. I honestly think one of the problems he had with coaching the Washington Redskins in the NFL was not being able to handle a D.C. winter, or handle playing on the east coast in cold weather. You get the idea that if Spurrier were coaching in Green Bay, he'd throw down his clipboard at about halftime, march off the field, and say, "Football's not worth getting cold for."

On the final play of the first half, Vandy quarterback Chris Nickson scrambles in for a touchdown. It's a huge play and the score is suddenly a manageable 17–10. Had Nickson been tackled before the goal line the half would have expired. In years past, there is a 100 percent chance Nickson would have been tackled and the half would have ended with Vanderbilt facing a near insurmountable deficit. Yet, somehow, Vanderbilt coach Bobby Johnson has instilled a degree of optimism that has continued to grow during his tenure. This optimism has been further fueled by upsets of Tennessee and Georgia in each of the last two seasons. Vandy may not be able to win every game but you get the feeling they think they can.

At halftime I talk to another Vanderbilt law grad, Steven Simmons, whom I ridicule for being a cheerleader at Vanderbilt from 1996 to 1997, and then again from 1998 to 1999. "I quit twice," he says by way of defense. I inquire what financial gain he received for cheerleading, "We got scholarships for books and food." This seems like a very cheap price for which to sell the soul. Then, he continues, "The quality of the cheerleaders has gone down and the weight has gone up since my time." I believe this qualifies as a cheerleading shot across the bow. Torrance Shipman of *Bring It On* wouldn't stand for talk like that.

Vanderbilt gets an interception to start the second half, but can only put up a field goal. It's 17–13, South Carolina. Then, South Carolina scores to go up 24–13 and scores again on the first play of the fourth quarter to take a 31–13 lead and send Vanderbilt fans to the exits. For yet another season, Vanderbilt will lose more games than they win.

Later, Vanderbilt students and alums across the city will regroup and dive once more into the Nashville night. Football losses fade fast when you've already had so many. This is a place where a night out is rarely, if ever, spoiled by gridiron defeat. So, the Vanderbilt crowd pours forth into the city and fills up bars with names like Dan McGuiness, Lonnie's, The Stage, The Tin Roof, and countless others. And, once more, the city of Nashville drowns in music from all over the world . . . and just down the block. If you come to Nashville, you will almost certainly have a good time, hear a sad song, and share a beer with someone you don't know.

And there's also a decent chance that if you come in the fall you'll see Vanderbilt lose a football game. So be it. In a city and university of countless rhythms, cadences, and songs, Vanderbilt football is one of the few consistently mournful notes and the last few verses suggest, perhaps, good fortune is even forthcoming for the football team as well. After all, on the buckle of the Bible Belt in a city with more churches and strip clubs than any other per capita, every sinner is a saint, every downtrodden songwriter a hit artist to be, and football redemption is only a weekend away.

MY LIFE AS A FOOTBALL PLAYER

My family has an old, faded program from a 1933 Tennessee-Vanderbilt football game. My grandfather Richard K. Fox is listed in the program as playing tackle at six feet and two inches and 185 pounds. Near the back cover, there is a team picture in which my grandfather appears on the last row. At the age of twenty, he is staring into the camera without smiling.

Official Program

University of Tennessee
Vanderbilt University
November 18th 1933   25¢

By the time I was born, my grandfather was sixty-six and his aged gait told the story of one too many lost battles on the line of scrimmage. For most of my youth, I can remember seeing him limping on his left leg due to an old football injury to his knee that had worsened with age. I was so young then, I remember envying my grandfather the battle scars he bore from long ago fields of gridiron glory. At that age, I wanted my own sports injury because, for some reason, it seemed to me that football injuries were the ultimate sports badge of honor, a true testament to adulthood.

I've been injured twice playing football. Touch football, that is. These injuries I incurred on different Sundays during college in the midst of our weekly two-hand-touch football games alongside the Lincoln Memorial. It was an august setting for games that were decidedly lacking in majesty, but it was the highlight of our week.

Each Sunday, my friends and I would drag ourselves out of bed to the exhortations of my friend Jason. Jason had an inexhaustible supply of pluck, and a singular capability to bounce back from a night of debaucherous drinking with nary a hangover. We gridiron stars would emerge from our northwest Washington dorm rooms and assemble on the streets of George Washington University's campus (usually in the vicinity of GW's Madison Hall on 23rd and H streets), and then begin our trek down to the fields. We always walked. Down 23rd Street we would stride tossing footballs in the direction of wayward pedestrians and scattering the late-morning joggers with reckless glee.

Derisions and taunts bounced off the empty buildings of our federal government and, occasionally, we ran patterns that approached the front door of the State Department. These were in the days before 9/11, when young, unwashed men who reeked of last night's alcohol were not likely to be seeking the destruction of the edifice. Now, wayward post patterns to the front door would likely get us shot.

Eventually, my roommate of two years, and eventual companion on the DDT trip to Mississippi State, Krishna Tripuraneni, would drop a pass and the football would skitter into the street. Everyone would groan. "Hands" Tripuraneni was always good for at least two or three drops in the open field. (I still encourage every group of guys who play a sport to adopt the moniker of "Hands" for whichever player has the most questionable catching ability. I personally guarantee you that this irony never becomes stale.)

We played in all weather. On my desk at home, I have two

pictures from these Sunday mornings—one photo of us playing in sweat-drenched T-shirts and shorts in the heat of summer, and another of us playing in almost a foot of snow. Usually it was cold, though, and sometimes it was raining. During my sophomore year it seemed to rain every weekend for almost a semester. Even still, we dutifully trudged through the games.

As time passed, we added new objects to the arsenal of our games. First cleats, and later football jerseys (worn in mock jest), and cones to mark our end zone (to replace the tossed off T-shirts, bags, and Gatorade bottles that had previously served as the boundaries of our game).

We were not a talented bunch. In fact, of all the people who ever played in our games, I believe only one person had ever played organized football in his life. Yet, each Sunday found us ready to play and eager to grasp the fundamentals of touch football. The rules we followed were simple:

1. Two passes equaled a first down. The distance of these passes did not matter.
2. There was one blitz every four downs. Otherwise the quarterback could not be rushed until five Mississippi had been audibly counted. Only upon being rushed, could the quarterback run.
3. Arguments were necessary since we self-refereed all games. Jason and I were often the verbal combatants because we were on different teams. Later we both became lawyers. Surely, this is coincidental.
4. Two hands meant two hands. But, without the benefit of say, instant replay or any impartial observer, it was impossible to resolve disputes as to whether or not someone was touched. To this day, my friend Sam Giller will occasionally bring up a kick-return

touchdown (ultimately brought back to where I said I touched him) that he alleges I did not touch him on. It's still a sore subject between us.

We only played tackle football once. The result was disastrous. On our first offensive possession I threw a pass directly between two of the players on my own team who were running patterns in opposite directions. Shaw and Kevin ran into each other at full speed and dropped to the ground clutching their knees with howls of pain.

Almost immediately, my then-roommate, Justin Pierce, channeled the voices of the Madden 2001 video-game announcers which we had spent an inordinate amount of time playing in our apartment. "Not only is that pass off target, but it's a good way to get your receiver decked," he deadpanned. Fortunately Shaw and Kevin were not killed, just knocked out of the game. Shaw's left knee swelled up to the size of a grapefruit, and later had to be drained at the hospital. Kevin limped for a month.

The game continued for one more series during which time Sam Giller made a tackle and his shoulder popped out of socket. Giller stood amidst our plaudits for a great tackle, shoulders slumped unevenly, walked off the field, sat down, and began trying to put his shoulder back into socket. "I'm out," he said quite simply. We never played tackle football again.

Given the limited nature of my own football endeavors, combined with the relatively gentle version of the game I *did* play, it's no small wonder I never incurred an injury as valiant as my grandfather's. But there were two that I ought to mention, if for no other reason than to lend a sense of legitimacy to my own football career: a strained right hamstring and a tooth that almost went through my lip.

The first injury happened in the latter part of my junior year. For some reason, I decided to work on my punting on one of these Sunday mornings. After booming a few and shanking several more, I made contact and felt an unexpected yank from the rear of my leg. When I attempted to run a few seconds later, my hamstring tightened, and I felt like I had been shot with a paintball gun. I had to pull myself out of the weekly game. But, after some coaxing I agreed to play all-time quarterback for both teams. I was like Dan Marino, wheeled out onto the field and standing completely immobile in the face of an angry mob of defenders. Ok, not so much . . . more like a bunch of people who wanted their darnedest to put two hands on me and end every play.

My hamstring injury restricted my activity for two weeks, then I returned, careful not to turn on my afterburnerlike speed for another month. When the afterburners were finally ready to be let loose again, no one who caught me from behind even noticed that I was fully recovered.

My other injury was more serious. During my senior year, while leaping forward to cover a crossing route, my mouth met the head of one Anthony David and blood immediately came pouring forth. I sunk to the ground and filled up one hand with blood and then spit out the rest onto the grass of the field. I imagined that even Abraham Lincoln, nearby cast in stone in his memorial, groaned at the violence.

One of my incisors had sliced into my lip and was almost coming out the other side. The wound was deep, painful, swollen, and probably needed stiches but, instead of going to an emergency room, I simply pulled myself out of the game and sat spitting blood on the sidelines. Later, I inspected the wound in the mirror of our apartment. "Dude," my roommate Justin said, "that was nasty."

Each injury was a small price to pay. As we played football in the shadow of the Lincoln Memorial, several Jews, a couple of Indians, a few Asians, northerners and the southerner, me, it would occasionally occur to me that there are few things more quintessentially American than a love of football. No matter where we had come from or how little, if at all, we had played the game according to organized rules, my friends and I loved these Sunday mornings together. In the sunshine, in the snow, and in the rain we played football and, arguments and on-field disputes notwithstanding, formed lasting bonds.

However, unlike my grandfather, I bear no lasting scars from playing football.

I didn't know it at the time, but GW's football team disbanded in 1966, thirteen years before I was born. Prior to that, George Washington University and the University of Tennessee met in football just one time. That game was played in Washington, D.C., on November 4, 1933, the only year that my grandfather played varsity football for Tennessee.

Sometimes, coincidences are so eerie they make you hold your breath until you've forgotten you were supposed to breathe. And the threads of your own life somehow seem not as distinct or random as they have before. As we played in Washington, the echoes of my grandfather's game were never far away. And I didn't even know it.

SOUTH CAROLINA

My parents have decided to come with me to Columbia, South Carolina, for stop eight on the DDT. All week, leading up to the trip, I felt like we were planning a trip to go look at colleges. Actually, this entire trip has me feeling like I'm going back in time since, once more, my Tennessee Vols will be taking on Steve Spurrier. Except now Spurrier's in South Carolina and I'm a completely mature adult.

Steve Spurrier began coaching Florida in 1990. In the twelve seasons he coached the Gators, Spurrier won six SEC titles, made the visor a fashion statement, and gave the rest of the SEC fits with his perceived cockiness and arrogance. A Heisman Trophy winner at Florida in 1966, Spurrier was a dark-haired assassin whose sideline twitching and fidgeting always seemed accompanied by one spectacular offensive play after another.

Spurrier delighted in gigging other SEC coaches with artful

putdowns (you can't spell Citrus without UT) and sarcastic one-liners (dubbing Florida State Free Shoes University after a scandal about a player accepting free apparel). Somehow, this pain was made all the more intense by the fact that Spurrier is a native Tennessean, having played his high-school football in Johnson City, Tennessee, before leaving to play in college at Florida.

Back in the days when I was less mature, Steve Spurrier was the cause of more cursing fits of mine than any other person in my life. In fact, it's still not even close. When I was a senior in high school in 1996, Florida came into Knoxville and scored thirty-five unanswered points on UT to begin the game. As Florida scored the thirty-fifth point on a fumble return for a touchdown, I let loose a torrent of curses that still makes my parents shiver. Then, I slammed the front door and went on a barefoot walk in my neighborhood. I spent the entire walk cursing aloud to myself while I gesticulated violently with my arms. After a time, I even started skipping around from one foot to another because I was stepping on sharp rocks that were hurting my feet. I looked like I was leading a primordial Native-American rain dance. It's a wonder I wasn't committed.

The 1996 game was the Steve Spurrier *coup de grace*. It represented five consecutive losses to Florida for my Vols, and it cemented my hate for Steve Spurrier. Sometimes, I had nightmares where Spurrier was standing on the sideline laughing maniacally as his team scored point after point after point on my Vols. Eventually, when I would wake up covered in sweat I could still see Spurrier grinning on the sideline wearing his visor and holding up the play chart in front of his mouth. I pictured him sending in a play called "make Clay Travis sleepless for a month." And, inevitably, the play worked.

After the 1996 debacle, I headed to college in Washington, D.C., where, during my freshman year, I wore a shirt that featured a quote from Will Rogers on the front, NEVER MET A MAN I DIDN'T LIKE. And on the back, it said: WILL ROGERS NEVER MET STEVE SPURRIER. This shirt gave me great solace after Spurrier beat my Vols again in 1997. Until, that is, I wore it to a party in Dupont Circle during National Coming Out Day. Every guy was winking and waving at me and I had no idea what was going on, until I looked down at the lettering on the front of my shirt. Score another one for the Old Ball Coach. I couldn't even insult Spurrier properly.

During my senior year of college, Spurrier won again when Jabar Gaffney caught a touchdown past for just four one-hundredths of a second with under a minute to play. My roommate Justin returned home and commented, "As soon as Florida scored, I turned to everyone and said, 'I hope Clay doesn't break anything of mine.' " He needn't have worried. Instead of doing violence to my possessions I walked to our fourth-floor balcony and contemplated jumping. I didn't jump, because somehow I was convinced Steve Spurrier would end up the beneficiary of my life-insurance policy. Put simply, he owned me.

Then, in January 2002, barely one month after a life-reaffirming 34–32 victory for my Vols in Gainesville, Steve Spurrier abruptly left college football for the NFL. It was sweet redemption; I could pretend my Vols had finally sent him packing. My psychological well-being soared. It never rained, birds always sang, and it wasn't even that cold in winter. At long last, my team and, by some odd calculus even if it made no logical sense, I had triumphed. Fought the good fight for so long and taken so many bruising body blows (like Ali against Foreman), that finally, God rest Spurrier's soul, we had won the war.

But then, like all villains in scary movies, Steve Spurrier came back for one final scare. Yep, he took over the South Carolina head-coaching job.

In the fall of 2005, Spurrier once again came into Knoxville and left victorious by a score of 16–15. On the night Peyton Manning's jersey was retired no less. I watched the UT–South Carolina game from a bar in San Juan, Puerto Rico. By the end of the game, I felt like Steve Spurrier had taken one gigantic ocean-sprawling step across the Atlantic and kicked me in the balls once more. Yep, I wasn't even safe from him in the Commonwealth of Puerto Rico.

And yet, despite all the abuse he's heaped upon me, I still like Steve Spurrier. And everywhere I go in the SEC there are fans of other vanquished teams who feel the exact same way. Which leads me to conclude that, if you want to analogize how abusive relationships work to Southern men, explain to them that it's the equivalent of still liking Steve Spurrier, even though he's done their teams wrong so many times before. You know you shouldn't, but you just can't help yourself.

So, it was with a great degree of trepidation that I set out for Columbia, South Carolina, to watch the Vols take on Steve Spurrier and the Gamecocks for stop eight of the DDT.

My dad insists on driving as we leave Nashville, which means for the first time on the DDT I'll be riding in the back seat of my own car. This is vaguely uncomfortable, primarily because my dad is not a particularly fast driver. I toss these concerns into the recesses of my mind and begin fiddling around with all the buttons and gizmos in the back seat of my car that I've never gotten to play with before. Pretty soon, I've constructed an odd weather pattern whereby cool air is hitting the top of my head and hot air is slamming into my shins. It's entirely possible I'm about to artificially create rain. Cars are whizzing by on both sides of us completely unaware of the scientific breakthrough currently taking place in my car.

The trees of Tennessee are bathed in vibrant shades of orange, red, yellow, and brown. Last week, while watching the Tennessee-Alabama game on television, I kept thinking that the overhead shots of the fans in their oranges and reds resembled the colors of fall across the South. During this drive, I'm sure of it. Tennessee in late fall is one of the most beautiful places on earth.

I read for what seems like nine hours. When I finally stop reading we're stuck in Knoxville traffic and only 180 miles from Nashville. "What happened, Dad?" I ask. "This Knoxville traffic is rough," he says, confidently skipping over the preceding eight hours and fifty minutes of his driving. Once through Knoxville, I am handed the keys. Night is approaching and we are still in Tennessee. As we cross into North Carolina my parents become fixated on the number of semitrucks on the road.

"Look at them," my mom says, "just look at all of them." Her eyes are slit like a cobra's right before it pounces. It's possible there is not a person on earth who dislikes semitrucks more than my mom. She's been antisemi for my entire life. "Why do they all have to be going the same direction as us? We need to make them all go back to the railroads again," she says. My dad is silent in the back of the car. I used to argue with her about how no one would be able to afford anything without trucks transporting our goods and that the wheels of American commerce would come rolling off. But this argument is eternally ineffective. My mom doesn't care. She would rather live in a

cave and roast captured squirrels for every meal than ever have
to drive alongside a semitruck.

I receive two telephone calls and chat for a bit. When I
hang up, my dad reports, "Eighteen of the last twenty-one ve-
hicles we've passed have been semis." "I told you," my mom
says, vindicated.

My parents are united in their antisemism, thanks to thirty-
seven years of marriage. I was their first-born son, in 1979. My
parents are lifelong Southerners, and so were their parents and
their grandparents and their great-grandparents. In fact, my
family tree is conspicuously absent of Yankees. At least as far
back as we can trace our family history, everyone has lived below the Mason-Dixon Line.

To a large degree, my love of sports comes from my dad,
Norm Travis, who has never met a game or a competition that
he wasn't fascinated by. Throughout my entire childhood any
time he was asked to play kickball, wiffle ball, basketball, baseball, football, or any other game, my dad participated whole-
heartedly. My dad even invents games where they otherwise
don't exist. When two of my college roommates visited us in
Nashville during college, they returned from an airport trip to
inform me that, to kill time while waiting for their flight, my
dad had hidden quarters on the carpet and had them compete,
as twenty-one-year-old men, to see who could find the quarters
first. Once, my uncle sat on the porch watching my dad create a
new game out of a single Wiffle Ball, a beanbag, and one dart
from a broken dart board. "There has never been," my uncle
told me, "a man who loves games more than your dad."

Conversely, there has rarely been a game my mom really
liked. Once, when my dad was out of town and I was eight or
nine, I persuaded my mom to throw me ground balls to field in

the backyard. Mom agreed. She walked outside, threw two ground balls that barely reached me and came so slowly I could field them with my bare hand, and then pronounced her shoulder to be injured. After that, mom never participated in outdoor games as much.

Before she threw out her shoulder tossing me grounders, Mom attended the University of Tennessee to work on her master's and she still complains about the fact that she couldn't use her parking-lot pass on football Saturdays in Knoxville. She has always cast a wary eye upon my and my dad's interest in sports, considering it, I believe, a bit too passionate for our own good. Once, when I was fifteen, after UT had squandered a football lead against Mississippi State, I was so angry I rushed to my room, slammed the door, and punched the wall with such force that my mother's ire was provoked. She followed me to my bedroom, ripped open the door and shouted, "Richard Clay Travis, you are not going to grow up and become one of those Tennessee fans who beats their wives when UT loses a football game." When my mother addressed me by all three names, I knew it was trouble.

But, as we've aged and avoided committing felonies in the wake of our team's crushing defeats, Mom has become much more of a sports fan. In fact, at this point, she's a legitimate Tennessee Vol fan. Even if she still resents the invalid parking pass of her early twenties.

Back on the road, our travel schedule is throwing my parent's own schedule for a loop. We eat dinner in Hendersonville, North Carolina, at a place called Binion's at around nine. This is roughly four-and-a-half hours later than my parents typically eat dinner. As we pull into the parking lot, my mom asks, "Who are all these people out at nine at night on a Thursday?" I'll tell you Mom, hooligans, each and every one of them.

Our destination is actually Charleston, because we're going to spend Thursday and Friday nights there before coming back to Columbia for the football game. We don't arrive in Charleston until after midnight eastern, making this the sixth latest night my dad has been awake since I was born.

We get a suite at the Fairfield Inn in North Charleston, which is really just a single room with a column down the center. I get the pull-out couch, upon which I can lie down and still wave to both my parents ten feet away. I have no idea how this is considered a suite. By this logic, my 900-square-foot condo is an eight-bedroom Tuscan villa. All night long, I dream that I am bombing a college interview.

We spend Friday in Charleston. I had never been to the city before. It is spectacular. Of course, on the day we visit, I wear a T-shirt, and it's freezing and the rain doesn't stop falling. Who would have figured you could freeze to death on an October day in Charleston?

Confession time: I'm a Civil War history buff. Have been all my life. In fact, I once went to Civil War camp in high school. I made the mistake of telling my wife this story once and she hasn't stopped making fun of me yet. Even worse I tried to defend myself by pointing out that I got a scholarship. "A scholarship to go to Civil War camp, I mean, that's useless," she said, "I'm surprised they don't have to pay people to go." Then, I made the further mistake of telling her that there were other high school students my own age also there. "There were other people who were Civil War camp nerds like you?" she asked, incredulous. Then she didn't stop laughing for five minutes.

At Civil War camp, we lived in the dorms at Gettysburg

College, took tours of battlefields, attended frequent lectures, and debated Robert E. Lee's strategy on his invasion of Pennsylvania. Seriously. I loved every minute of it. One day, my roommate and I slept through the opening breakfast and missed a bus departure to tour a battlefield in northern Virginia. We didn't arrive until the afternoon. When the other kids saw us, you would have thought we had robbed a bank and been involved in a massive gunfight with a cabal of syphilitic prostitutes. "You mean you just slept right through breakfast and the bus," asked one of my bespectacled sleepaway camp brethren. His eyes were agape. Yep, after that no one ever had greater Civil War sleepaway camp street cred than I did.

So, anyway, my parents and I take a trolley tour of Charleston. Which is great. Primarily because I am the only person who is not a senior citizen on the tour. This makes my mom very happy. I'm twenty-seven and she is still impressed by how mature I am for my age. "Isn't this tour great?" she asks. I nod my head and she beams at me. I am the best son in the entire world. Not only that, there isn't a close second. I'm sorry, it's the truth. Ask my mom.

Per Civil War sleepaway camp blood-brother rules, you have to visit any Civil War site when you have the opportunity to do so. So, I went to Fort Sumter in Charleston Harbor. We ride out in the pouring rain on a ferry that is full of seventh- and eighth-grade kids who are racing around the boat playing tag. My decision to wear short sleeves is making less and less sense as the cold wind snaps off Charleston Harbor. These kids are rushing around like hungry tigers and I'm beginning to seriously question how much actual Civil War knowledge these seventh and eighth graders have.

My wife calls as our boat docks in the pouring rain. "We're

at Fort Sumter," I say. "Where?" she asks. "That place where you Yankees started the War of Northern Aggression," I say in response. "Oh, jeez," she says, "the Civil War again?" I hang up after informing her that she is missing a great time. This is a lie. Everyone is freezing. Fort Sumter is on a small island and resembles a decrepit open-air mansion.

Onshore, I get my picture taken alongside a cannon. Actually, my mom has to take six or seven photos with my digital camera before both the cannon and I fit in the frame. Several of her photos appear to capture the sky and nothing else.

Once inside, we listen to a park ranger give a presentation about life in Fort Sumter. The seventh and eighth graders are pinching one another. My mind is made up: These kids are not future Civil War sleepaway camp material.

Per Civil War sleepaway camp rules, fort visitors must be photographed alongside a cannon.

Doing my best to dodge the freezing, plump rain drops, I take a tour of the outside of the fort. For a time I close my eyes and try to imagine what it would have sounded like for huge, booming cannon balls to slam into its brick walls. When I open my eyes, I see a dolphin frolicking in the water in front of the ramparts of the fort. This seems like a favorable omen. Also, it obsesses me, and distracts me from my physical discomfort during the return trip to shore.

Am I the only person who is completely shocked that dolphins can swim in regular freshwater rivers? Or that you can just randomly see dolphins in Charleston Harbor? Why does Charleston not take better advantage of this magnificent anomaly? Abysmal marketing, absolutely abysmal.

I will say this for the state of South Carolina, though: Every place we go to eat has Mello Yello to drink. Except a restaurant called Sticky Fingers which has awesome barbecue, and so makes up for the soda error. Plus our waiter seems generally pained when I request Mello Yello and they don't have it. "Awww, man," he says, "we had it until last week and then we replaced it with Mr. Pibb." The disdain in his voice is palpable. *Who even drinks Mr. Pibb?* he seems to be saying in sympathy.

South Carolina definitely has its share of 'Bama Bangs. The most interesting is on the front of a weekly newspaper in Charleston. Two men are canoodling and the article is about South Carolina's amendment to ban gay marriage, which, I would imagine, will receive 99.9 percent of the vote. Yep, 'Bama Bangs are so ingrained in South Carolina that they've made the leap from fraternity staple to gay men's fashion. Some would argue that this is no leap at all.

We return from Charleston and get back to the hotel room. My dad turns on the television and scrolls through the channels looking for the St. Louis Cardinals-Detroit Tigers World Series game. "Must be another rain delay," he says. I tell him it's too early for the game to have started. My dad brushes his teeth and reads the paper for a little while. Then, he turns on the television again. "What's the score?" I ask. "Nothing, nothing, bottom of the first," he says. Then, he turns off the television and the overhead light.

"What are you doing?" I ask.

"We're going to bed," says my mom. It is, and this is the complete truth, eight-forty eastern. This makes it seven-forty in our own time zone back in Nashville. I don't even know what to do. "Don't let us bother you," says my mom from the darkness of her bed ten feet away.

I feel like Bart Simpson when he spent the night with Ned Flanders and the whole family went to bed while it was still daylight. I sit on the pull-out sofa ten feet away from my parents and am silent. I can't turn on the television so, instead, I put on my gym shorts and go downstairs. While I ride the bike, I determine that the pool and Jacuzzi outside are going to be open for over two hours after my parents have gone to bed. This is the first time I've ever known anyone to go to bed in a hotel room before the pool is even closed.

I make several calls on my cell phone and hang out for a while in the lobby. No one is around. I read a couple of brochures about Charleston attractions. The few people who do enter the hotel look at me strangely. Eventually, I tire of hanging out by myself in the lobby and go upstairs. My parents are sound asleep, and my dad is snoring.

I go into the bathroom, shut the door behind me, turn on the exhaust vent and call my wife. "What do you think of the game?" she asks. I tell her I can't watch the World Series because my parents are already asleep. She starts to laugh. Then, she gives me a play-by-play from the bottom of the eighth on. We talk for a half hour and this entire conversation takes place while I'm sitting on the floor in the bathroom with the door closed and the exhaust vent running. Yep, I'm twenty-seven, going on sixteen.

Predictably, my parents wake up at the crack of dawn. Luckily, they let me sleep. My parents have recently retired, so their schedules are completely up to them. Despite this scheduling freedom my dad often wakes up at four thirty in the morning when he hears the newspaper land in the driveway. My mom says a few times she has woken up and found him sitting in the den reading the newspaper while it is pitch black outside. "I'll say, 'Norm, what are you doing up already?' and he'll say, 'The paper's here.' "

We arrive in Columbia by noon for the seven forty-five eastern kickoff of Tennessee-South Carolina. Alongside my parents I take a stroll through the Horseshoe (old quad) of the University of South Carolina. The buildings date from 1805, and the live oaks lining the center of the campus are majestic. All around us tiny acorns are pinging onto the brick walkways.

No state in the South is anywhere near as attached to their state tree as South Carolinians are to the palmetto tree. The thing is everywhere—on the really cool state flag with the crescent moon and blue background, on the flags flown above Fort Sumter back in 1861, probably in hidden (and not so hidden) areas on South Carolina girls' bodies. In South Carolina, there are even lots of people named after the palmetto. Or, at least, this seems likely. I bet most Americans couldn't tell you what their state flag looks like, but if you ever questioned whether someone was actually from South Carolina or not, just ask him what the state tree is. If he answers incorrectly, there is a 100 percent chance he isn't from South Carolina.

My favorite fact from the South Carolina pamphlet I'm reading as we walk is: "The brick wall, which today borders the old campus area, was originally built to confine the unruly students, who sometimes entertained themselves by firing weapons, drinking, gambling and burning the wooden steps of the architectural treasures you view today." Yet we're supposed to react with indignation when some current college athlete gets

arrested for having an open container? Please, college kids today are miscreant slackers when it comes to the cats from the
early 1800s. They used to burn the school . . . for fun.

At three in the afternoon, we arrive at Williams-Brice
Stadium, which is two miles off South Carolina's main campus
and connected to the South Carolina State Fairgrounds. Based
on my corn dog research, this makes Carolina fans ripe for corn
dog jokes as well. There are grass tailgating spots that are identified by hanging wires with numbers written on them. The stadium itself is in a sort of industrial zone that is zigzagged by
train tracks in every direction and consequently the stadium
almost looks like the center of a train-track roundabout. All
around me, literal gamecocks have been recorded and are crowing on loudspeakers outside tailgates.

I meet up with Drew Toney, who will be my tour guide
around South Carolina's stadium. Drew practices law now in
Columbia and is a friend of my law school classmates John and
Heather, who were with me for the Vandy-South Carolina
game. Drew has graciously agreed to show me the proverbial
ropes. We immediately head to the tailgate of Darby Plexico,
who is in the process of steaming 110 pounds of oysters. For the
first time in my life, I eat oysters that appear to be hidden in legitimate rocks. Pretty tasty.

I learn that, a couple of times a year, Carolina football
games coincide with the South Carolina State Fair. Plexico
says it is an unbelievable scene. "I mean when you're a kid and
you go to the state fair you go for the rides, and you don't really
notice the other people there. Then, you go when you're an
adult and realize that there are all these twelve-year-old-
mothers everywhere." For the record, this also pretty much
sums up the Tennessee State Fair. My favorites are the people

who go to the state fair on multiple days, as if there's too much excitement to take in during a single day's visit. (Also, for the record, when I was a senior in high school, a man got beheaded at the Tennessee State Fair by one of those swinging boat rides. He was trying to pick up change that had fallen out of a patron's pockets. No word on whether he could still see after the beheading.)

I buy tickets for myself, my mom, and my dad for ninety dollars each. This is twice the forty-five dollar face value and I buy them too early. But you know how things get when your mom is around and keeps wondering whether you know what you're doing. Earlier we had driven by some guy three miles from the stadium, a professional scalper it seemed, and my mom had wanted me to pull over and negotiate with him from the car. Finally, my dad stood up in my defense, "He's done this a few times, Liz, just let him take care of it." But, by that point, my mom was in my head. So, I pulled the trigger early on the ticket buy. This is the first ticket-buying error of the DDT and, of course, it's the only one my parents see.

With tickets in hand, we continue our tour of South Carolina tailgates. Eventually, we make our way to a group of tailgaters who are flying the English flag. Yep, Dan Blackmon and friends are not only huge Carolina fans, but also follow English soccer with a passion. The group has a trip to England to watch games planned for April. Blackmon immediately apologizes for the food situation. "There are eight of us and one person is supposed to bring food each week. This week our food got left in Aiken. So we've been eating salsa and candy corn all day."

Conversation at the tailgate centers around a movie called *Who's Your Caddy?* which is currently being filmed in nearby Aiken, South Carolina, and will star, prepare yourself, Queen

Latifah and Andy Milonakis. I'm not sure if they're going to rush this one out this fall for Oscar season or not. Former South Carolina tennis star Ben Cook joins the conversation, "It was wild. Andy Milonakis was buying shots for everyone in the bar the other night," he says.

Blackmon is wearing khaki pants that are popular in South Carolina. They have the gamecock insignia sewn in all over them and I've seen at least ten guys wearing them so far. Somewhere, Vanderbilt Chancellor Gordon Gee is angry that others are stealing his pants' glory. I ask Blackmon how much they cost. At first, he won't say, then finally he relents. "One-hundred fifty-two dollars," he says, "and they screwed up the hem." Where can you find them? www.stadiumpants.com, of course. Interestingly, the Florida Gator pants don't even come in khaki, just jean shorts.

Dan Blackmon's fashionable Gamecock-covered khaki pants.

Visors are everywhere among South Carolina fans. I ask my English-soccer fan hosts whether the visors were popular before Spurrier arrived. "We liked Spurrier even before he came here, back when he was beating our ass in the 1990s," says Bob Cook. "Three of us (he gestures to two of his buddies) started wearing them in the late 1990s as a show of respect for Spurrier." They were in the vanguard. Since Spurrier's hiring, sale of Gamecock visors have increased by, conservatively, 19,000 percent.

It's also not an exaggeration to say that South Carolina fans see Steve Spurrier as a messiah. "It's divine intervention that Spurrier is here now," says Dan Blackmon, grinning. "God smiled on the Cocks."

Ben Cook explains that South Carolina fans have had it rough in past SEC seasons. "I was here when Tee Martin (former Tennessee quarterback) completed 742 consecutive passes against us." Actually Martin completed only twenty-three consecutive passes back in the miraculous 1998 Tennessee national championship season but that set a then-NCAA record for consecutive completions by a quarterback. But this is par for the course, when it comes to South Carolina football. In their entire history as a football program, South Carolina has won only four bowl games.

Cook also tells us about the Tennessee-South Carolina game in Knoxville during Peyton Manning's senior year in 1997. Jim Bethune, the former South Carolina ticket manager, had procured sideline passes for several of the guys. During that game, Carolina quarterback Anthony Wright suffered a knee injury, and backup Vick Penn was placed in charge of the offense. According to Cook, when he and his buddies entered the locker room at halftime, Carolina was losing and the entire team was eating Reese's Peanut Butter Cups and paying no attention to then-coach Brad Scott. Ultimately, Scott attempted to rouse the team by asserting, "Vick Penn makes plays," and clapping his hands furiously. The players picked at their chocolate cups, stared off into space, and returned to the field to lose 22–7. Not surprisingly, Gamecock fans still react bitterly when reminded of the Brad Scott era.

All around us there are season-long parking passes that can be purchased. Some of these parking places could literally include the directions, "Turn off the paved road, drive across two different train tracks, enter through the chain link fence, drive over the dry creekbed, and stop when you hit the barbed wire." For this privilege, people pay well in excess of one hundred dollars per year.

If you want to avoid the expense and difficulty of obtaining parking passes, however, alongside Williams-Brice Stadium there is a brand new tower featuring condos. The condos have balconies, and are a long pass away from the stadium itself. Many an envious eye is cast in their direction. Supposedly, there are three other condo towers in various planning stages. Compared to how much parking costs, several hundred thousand dollars for a condo seems like a bargain.

Currently, prime tailgating locations in South Carolina are at a premium. For instance, some UT fans are tailgating on the actual train tracks. I ask my host, Drew Toney, whether trains come through very often. "Yeah," he says, "pretty often actually." This may be the first recorded version of tailgate chicken.

Leaving behind the train-track tailgaters, Drew Toney and I arrive in the vicninty of the famous Cockabooses. The Cockabooses are railroad cars that sit on abandoned tracks directly behind the south end of Williams-Brice Stadium. We enter Cockaboose #3, which is co-owned by Raj and Bhavna Vasudeva. The Cockaboose is one slender room with a single bathroom. It features a stocked bar and is decorated nicer than my condo. It's packed with both Tennessee and South Carolina fans who are eating and drinking heavily. While I'm inside I keep thinking about the Boxcar Children books I read as a kid. Unfortunately for me, and unlike the Alden children, I have no rich grandfather to spring for a Cockaboose, since they sell for $200,000 or more.

The Vasudevas welcome us with open arms, and their food is excellent. I ask Bhavna how they ended up Cocks fans. "We came down from Illinois and then . . ." she shrugs with a warm smile on her face. Somehow this answer suffices.

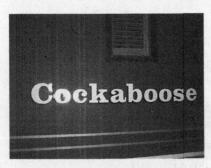

For two hundred thousand dollars or more, this Cockaboose could be yours.

While there I meet Vol fan R. D. Singh, who was born in India and received his master's from the University of Tennessee in 1977. Singh now lives in Memphis and sees the Vols play several times a year. I ask him what turned him into an SEC football fan. "I've always loved sports," he says, "but prior to 1974 I had no real knowledge of American football. Then I got to UT and that was my indoctrination. I've been suckered ever since." Welcome to the twenty-first century South, where SEC football will seduce you no matter where you're from.

We go to the upstairs Cockaboose deck where you can stand and watch the crowd filing into the stadium. South Carolina's teams have been known as the Gamecocks for over a hundred years, due in no small measure to the fact that for a long time the state of South Carolina has been known as a breeding and training ground for the gamecocks used in cockfighting. South Carolina's own General Thomas Sumter was also known as "The Fighting Gamecock" during the Revolutionary War. Over two hundred years later, the popularity of the moniker remains, even though cockfighting is now illegal in every state but Louisiana.

All around us chants of "Game" and then the answered "Cocks" echo into the night sky. Naturally, this chant appeals to my sophomoric sense of humor, particularly in light of the recently learned fact that gamecocks don't have penises.

Leaving the Cockaboose and my host Drew Toney, I meet my parents amid the onrush of humanity, and we enter the stadium. We are in the upper deck, section 501, and start our walk upstairs. Shortly after we are seated, the Carolina Jumbotron shows highlights from the season, which are accompanied by the music from *Pirates of the Caribbean*.

There are lots of drunk people in this stadium, which makes using the urinal trough an absolute adventure. Incidentally, I think SEC football stadiums, along with elementary schools, are the last bastion of the urinal trough. People are swaying in every direction alongside you while they pee. Urine is bouncing off the porcelain like liquid mortar rounds. Standing in line for the bathroom, a man begins a "Big 10 sucks" chant. Vols and Gamecocks join in the chant together. About this time, I suffer the first casualty of the DDT: I lose my pen into the urinal trough of Williams-Brice. And there it stays. No way I'm reaching down into one of those things.

South Carolina's football team enters to the chords of *2001: A Space Odyssey*. The song isn't that audible up in my section, and I'm not sure if the problem is that the band isn't very loud or that the audio system has malfunctioned. Nonetheless, I am entertained by the fog that surrounds the team as they enter. Somewhere, Jake "The Snake" Roberts just flexed his bicep.

The "Cocks" portion of the chant is beginning to overwhelm the "game" half, so that soon it sounds like the entire stadium is screaming, simply, "Cocks!" I attribute this imbalance to every South Carolina man embracing his inner seventh grader. In fact, the whole Cocks business reminds me of algebra at Martin Luther King Magnet when we used to sit in the back of the class and compete to see who could say penis the loudest without getting in trouble. You know, somebody starts off really soft and then it keeps getting louder until you or your friend gets kicked out of class. (For the record, this game also caught on again for just about two weeks when I was at Vanderbilt Law School. And I won. But I'm not bragging or anything).

South Carolina is a pretty flat state, and Williams-Brice is a pretty tall stadium so, sitting in one of the top rows, I feel like I can almost see all the way to Charleston. At least I try to see Charleston because I don't want to look onto the field and see Steve Spurrier clapping his hands together on the opposing sideline. It hurts too much.

The only thing that consoles me, when I look at Spurrier, is thinking about the ridiculous Digiorno Pizza commercial he appeared in. In the commercial, Spurrier flits about the sideline calling plays, while before him a team of men wearing dresses faces off against a team clad in normal apparel. Worst of all for Spurrier, I'm not even sure whether he's coaching the guys in the dresses or the guys in normal uniforms. It's a ridiculous commercial, and I relish the fact that he is in it. Now, if only Steve Spurrier had to coach in a dress.

There's a really strong wind blowing south to north. Up in the top of the stadium it's officially South Carolina cold. How do the dolphins survive? The cold is suddenly less bitter once the game begins, as Tennessee's defense scores on the second play of the game. I had barely returned to my seat from the urinal trough when I was leaping up and cheering amid the other UT fans. We're so far up that my dad doesn't realize it was an interception returned for a touchdown and not a fumble returned for a touchdown until I tell him at halftime. "Really," he asks, "I could have sworn it was a fumble." But even though he doesn't know how we scored, my dad still whoops with ardor.

On the next possession, Tennessee intercepts a tipped pass in the end zone, which sets off a raucous celebration in the section around us. We're so far from that end zone that I can't even tell for sure what happened for several seconds. UT then drives all the way to South Carolina's end of the field and scores on their own tipped ball for a touchdown. As Erik Ainge threw this pass across his body into the end zone, I was screaming for him to throw the ball away. But, crazily, this tipped ball also bounced in our direction. At the end of the first quarter, the Vols are leading 14–0 and Steve Spurrier is in misery on the opposing sideline. But I still don't want to look at Spurrier because it would take at least a forty-point lead for me to feel at all comfortable against a Spurrier-coached team. Indeed, South Carolina proceeds to score ten unanswered points to slice into the Vols lead.

It's still 14–10 Vols at the half and my shins are bruised, thanks to the smallest walkway between seats that I've ever seen. The bleachers have chair backs but, somehow, this makes someone actually passing you in the aisle a near impossibility. Even if you stand up, it's still a complicated maneuver. If a fat person tries to pass you, you might as well just stand on the seat itself and brace yourself. And if the fat person is carrying nachos, as they always are, you're done for.

My dad turns to me, "Well," he says, "if you'd told me at the beginning of the game that we'd have had a four-point lead at halftime I would have taken it. Wouldn't you?" I agree with him that I would. Particularly against Spurrier. My dad loves to say things like this. He is the most optimistic fan on earth. The Vols could be losing by thirty-five with five minutes left and my dad will say something like, "I think we've really played hard in the fourth quarter." But both of us are nervous about what might happen in the second half. My mom is not. "It's cold up here," she says shivering. The only thing my mom hates more than semitrucks is the cold.

As the third quarter begins, everyone agrees that we can't see the player's numbers, hear the announcer, or hear any explanations of penalties from the referee. It's like watching a game from the blimp. Worst of all, Steve Spurrier is on the opposing sideline, so I keep expecting a receiver to miraculously appear wide open somewhere on the field with the ball already headed in the air in his direction. And then it happens, South Carolina scores first in the second half to take a 17–14 lead when UT leaves a South Carolina receiver all alone in the end zone. As a general rule, it's almost impossible for twenty-one men to be nowhere near the twenty-second player on the limited expanse of a football field. Spurrier makes this play an art form. At least, against Tennessee he does. No one creates offensive space for his players better than Steve Spurrier. In the immediate aftermath of this wide-open touchdown pass the stadium is rocking. Literally. The upper deck is swaying a bit. This is not the least bit troubling. I mean, we're only in the open air in the tallest structure in South Carolina. The cock is crowing, as it does after big plays or to get the crowd in Williams-Brice fired up. As I stew over South Carolina's touchdown, I realize that it's sort of surprising that this cock-crowing trend could catch on in the South. After all, didn't the cock crowing mean that Peter had failed to acknowledge Jesus? Maybe this accounts for South Carolina's poor showing in football. After all, if you were Jesus would you want to be reminded about your friend betraying you? How could He possibly favor the Cocks?

However, with every South Carolina fan standing and screaming as loud as they can, UT takes possession and scores to take a 21–17 lead. At least we hope it's a touchdown. That's because there's a penalty flag on the field. Seeing a penalty flag on the field immediately after your team scores makes the ensuing penalty announcement seem like it takes eons. In the upper deck, there are tons of Vol fans alongside us and all of them groan in unison when they sees the penalty flag on the field. But, sweet justice, the penalty is against Carolina and the crowd around me exults. Now, it feels like the upper deck is moving even more. But I don't mind. If I'm going to die in a terrifying plummet to the concrete below, at least my team will get the win when officials cancel the rest of the game. My dad and I exchange fives and the band's playing of "Rocky Top" carries across the cold South Carolina night into the shaking upper deck. "That was big," I say to my dad, "Really big."

With the score still 21–17, UT's Jonathan Hefney returns a punt to the Carolina five. As Hefney jukes across the field all of the fans around me stand as one. Poised on our toes, fingers clenched tightly in gloves, we're all ready to scream with blood-curdling fury should the play end as we hope. When Hefney is tackled just five yards from the end zone, I quickly scan the field for flags and see there are none. On the next play UT scores to take a 28–17 lead. My dad and I are whooping with joy in the Carolina cold. Even my mom is cheering loudly. For a moment, she seems to have forgotten how cold it is in the upper deck.

Shortly thereafter, UT's Jonathan Wade absolutely mugs South Carolina wide receiver Sidney Rice and there is no call. It's really saying something when I can see the penalty on the field from where I'm sitting. Every UT fan around me acknowledges that we got away with one. The South Carolina student section comes undone, raining debris into the end zone nearest them. The cock is not crowing.

When, on the next play after the South Carolina punt, Vol quaterback Erik Ainge goes deep to Robert Meachem for sixty-three yards, the South Carolina fans begin to file out of the stadium. Every one around me is surprised so many people are leaving with so much time remaining. And with Spurrier as their coach. Do these South Carolina fans not remember what Steve Spurrier has done to my Vols in the past fifteen years?

Erik Ainge rolls out on a called quarterback sneak (the dumbest play call of the year) and gets tackled. The tackle is awkward and Ainge rolls up his ankle and hobbles off the field. My friend Bryon Smith describes Ainge going down in a heap during the tackle as resembling "an octopus falling out of a tree." Despite this injury, UT holds on to win 31–24. We celebrate the victory in the upper deck. My dad says, "When you can beat Spurrier, it doesn't matter how you do it, you take it." Dad is right. We exchange fives with the hordes of UT fans climbing down the concrete steps singing "Rocky Top" as they walk. Even my mom is excited. "Whew," she says. "Your grandpa would have liked to have seen this one." Which is true, of course. Only he would have been watching it on tape delay.

After the game, we make our way downstairs closer to the field and watch as Spurrier's somber press conference is played on the Jumbotron. UT fans enjoy taking Spurrier's picture alongside the scoreboard that records our victory over him.

Victory, no matter how ugly, is always treasured by Vol fans when Steve Spurrier is on the opposing sideline. I take my own picture of Spurrier and hope he can't sleep for a month.

But Volunteer fan antipathy for Spurrier is canceled out by Gamecock adoration of their new coach. How much do South Carolina fans love Steve Spurrier? After the loss, there are many more calls to the Gamecock Radio Network calling into question the band's performance than the head coach's.

Back outside the stadium, after sitting in traffic for over an hour, as my parents and I begin the long drive back to Nashville, I know that somewhere, the mad genius Spurrier is already concocting plays or talking to recruits that will make me miserable in the future. And, no matter how much I'm going to hate him when that time comes, I wouldn't have it any other way. Spurrier helps make the SEC special. Even if he also gives me nightmares.

WHY CAN'T WE ALL JUST GET ALONG?

As evidenced by the anti-Big 10 chanting in the bathroom at South Carolina, no two conferences in America hate each other more than the Southeastern Conference and the Big 10. I learned this in college when I traveled north of the Mason-Dixon Line and experienced bromides like these each Saturday afternoon: "The teams down South would be so much better if they could afford shoes." "Seriously, people in Mississippi, they have outhouses, right?" And worst and most grating of all, "Charles Woodson deserved the Heisman Trophy over Peyton Manning." I never thought I would get over my anger at the University of Michigan . . . and then I went and married a Michigan grad. Sometimes, irony is knowing that, in the event of divorce, half your assets are heading back to Ann Arbor. It's okay though, really, the band played "Rocky Top" at our Michigan wedding.

Notwithstanding the détente in my own life, the tides of anger and retribution have not lessened over the years between the two conferences. Instead, the hate has continued to boil producing a proverbial witches' brew of callous insults, intended and perceived slights, and head-to-head matchups that only materialize in bowl games. (For purposes of this analysis I'm discarding Kentucky and Indiana's so-called football rivalry.) And now I come not to bury the conference discord, but to inflame it.

Without further ado, here are eleven arguments and counterarguments on behalf of both conferences to anger everyone and settle nothing. The Big 10 gets five and the SEC gets five, and I get one to decide it all for eternity.

Big 10 Arguments

1. All SEC schools cheat. This is completely inaccurate. Only the following SEC schools have been on probation in the past twenty years: Alabama, Kentucky, Georgia, Florida, Mississippi State, Mississippi, Tennessee, South Carolina, Auburn, Arkansas, and LSU. Vanderbilt has not. So, clearly, this whole cheating argument is blown way out of proportion. Also, the SEC has been penalized by the NCAA for rules violations forty-three times since the early 1950s, which is more than any other athletic conference. But that's unfair, because most athletic conferences did not exist in the 1950s so, of course, the SEC is going to have more.

2. Most SEC players cannot read. Again, this is just not true. Most SEC running backs cannot read but they hardly make up the entire team.

3. SEC fans aren't even smart enough to get into their own shabby state schools. Touché. That's French for touchy. You wouldn't do very well on the SAT or ACT either if your bangs kept dropping down into your eyes and blocking out the answer sheet. Also, if our schools are so bad, how come so many people keep moving to the South from Big 10 country?

4. SEC schools exist almost entirely for football, ergo culture, learning, and literacy never make it inside the doublewides. Again, simply not true, the SEC has Vanderbilt. Also many SEC fans live in singlewides and there is not room for much of anything in a singlewide.

5. SEC fans always argue there is a northern bias. The northern bias is this: Our schools are better than yours at academics, intelligence of students, facilities, and football. Ouch. Who's talking about academics, intelligence of students, and facilities?

SEC Arguments

6. There is a northern bias. Of course there is a northern bias. It exists because newspapers and Internet columns are written for the literate. If everyone still communicated with hollers from one valley to another things would be equal.

7. Big 10 girls are ugly. Admittedly, this has nothing to do with football and is blatant name-calling. Also, I am not the best judge of this question because I am married to a Big 10 girl and would like to continue to share the same bed with her. Having said that, this is the only argument SEC schools ever make outside of football, so its universal status may have some credence.

8. Big 10 players are slow and fat and work in Detroit factories producing manhole covers when they graduate. Is "manhole covers" a *double entendre* here? Even I'm not sure. And anyway, this is not true. Some Big 10 players go to work in meat-packing plants when they graduate.

9. Big 10 schools are pompous and arrogant. No SEC school calls itself "*The* anything" like *The* Ohio State University. This is a ridiculous argument, the *The* is very important. Otherwise *The* Ohio State University might be confused with plain ole Ohio State University, which everyone knows is a school filled with tons of male students with small penises.

10. The Big 10 actually has eleven members so don't lecture us about reading and writing when arithmetic is clearly not your conference's strength. If SEC schools ever added calculators to the school supply list and put down the abacus, you would be aware that we are eternally waiting for Notre Dame to return our whispered words of endearment, then we'll be the Big 12. Plus the A-10 is much worse, it actually has fourteen members. But Big

11, what kind of idiot chooses to go with eleven numbers when there is another option?

And Now to Decide Things for All Eternity

11. These conferences are mirror images of one another: The SEC and Big 10 are each made up of all state schools with one private school (Vanderbilt and Northwestern, respectively), have huge football stadiums with demanding alumni and substantial fan bases, have athletic departments that are money-making machines beyond compare, have players who consistently fill the rosters of NFL teams, have the colors of the teams duplicating themselves, and finally both have fans who would sooner marry a first cousin than lose to a rival . . . okay, I guess in the SEC this isn't even a tough decision. Ultimately, these similarities are much more grating than the differences. For instance, no one fan of the SEC or Big 10 lies awake at night thinking, "My team could run wild if they played in the MAC, or Mountain West, or Conference USA, or the Big East."

In the end, if you can lie down at night with the enemy (as I do), you find out that cross-pollination can be a good thing. Sometimes, you even think, maybe a football fan can even appreciate both conferences for what they bring to the college football smorgasbord.

Of course, then you come to your senses. I still hate the Big 10.

KENTUCKY

LEXINGTON, KENTUCKY
THE UNIVERSITY OF GEORGIA VS. THE UNIVERSITY OF KENTUCKY
NOVEMBER 4, 2006

Everyone has a friend whose college football team never wins. And I don't mean *never wins* in the sense that they never win a championship. I mean *never wins* in the sense that each time their team plays Louisiana-Lafayette or Eastern Michigan or Akron, they are legitimately afraid of what might transpire. For me, these friends are Kentucky football fans.

My law school classmates Daq Tardio and Tim Weatherholt spent three years regaling me with fanciful stories about contending for SEC East titles, how the latest unheralded recruit that they stole away from Furman was destined to be an All-American for multiple seasons, how Kentucky was always close to turning the proverbial corner, and instilling fear into the hearts of college football fans everywhere. No matter who Kentucky played, these two would construct lavish and detailed analyses proving the Wildcats were going to win. It didn't matter if Kentucky was a four-touchdown underdog;

every outlandish upset was always, eternally, right around the corner.

You know how this story plays itself out. Week after fall week, these two guys were constantly disappointed. One of my favorite stories reinforcing this fact was when Weatherholt attended a Vanderbilt-Kentucky game in 2003, watched his beloved Cats lose to Vanderbilt, then told me that an offensive lineman literally laughed at him when he called out, "Good luck next week against Tennessee." Tardio was unable to speak that same season after Kentucky allowed LSU to complete the most unnatural Hail Mary pass I have ever seen. It was so shocking and unexpected that some Kentucky fans actually stormed the field as LSU scored to defeat them.

That season taught me that being a Kentucky football fan was sort of like being one of those guys who ends up getting struck by lightning eight times in his life. Despite the terrible odds, there comes a point that whenever you hear thunder you don't want to go outside. Welcome to Kentucky football, where every kickoff should be accompanied by an air-raid siren alerting all to duck and cover underneath the bleacher seats.

Yet, after the crushing arrival of each mortar round, both Tardio and Weatherholt stood and dusted themselves off. By Wednesday, even after the most debilitating of defeats, once more their optimism had returned, and new theories of an upset were percolating in the law school environs. It was a stoic fatality grounded in an absolute leap of Kentucky football faith. In short, Tardio and Weatherholt were the faithful and the rest of the SEC were the lions.

So it was that I headed for Lexington, Kentucky, for stop nine of the DDT, to see the Georgia Bulldogs travel to the Bluegrass

State. My hosts were Tardio and Keven. Previously, they accompanied me on my trip to Baton Rouge, where Kentucky distinguished itself by managing to keep LSU from scoring fifty points in the first half and Tardio distinguished himself by being unable to finish a daiquiri and wearing boat shoes. They also hosted me at their apartment for the Vanderbilt-South Carolina game a few weeks prior. So, at this point, they are DDT veterans.

After driving the 215 miles to Lexington on Friday night, we go to a bar called Saddle Ridge, which, in the past eight years, has gone by the names Lexington City Brewery and Varsity Blue. Every college town has a bar like this that seems to constantly reinvent itself while always ending up essentially the same kind of place it was before. It's the sort of spot where camouflage pants on girls are cool.

"Back in '99, this place was awesome, when it was Varsity Blue," Tardio tells me, his claim falling on disbelieving ears. While we are at Saddle Ridge, we run into Eric from the current *Real World/Road Rules Challenge*. (Later, when I told my wife about this, she had no idea who I was talking about. After some descriptive work on my part, finally, she said, "Oh, you should have said Big E, I thought you were talking about Eric Nies.") I talk to Big E and he tells us, "Man, sorry about the crowd here. At UK you need to go out on a Tuesday, Thursday, or Saturday." It's Friday and the crowd is dancing to both hip-hop and country. After many beers and Jager shots, we make our way up on to the stage. Here, Keven and a random fat girl dance wildly while Tardio and I dance by ourselves. Eventually, we get off the stage and Keven joins us for more shots.

"You were going low," Tardio says to Keven, with an accusatory tone.

"I did not go low." Keven replies indignantly.

"You went fat," Tardio says.

Keven opens his mouth to reply but then shuts it.

"Okay," Keven says, "I went fat but I didn't go low."

Tardio is fond of accusing his friends of going low when they dance. By low he doesn't mean low class, or low brow, or low down. Those are all fine. He literally means low. As in dropping down so far while dancing with a girl that your own ass touches the ground. All around us guys at the bar are going low. To Tardio, this is a mortal sin. Like hooking up with a girl missing an arm or leg. Wake up after a night out with Tardio and there's a solid chance the first thing he'll say to you is, "Man, I saw you. You were so wasted you went low."

Some time well after two, we make it home abandoning the dancing crowd to a solid rendition of Montel Jordan's greatest hits. The highlight of the evening is Tardio, dancing alone in a spotlight on the stage while Jordan's classic "This Is How We Do It" echoes over the bar.

Somehow, we lose each other in different cabs on the way home and Keven and I end up without Tardio. We are staying with another UK grad from the class of 2001, Dave Wolfrom, whose house is in the suburbs of Lexington. "There's lots of old people out here," Dave says when he is questioned about how he likes living in the suburbs. He has a lawn, vaulted ceilings, and lives with his sister.

Our cab ride to the suburbs is so twisted and convoluted that I almost throw up. Thankfully, I handle myself like the upstanding officer of the court that I am. When we make it into the house I immediately rush upstairs and claim Dave's sister's bed where I pass out.

Luckily for Dave, his sister is out of town. Within ten minutes of arriving at his house, Keven has found a pair of Dave's sister's pink panties and Tardio has hung them from the chandelier in the living room. We are very mature.

There's a minor miscue on our morning tailgating plans, due to the fact that none of us have any idea what time it is. One of the rules of suburban living is that you have to have at least three different clocks in each room. This means at Dave's house there are approximately fourteen different clocks, all of which have different visible times. Daylight savings was the week before and, while some clocks have been adjusted, some have not, and others are just supposed to be decorations and are completely off anyway. Against all odds, we manage to do the math, figure out what time it is, and leave the house by ten-thirty.

It's supposed to be cold, so I wear flannel pants underneath my jeans. "It's not sleeting," Tardio says derisively. Then he walks downstairs and opens the door to confirm this fact. Keven turns to me, "Whatever he says, subtract fifteen degrees." Tardio stands in the doorway and claps his hands. "It's like fifty-five degrees out here," he says impatiently.

Dave gives me a gray UK sweatshirt, which would be loose on Hurley from *Lost*. I call an audible and end up in a hooded UK sweatshirt. "You look like *Willow*," says Tardio. We step outside and immediately begin shivering. "It's going to feel fifteen degrees colder at the tailgate because of the wind," Keven says. Tardio assaults this declaration with complete tenacity using all of the logical reasoning skills he acquired while at Vanderbilt Law School. Keven shrugs and shivers.

In the car on the way to the game, I say, "I think it's going to rain today."

Tardio erupts in the front seat of the car. "It is not going to rain today," with all the force and innate faith of a southern evangelical preacher. Keven and I disagree, "It's going to rain," he whispers to me.

When we get to the tailgate, it's absolutely freezing and Keven is vindicated. It definitely feels fifteen degrees cooler. There is nothing to restrain the wind around Commonwealth Stadium. A few tailgaters have actual stoves set up—to warm their hands, not for grilling. We arrive at our tailgate and begin eating single meatballs with our fingers because we have no utensils. In the coolness of the Kentucky morning, the meatballs are steaming. We can see our breath.

We have no women at our tailgate either. This probably accounts for the absence of utensils. "We haven't really had that many girls around our tailgate since the late 90s," Tardio explains.

All around us, Kentucky flags are snapping in the breeze. Kentucky fans are very fond of blue flags with white stripes that are made to resemble the American flag only in place of the stars

"I pledge allegiance to the United State of Kentucky ..."

are the letters "UK." Many people even hang these Kentucky flags above the American flag. It's like the Civil War all over again, "I pledge allegiance to the United State of Kentucky . . ."

Our tent blows over in a gust of wind. By tent, I think what I actually mean is canopy with four legs and no sides. It's basically a large umbrella. People grab rocks from the roadbed to hold up the tent. Everyone is standing around shivering. I contemplate holding a meatball in each of my hands for warmth.

Keven asks Tardio to loan him one of his gloves. Tardio refuses. "You only need one for the beer and the other one you can put in your pocket," Keven argues. Tardio relents and passes over his left glove. Keven goes leftie with his beer.

There is much talk about the top-ten-ranked Louisville football team's win over West Virginia on Thursday night. Kentucky fans are very bitter. It's as if their younger brother is suddenly dating Jessica Alba and they are stuck married to Cameryn Manheim. Tardio says the two most common statements are, "Screw 'Tino" (no one pronounces the Pi, he informs me) and " 'Trino sucks" (ditto on the Pe). The odds of a Kentucky school having a Petrino and a Pitino as their top two coaches have to be really high.

Kentucky football has never really recovered from the fact that they once had legendary Alabama coach Bear Bryant as their own head football coach. For eight seasons, from 1946 to 1953, Bryant coached at Kentucky. Included during this stay was Kentucky's only SEC football title, in 1950. Bryant left the Kentucky football program after an awards banquet in 1953. To commend his achievements as football coach that year, Bryant was given a watch. Kentucky's basketball coach at the time, Adolph Rupp, was presented with a brand-new car. Incensed at the disparate treatment and finally convinced that football was never going to be as popular at Kentucky as basketball, Bryant left for Texas A&M. When he returned to the SEC to coach at Alabama in 1958 Bryant didn't lose to Kentucky for the next twenty-four years. By the time his career was over at Alabama, Bryant had won thirteen SEC and six national titles.

Lots of Kentucky fans are wearing basketball jerseys to the football game over their sweatshirts. The jerseys are like a metaphorical bulletproof vest. Actually, several Kentucky fans I meet have suggested I would have done better to forgo the football game and gone to the basketball exhibition game on Thursday instead. These fans infuriate my friend Weatherholt who believes they are the reason the football program always loses. "I don't accept that we can't be good at both football and basketball," he says. In fact, if Weatherholt died tomorrow this would be an excellent inscription for his tombstone.

As we stand shivering in the brutal wind, Jason Baker, a Kentucky fan and lawyer I meet, suggests that November is not the best time to come to a game at Kentucky. "Come when there are horse races at Keeneland," he says, "there's an unbelievable talent level then. You can throw a rock into the air and no matter where it comes down it hits a hot chick."

As we stand shivering in the cold awaiting kickoff, Weatherholt arrives at the tailgate. Weatherholt is the kind of sports fan who makes you feel guilty about your own fandom. And, trust me, it takes a lot of knowledge to make me feel guilty. If you miss a game featuring your favorite team and there hasn't been a death in the family, Weatherholt looks at you with a very subtle and contempt-laden gaze. He is married now, and can honestly trace the intimate history of his relationship with his wife based on the individual Kentucky sports games he has been watching in close proximity to their encounters. In vivid detail. During law school, a professor once made a passing comment in class that Kentucky's upset loss in the NCAA Tournament to UAB was a joke. Weatherholt stormed out of the classroom and sat outside until he cooled off. When asked whether he thought he might have overreacted, Weatherholt responded: "Hell, no, there was no reason for that joke. No reason at all."

As we walk around Commonwealth Stadium in an effort to stave off hypothermia, I realize there aren't that many 'Bama Bangs at Kentucky. Instead the sideburns seem to retain an irrational appeal. I ask Tardio about this. "Burns are big up here," he says. You can imagine then how significant it was to Tardio when Supercuts recently lopped off his sideburns all the way up to midtemple. His roommate Keven claims he found Tardio curled up in the fetal position shivering, his temples having been raped by the haircutting chain.

Weatherholt and Keven at the Bush.
(Insert eighth grade giggling.)

Just outside the orange tailgate zone is a huge bush that forms a large canopy around a utility shed of some sort. This area is known both universally and inventively as the Bush, and, aside from lending itself to a constant stream of double entendres, it also serves as an effective hidden bathroom. If the Lexington police ever put up a sting here, they could bust every man in the orange tailgate zone for public urination.

Emily Melton of College Sports Television arrives at the tailgate and interviews us. She offers commentary on Tardio's not being able to finish his daiquiri. "I mean, it's kind of an understood thing that when you get a daiquiri, you finish it." Daq

Tardio declines his head in shame. When she asks him about his favorite college football traditions, Tardio is visibly rattled and accidentally conflates Clemson's tradition of running down the hill with South Carolina's entering to *2001: A Space Odyssey*. As he realizes his error, I stand over Emily's shoulder and signal that Tardio needs a twenty-second timeout because he's flustered. The interview tape is reset and Tardio answers without error. When he finishes, Tardio points out that Emily is wearing boat shoes. "Boat shoes, bang," he says pointing at each of us in turn.

When others find out that I am a Tennessee fan, it becomes readily apparent that Kentucky fans hate the University of Tennessee. This is odd to me, because I don't know a single UT fan who legitimately hates Kentucky. Maybe a few diehard basketball fans love to beat Kentucky, but no one who truly despises them. In terms of football, I don't think there's a single UT fan who has any real opinion of Kentucky at all. At least now that Tim Couch is gone.

Mercifully, game time arrives and Weatherholt and I buy tickets outside the stadium for twenty dollars. There are tons of tickets available and, if we had waited longer, we could have probably gotten in cheaper. This is despite the fact that it is UK's homecoming. Tardio is a season-ticket holder and insists that we walk all the way around Commonwealth Stadium to the east endzone before we enter because this is his good luck gate. Given the history of Kentucky football, good luck is used in a very loose, "We beat Central Michigan"-esque, manner.

We sneak into the half-filled student section because the seats there are better than the ones we paid for. Almost immediately, the UK students begin an "overrated" chant directed at

Georgia. How a team can be overrated when they are not actually rated remains a mystery.

Georgia misses their opening field goal and the football that lands in the crowd gets tossed around the stadium. The student section chants for the football to be thrown out of the stadium but the football rapidly caroms its way around the seats and into the upper deck. Then we lose sight of it. This is a fairly entertaining trend, so long as it is not your wife who unexpectedly gets decked in the side of the head by the football.

I am happy to report that Commonwealth Stadium is the first place I have visited in the SEC that does not have a single hedge. After eight consecutive stadiums featuring a hedge of some sort or other, Kentucky breaking the trend seems almost epic. Maybe commonwealths can't have hedges, we wonder. Then again, none of us even know what it means to be a commonwealth. All we know (okay, all Weatherholt knows) is that there are four of them in the U.S.: Kentucky, Virginia, Massachusetts, and Pennsylvania. On the flipside, we figure that maybe the lack of hedges in Commonwealth Stadium has something to do with its being a relatively new football stadium. Then again, *new* in the tradition-bedecked SEC means thirty-three years old.

It's 7–3 Georgia at the end of the first quarter, and the student section is almost full now. Incidentally, the entire student section is blanketed with blue pompons; someone must have had the delightful job of walking around the section before the game started and scattering them on the ground. Most of the pompons lie limp on the ground until Kentucky scores to cut Georgia's lead to 14–10, and then the students around us begin picking them up and waving them. Due to the fact that they've been lying on the concrete beneath the bleachers, many of the pompons are sodden with spilled drinks and other detritus. We get sprayed, as the men around us merrily shaken them—in a very bicurious manner, might I add.

The Kentucky Wildcat mascot is wearing overalls. And, worse than that, he's wearing overalls with only one shoulder buttoned. The other is hanging off. Evidently it is perpetually 1992 in Lexington. I'm halfway expecting for the mascot to come out for the second half with the overalls on backwards dancing to a Kris Kross song.

Georgia's freshman quarterback Matthew Stafford throws an interception at his own three, and the UK student section truly comes alive for the first time. Kentucky is only three yards away from claiming the lead. So far this season, Stafford has been one of the most infuriating players in the SEC. It's clear he's got a strong arm and tremendous talent but he has also proved capable of losing the game on every play. It doesn't help that his eyes look perpetually half closed. You get the feeling that he might take legitimate naps on the sideline during the games. But Stafford's interception goes for naught because, three plays later, Kentucky's Andre' Woodson throws an interception of his own.

I am standing between Tardio and Weatherholt. Tardio reacts to this second interception with stoicism. Like a man entirely comfortable being kicked in the groin. Weatherholt collapses to his seat, lowers his head, and begins talking to himself. Of course Weatherholt also puts tape over the bottom of his television screen so he doesn't see the scores of games he TiVos passing on the score ticker at the same time he watches another game. Weatherholt also, and this is completely true, ate a lunch of crackers and soup every day during law school and lived in such a dingy apartment during those years that his then-girlfriend, now-wife wouldn't visit after dark. So, this is actually pretty normal behavior for him.

No one around me in the student section can explain why Andre' has an apostrophe at the end of his name. I ask several people. Tardio suggests that perhaps it is because Andre' presumptively owns everything.

Tardio is absolutely certain that Georgia is going to score a touchdown even though they are only at their own thirty-one-yard line and there are less than forty seconds remaining in the half. "You haven't seen our defense play eight games," he says. On the next play Stafford completes a long pass to the Kentucky two. Tardio just shakes his head. But then, incredibly, UK picks off Stafford in the end zone and the half is over. Georgia leads, but only 14–10. Matthew Stafford is relieved. He can take a nap during halftime.

The Kentucky band comes out and plays. They have a midget on the flute.

Since it is homecoming, we watch the crowning of the king and queen. This whole concept just seems so 1950s to me. It would seem to me that being named the homecoming king actually lessens your appeal to women. I can see girls hanging out at the bar and one of them saying, "Yeah, he's okay, but, you know, he was the homecoming king." Then everyone just sort of nods and the guy goes home alone and smashes his crown on the front porch. Of course, I also picture girls taking whipped cream shots off each other while wearing skimpy underwear before they go out to bars, so take my opinion for what it's worth.

Unfortunately, Kentucky has given up on the scepters and the capes, but I'm surprised to see that they still give the so-called king and queen actual crowns. I think if you're going to stick with the crowns, you should have to give the king a sword and the queen a chastity belt as well. Also, they should be given fiefdoms and the king should have the right to take the virginity of every woman who farms on his land. Like in *Braveheart*. But maybe that's just me; I'm all about historical verisimilitude.

Then, the real homecoming king arrives in the student section. Yep, none other than Tubby Smith, the steely-eyed legend himself, who is in his tenth season as UK's head basketball coach. Tubby materializes suddenly in the upper section of the student section as if he's been sitting there all along. Either that or Tubby is like Great Tiger from Mike Tyson's *Punch Out!!*, and can throw down some powder and suddenly appear. "I have purred long enough, now hear me roar." Chants of, "Tubby, Tubby, Tubby," rain down upon him as he makes his way down the aisle. Tubby is wearing a sleek leather bomber jacket and looks like he might be en route to his F-16. It seems odd to see Tubby Smith without CBS announcer Billy Packer walking alongside him with a microphone, telling the audience the oft-repeated story about how a baby born Orlando Smith ended up with the name Tubby. (For the record, the nickname arose because Tubby enjoyed taking baths so much as a child.)

In Tubby's wake, I ask Tardio and Weatherholt when the last time they beat Georgia was. Both are silent for a moment, thinking. Then Weatherholt says, "It hasn't been that long. Nineteen ninety-six, I think." Welcome to Kentucky football, where ten years in a row of losses is the blink of an eye.

The second half opens, and Georgia running back Danny Ware gets a few carries. Danny Ware, of course, is the 431st heir apparent to Herschel Walker at Georgia. As much as Georgia fans love Herschel, give any freshman the football and they will proclaim him the second coming.

Both teams squander scoring opportunities for the entire third quarter. Included is a nifty fake field goal by Kentucky, which is run to the short side of the field and manages to re-semble what yours truly would look like running the football. Then, at midfield, Kentucky decks Georgia wide receiver Mario Raley and recovers his fumble. This is a serious injury, and Raley is ultimately carried off the field on a cart. But, for some reason, the referees feel the need to announce to the stadium the outcome of the play's review while Raley is being immobi-lized on the board. I mean, couldn't they have walked over and told each coach and waited to make the announcement until he was off the field?

On the ensuing play, Kentucky runs the flea-flicker and Andre' Woodson waits just a fraction of a second too long to hit his open receiver. The ball falls to the turf in the end zone. Around me, the students explode in cheers believing, for an instant, that the ball has been caught.

Some idiot with a huge fraternity flag lifts it up and blocks half the student section as Kentucky is driving. All of a sudden, any object that can be hurled is traveling in the direction of the guy with the flag. I nominate this guy to be the indentured ser-vant of the homecoming king.

Back on the field, which I can once again see, Woodson rolls right and throws all the way back across his body to Ken-tucky's top receiver Keenan Burton and suddenly the Wildcats lead 17–14 with 8:28 left in the fourth quarter. The entire stu-dent section is a jumbled mass of joy, and blue pompons go sail-ing into the air, spraying stale beer and peanut shells every which way.

The guy in the Cat suit is lifted onto a platform and cranks out seventeen one-armed pushups. I have some issues with this because one-armed pushups are pretty tough, even if you aren't wearing a furry costume and on top of a platform. In fact, I just stopped writing the book and tried to do one myself. I failed miserably. So, I really doubt the mascot can do them this easily. I'm beginning to wonder if the mascot isn't just putting both of his arms into the same furry mascot suit arm and doing one-armed pushups with two arms cleverly disguised as one?

Go ahead and try to do a one-armed push-up yourself if you don't believe me as to how hard it is. Also, what if Kentucky scored fifty points, is the Cat going to do two hundred or so one-armed push-ups? And, if he's truly doing all these push-ups, is the Kentucky Wildcat the strongest mascot in the country? At the tryouts for the Wildcat mascot do they just lock the gym doors and not open them again until only one person is still doing one-armed push-ups? I'm filled with questions and buoyed with extreme skepticism about this whole process.

While I ruminate upon mascots and one-armed push-ups, Georgia takes the ensuing possession and marches down the field to score a touchdown, but their extra point is blocked. It's 20–17 Georgia, with about four minutes remaining in the fourth quarter and the tension in the Kentucky student section is palpable. It's like going to Supercuts and waiting to look in the mirror to see if your sideburns still exist.

Weatherholt, defying all fears and turning remarkably cocky, says, "You'd better put in your book that Andre' Woodson is the best quarterback in the SEC." We debate this as Kentucky takes possession, and works their way down the field. Primarily, Kentucky is moving the ball by running. Ultimately, with 1:34 remaining the Cats have a first and goal at the Georgia five.

I take on the role of mosquito in Weatherholt's ear by telling him repeatedly that Kentucky is going to score too fast. Weatherholt asserts that when you are a Kentucky fan there is no such thing as scoring too fast. (Apparently, Kentucky football fans are not unlike virginal high school boys.) Both Weatherholt and Tardio are bouncing up and down on our bleacher row as Georgia takes two timeouts. Our bleacher row is wobbly, and I have to ask them to stop because already I've fallen into the two girls in front of us twice. And I mean legitimately fallen. The girls in front of us hate me and turn around to glare at us.

With 1:21 remaining, Kentucky scores on a running play and bedlam ensues in the student section. Weatherholt and Tardio are screaming, hugging and high-fiving everyone in sight. Keven turns and hugs a nineteen-year-old male freshman he does not know. We're in the midst of a huge blue mosh pit and it's 24–21 Cats. The fans begin chanting "C-A-T-S . . . C-A-T-S!" It's like 1996 all over again.

Georgia takes possession and, when Matthew Stafford throws his third pick of the game, there is a riot in the student section and on the Kentucky sideline. Ever wary of lightning Tardio screams with all his might for the Kentucky players to put their helmets back on before they get penalized. Kentucky takes the knee and Tardio and Weatherholt are swept down to the edge of the field in a tide of onrushing students. It is pandemonium in Lexington.

Students pour over the wall and rapidly attack the goalpost in front of us. For over twenty minutes, students will struggle with all their might to bring it down. The uprights will tilt left, will tilt right, and will ultimately take a very slow and ponderous circle while students alternately climb, fall, and dance on the yellow bars.

Kentucky's players are mixed in among the crowd, which is rapidly growing in size, at this point covering well over half the field. Thousands of blue-clad revelers are reeling and yelling in one large mass of redemptive ecstasy.

For a moment, I stand taking pictures from the edge of the student section, then, I, too, am up and over the wall to the field below following Tardio and Weatherholt. It's a pretty good drop to the field surface from our section and I contemplate the irony of the DDT coming to an end when I break my neck on the fall. But I land on the sideline and, for a moment, I think I might be one of the oldest dudes to ever storm a field. Then, I look around Commonwealth Stadium and realize that there are lots of old people on the field as well. I'm twenty-seven, and I think the average age of the people on the field is even higher than mine. I think one guy even had an oxygen tank. Tardio points out a couple of older guys who are smoking out at midfield like they are taking a break from work.

Keven reaches down and rips up a piece of the turf. Then he puts it into his pocket. Tardio shakes his head, "That's just stupid," he says, "what are you going to do with grass?"

For some reason, Keven claims a clump of turf.

Keven shrugs, "I think I'll put it into a baggie," he says.

We run into a couple of guys who apologize for the amount of time it took for the goal posts to come down. "This one cop had his hand on his gun like he was going to shoot some one," they say by partial explanation. The hard-working Lexington police have reclaimed the goalposts near the west end zone. Fans are stopping and having their pictures taken alongside the goal post. The police officers appear, unsmiling, in all the photographs. Kentucky's finest are not pleased with the trespassing of the masses.

The PA announcer requests that all fans who have stormed the field exit through the west end zone. As wild as the storming of the field was, the exit is remarkably calm. Everyone, it seems, stops to rub the goalpost which has been felled as a sign of victory. Somehow touching the goalpost makes the victory tangible for a fan base that has had far too few tangible victories.

Somewhere in the masses of Kentucky fans we have lost Weatherholt. When I eventually get him on the phone an hour later, he sounds like he is still out of breath. "I told you we were going to win," he says. Up above us the clouds have rolled in and the air is turning cold again. On the way back to our tailgate, no one is watching for lightning. "I told you it wasn't going to rain today," Tardio says triumphantly.

Tardio and I get acquainted with our newest friend,
the goalpost.

TIM TEBOW IS GOD

Florida quarterback Tim Tebow is immortal. At least that's what I hear from my friends who are Florida fans. It's possible that there is not a single man or woman in Gainesville who wouldn't like to have Tebow's baby. The love affair has gotten out of control.

A year ago, grown men in Alabama wept over the fact that Tebow chose to go to Florida (and that Mike Shula was still their coach), and now you get the feeling that there are about three million Gator fans who would gladly take a bullet for Tebow. Yep, he's nineteen years old and in the eyes of Gators across the country, Tebow can do no wrong.

Want more? Tebow's name is already a verb. My friend Neville has text messaged me lots of times this season with this simple word, "Tebow'd." Occasionally, he gets creative and writes, "You've been Tebow'd." I have to grin and bear this. Worse, I might have to grin and bear it for the next three years. Superman had kryptonite, Green Lantern had to carry an actual green lantern, and Jeremy Piven killed Kobe Tai while having sex with her in *Very Bad Things*, but what flaw does Tim Tebow have?

I'm just waiting for the article to be written about him scoring a 2400 on his SAT, and I live in constant fear that my editor is going to e-mail me and say, "Clay, Tim Tebow is going to be writing the ClayNation column for the next three years." The next e-mail will be from my editor at HarperCollins, "And he gets all the royalties from your book."

This year, his first season of college ball, Tebow has already managed to make the quarterback sneak an art form, shown that a left-handed Uncle-Rico-esque throwing motion can be effective, and executed a jump touchdown pass. Next year, I believe Tebow might just jump over the line of scrimmage at midfield and not land until he reaches the end zone. Either that, or he's going to bring back the goal line offense no matter where the Gators are on the field. Florida is going to announce that they no longer need wide receivers to take advantage of fancy offensive gimmickry like the forward pass.

Already, Tebow's the most difficult white man to tackle since Bill Clinton pulled into a parking lot featuring a rib joint alongside a strip club. In the process, Tebow has become every other SEC fans' least favorite football player. And he's only a freshman. I would bet you that by the time he's a senior (if he stays until he's a senior), Tebow is going to make Duke's J. J. Redick seem downright loveable in comparison.

There are many reasons why other fans will detest Tebow. Primarily, it's because after every successful play, Tebow jumps up and runs around like he just threw Hacksaw Jim Duggan over the top rope to win the Royal Rumble. But equally important is the fact that Tebow appears flawless, or as close to flawless as a nineteen-year-old can be. Each of these traits that conspire to make opposing fans hate him also coalesce among the Gator faithful to make him the greatest thing since Steve Spurrier won the Heisman.

Without further ado, here are eleven signs that Florida has succumbed to Tim Tebow fever:

1. Florida head coach Urban Meyer has forbidden Tim Tebow from ever flexing both his biceps at the same time. The last time Tebow flexed, the top of every coed at the University of Florida miraculously rose at the exact same time. This caused two plane

crashes, ninety-six fender benders, and all classes were canceled at the university.

2. The Florida Education Council is rewriting all textbooks to replace references to the bubonic plague with the Tebonic plague.

3. Governor Jeb Bush is rumored to be suggesting that Tim Tebow be named the replacement for both Bobby Bowden at Florida State and Larry Coker at Miami. Tim Tebow would then be head coach at both schools at the same time while still playing for Florida.

4. Tim Tebow has had to use 14,223 bottles of hair gel this season because once he uses the bottle, there is a riot outside his apartment to get the rest. Marie Antoinette once said to the masses, "Let them eat cake." Tim Tebow now says, "Let them use my hair gel."

5. Tim Tebow doesn't put popcorn in the microwave, he just stares at the kernels until they pop of their own accord under the piercing power of his gaze.

6. Florida forward Joakim Noah and Tim Tebow are forbidden from ever being in a campus building with a covered roof at the same time, for fear of the spontaneous combustion which would doubtless ensue.

7. Every time Tim Tebow goes on a date, the other girls on campus carry the girl he dated to Lake Alice wrapped in uncooked chickens and feed her to the alligators.

8. Word spread that Tim Tebow was thinking about getting a barbed wire tattoo on his arm, and they suddenly became cool again.

9. Once, Tim Tebow took out his mouthpiece and threw it into the stands. It sold the next day on eBay for $14.2 billion.

10. Tim Tebow once mentioned that he thought gondolas were cool.

Now Florida is constructing a canal between his apartment and the football practice complex so that he can glide in comfort. Also, current starting quarterback Chris Leak will be piloting the gondola in one of those striped T-shirts.

11. Tim Tebow is going to Halloween parties as himself. This means every man on Florida's campus will have the same Halloween costume this year.

11

FLORIDA

GAINESVILLE, FLORIDA
THE UNIVERSITY OF SOUTH CAROLINA VS.
THE UNIVERSITY OF FLORIDA
NOVEMBER 11, 2006

The War of the Visors came to Gainesville, Florida, on Saturday, November 11. Everywhere you looked, Florida fans who refused to relinquish their Steve Spurrier–inspired visors came face-to-face with South Carolina fans who have newly embraced the visor. It was bare-headed warfare, a Velcro'd Civil War, a golf-course tussle against par brought to a north Florida gridiron. At any moment, I expected a country-club–infused rumble to erupt on University Avenue. For ascots and sweater vests to go firing into the air and for a woman wearing a Burberry scarf to scream bloody murder as she tossed an already-lit martini in the direction of her foes. Welcome to the newest rivalry in the Southeastern Conference, in which both sides owe their football success to the same man.

And the game would be as even as the visor-clad heads. However, that was in the future—first the DDT had to manage to make it to Gainesville in time for the game.

• • •

I'm flying on this leg of the DDT. Southwest Airlines, to be precise, which means I don't receive a seat assignment. I've gotten used to this. What I haven't gotten used to is that Southwest now allows you to check in for your scheduled flight and print your boarding pass roughly ninety-six days in advance of your actual flight. And that, if you make a tremendous error in printing your boarding pass and wait until, say, ninety-four days before your scheduled flight, you will be in the B or C boarding group. This means all the A people will board, take all the aisle seats, and slow down the entire boarding process by then requiring every single row of people to stand and allow the B or C people to slide in.

And woe unto you if you are flying with a significant other and forget to check in ninety-six days before your flight. This spring, my wife and I flew to Ft. Lauderdale and I forgot to check in, which meant we were in the hated C boarding group. Lara had to sit in the center aisle between two fat men, one of who smelled as if he'd just rubbed tuna fish all over his flabby body. Every now and then she would turn and stare at me with such a chilling look that it turned three small children to ice.

As if this isn't bad enough, the people in the A and B and C boarding groups all line up in these cattle lines that Southwest has provided. Some people will stand in line for over two hours just staring straight ahead. Yep, doing nothing but staring. Nary a book, magazine, crossword puzzle, or iPod in their hand. How boring is your life if being first in line for the airplane is this important? If you're willing to stand in line to board a flight longer than your flight lasts, your life is going to be just as boring when you land as it was before you left. The seat choice really doesn't matter.

But, this time, I'm in the B group so I'm feeling a bit confident. So confident, that I stop and buy a barbecue sandwich, which I douse in enough mild sauce to sink a small boat. While drowning my food I run into my former classmate, Steven Simmons, who is coincidentally also a former Vanderbilt male cheerleader. Simmons came to the Vanderbilt Homecoming game with me a few weeks ago on DDT stop 6 and ridiculed the current roster of Vanderbilt cheerleaders. Simmons is eating barbecue with his pregnant wife, Brenna. We're all three on the same flight, so we make our way to the gate.

By the time we arrive at the gate for our flight to Tampa, the lines stretch almost the width of the terminal. I attempt to eat my pulled pork with limited success. Even worse, I have managed to sit down and stuff my face while the pregnant Brenna is forced to stand beside me waiting in line and making me feel like a royal schmuck. The barbecue sandwich is falling apart and my decision to go with corn on the cob is basically inexplicable. Eventually I give up and toss it out. Across the Yangtze River in front of us, it's possible someone is saying something at our gate.

As we wait, Simmons and I somehow end up in a discussion about the various physical trials necessitated by the NFL Combine and their intense training regimens. Brenna enters the conversation by explaining to us that when she was in seventh and eighth grade they used to spend PE class at Ensworth School in Nashville running laps with tires strapped to their backs. Neither Simmons nor I will accept the truth of this. When we land, the kid in front of us stands and tells Brenna that he goes to Ensworth. I ask him if he has to run with tires strapped to his back. He says he doesn't. His mother arches her eyebrows. "He's too young," Brenna says, by way of explanation.

• • •

I'm meeting my friend Neville in Tampa. Neville graduated from UF in 2001, and now practices law downtown. Unfortunately, he e-mails to say that he can't pick me up from the airport because his brother is using his car, and there are no cars to be rented in Tampa. "We're the equivalent of sixth-grade girls who have to wait after soccer practice," Neville remarks.

Neville invites me to keep him company in his office while he works. As occupations go, there are few jobs less scintillating to survey than that of a lawyer in a law office. Occasionally, my own wife would come wait for me at my office and, after waiting a while, would look at me and say, "You're really boring." As soon as I arrive, Neville takes me up to his office. We enter through the back door. "I always come in this way," he says, "so people can't tell when I leave."

We walk through a darkened and abandoned side of the office. Small cardboard boxes are strewn about and the footing is treacherous.

"Would anyone really care if you left through the front door?" I ask.

Neville is silent for a few steps. "Not really," he responds.

Neville introduces me to his secretary and we enter his office. I put down my bag. Neville walks around his desk and looks at his chair, out the large window behind him, then at his laptop. "Oh, man," he says. Then he sighs. "Let's just go."

Neville has been practicing labor and employment law in Tampa for over two years now. For most of this time, he has been fairly miserable. Not with the people he works with, but with the job of a lawyer in general. "Some nights when I'm working really late and no one else is here," he tells me, "I walk into the managing partner's office and sit down across from his desk. Then I act out conversations where I pretend to quit my job. I go back and forth for several sentences explaining my rationale and whatnot." I ask him how often he has these imaginary quitting conversations late at night in his boss's office. "Pretty often," he says. Every person who is considering going to law school should have to read this paragraph.

Predictably, we once more traipse out the back door of the law firm. We go to happy hour. It's a little before four in the afternoon.

Eventually, we get picked up and make our way to *Borat*. If you haven't already, please see the movie, if for no other reason than to watch the three South Carolina frat guys in action— quite possibly the worst imaginable advertisement for their school.

After the movie, we go to Neville's suburban house where he makes fun of me for not wanting to watch the Lakers play some other team that isn't the Lakers on television. "In two months, you're going to write some column making fun of Kobe Bryant, and not have even seen him play an entire game yet this season." Before I can defend myself, I start sneezing. Neville lives in the suburbs by himself with his cat, Lorenzo, named after Lorenzo Neal, the NFL fullback.

Neville's rented house is absolutely identical to what appear to be about fourteen million other one-level homes in the same neighborhood, yet he roars through the streets in his Mitsubishi Galant with reckless abandon. We squeal to a stop in front of his cookie-cutter paradise, which looks exactly the same in paint scheme, size, and layout as every other house we have just driven past.

"How do you know which house is yours?" I ask.

"Some guy with a garbage truck always parks next door," Neville replies.

Neville's house has three bedrooms and one bed. The name of his suburban town is Apollo Beach. When I ask Neville how close the beach is to his house, he says, "There's no beach anywhere near here."

In his VCR, a high school football highlight tape entitled *Shorecrest Chargers—1996* is protruding from the tape deck. I ask Neville whether he has watched his high school football highlight tape recently. He hastily replies, "No, why?" Then refuses to make eye contact. I inform him that I just saw it hanging out of his VCR. He comes clean, sort of. "When I was moving, I popped it in for a second and I haven't taken it out yet."

Neville was an All-State football player in Florida. He once tackled current NFL fullback Heath Evans eight times in a single game. In law school, he tore his ACL playing flag football; his Halloween costume the next day was an injured flag-football player.

Lorenzo the Cat is fat and affable. Unfortunately, I am allergic to cats. This necessitates a late-night trip in search of allergy medicine. The only available allergy medicine at the 7-Eleven in the Apollo Beach suburbs is Children's Benadryl which comes in a pink package and is bubble gum flavored. I am instructed to take two to four teaspoonfuls. Neville has no teaspoons and in his defense I'm not sure I've ever used a teaspoon in my life either. So, I just turn up the bubble-gum flavored benadryl and drink. Immediately, my throat goes numb.

At ten the next morning, I wake up on Neville's couch. I can barely open my eyes. My head is still numb and I can't swallow. I think Lorenzo the Cat may have spent all night sleeping on my face, shedding tiny poisonous hairs into my throat. But as soon as I remember that, today, I will see my foe Steve Spurrier in action again, I buck up and wipe my eyes.

Neville's friend, Jorge, who attended both high school and college with him, has arrived to go with us to the Florida–South Carolina game in Gainesville.

Jorge now lives in Seville, Spain, where he has started a travel company for American kids studying abroad, and where he occasionally gets to watch Florida games in bars overseas. "The NCAA Championship basketball game ended at three forty-five in the morning in Seville," he said. "It was me and a bunch of drunk Spaniards."

Neville has assured me that Gainesville is an hour and a half from Tampa. This might be because Neville drives approximately ninety miles an hour everywhere. Somewhere on the interstate, Jorge points to a single tree that appears to be losing its leaves, "Welcome to fall in Florida," he says. We have already been driving for an hour and a half and are nowhere near Gainesville.

Well over two hours later, on the outskirts of Gainesville, Jorge assures me that some dolphins live entirely in fresh water and, so, the fact that I saw a dolphin in a Charleston river is insignificant. Before my dolphin knowledge can be further ridiculed, his business partner Eric, also a UF grad, calls from Morocco. The phone number on Jorge's cell phone is sixteen digits long. Neville taunts Eric about going to see the Gators play. After a while, due to bad reception, Neville hangs up. When asked how Eric took the taunts, Neville responds: "He asked me, how many cobras have you seen today?"

We park in the midst of student off-campus housing. We're
going to be staying at Jorge's sister's house, which she shares
with several of her Kappa Delta sorority sisters. We're basically
the guys from *Old School* except not very lovable.

Immediately, we set out for the center of Florida's campus
in search of tickets for the game. We're all wearing shorts because, despite the November date, it's still very warm in Gainesville. Our walk to campus is completely flat and we constantly
pass Gator fans drinking on porches and patios. One of the
great things about Gainesville is that the bar and house patios
can be used for drinking and parties all year long.

We arrive on University Avenue where bars line the street
opposite the Florida campus. All of the bars are packed, and so
are the sidewalks. It's difficult to move. On University Avenue,
we come upon a sudden mob of people that have come to a
complete stop. A street vendor has been swarmed while selling
his SPURRIER IS A COCK T-shirt. There must be some double entendre or subtle wordplay here that I'm just not seeing, because
the vendor is selling these shirts as quickly as he can take Gator
fans' money.

Only twenty minutes into our Gainesville visit, Neville
pulls me aside. "Note the lack of jean shorts," he says. I don't
reply and Neville asks nervously, "Wait, have you seen some?"
Throughout the SEC, Florida Gator fans have achieved a measure of renown for supposedly wearing jean shorts, known to
most of us as *jorts*, in huge numbers. For several years, Neville
has been arguing this is not the case. Now is the chance for his
jort redemption.

It's approaching one-thirty in the afternoon and it's over
eighty degrees for sure. The jean shorts issue remains up in the
air, but there's no doubt about it: Gainesville has set an SEC

record for most male fans without sleeves. There are lots of wristbands and lots of hats worn by Gator faithful that are faced neither backwards nor forwards. Not coincidentally, rumor has it that Kevin Federline is considering relocating to Gainesville once his divorce is final.

In general, Florida seems the least Southern of the SEC schools I've visited thus far on the DDT. Florida as a state is much more like an amalgamation of the rest of the country. Only drenched in sunshine. As Neville so eloquently puts it, "Our white girls aren't really Southern white girls." Somehow, this makes sense. Put another way, Neville is a huge football fan but, occasionally, for big games, he would sell his student tickets and use the proceeds to buy a new shirt to wear out to the clubs in Gainesville. Somehow, I don't see this happening at Auburn.

I notice that most UF girls seem to be packing about six to eight extra pounds on the backs of their arms. I attribute this to the northern influence on the student body of the University of Florida. Either that or maybe their reputation has gone to their heads . . . or the back of their arms. Later, when we're back at the house with the KD girls, Rachel takes a break from making fun of my Facebook profile picture and how old I am to inform me that, "Since UF has become really selective with students the girls have gotten less attractive." According to Neville, the Kappa Delta sisters are "lean and sinewy." He is correct. They do not have excess fat on the backs of their arms.

Back on University Avenue our quest has yielded a bevy of available tickets. We buy three seats for sixty dollars each. Face value is thirty-five dollars. Lots of students are also selling their seats. Apparently, in Gainesville, you have to flash your student

ID to be admitted with a student seat. One student is deter-mined to get around the rules and seal the deal. "I'll sell you my student ID for ten dollars, too," he offers. This is evidently the replacement cost for a lost card. Neville is impressed with his entrepreneurship, "Ingenious," he remarks as we walk away.

We run into Florida fan Beth Justice who is modeling a shirt that says SOON TO BE MRS. TEBOW. I ask if she has ever met or seen Florida quarterback Tim Tebow. No on both accounts. "He has no idea about our future marriage," she says matter of factly.

Neville and I buy beers from the open window at Balls, a sports bar, and stand in front of a church drinking them. While we are drinking, a police officer walks past just twenty yards away from us. At this exact moment, a man carrying a long line of bratwurst pauses beside us, "You'll get a one hundred eighty five dollar ticket, and get arrested if you're from out of town, for drinking those," he says. We throw our beers away, though we can't help but wonder, why does Balls sell individual cold beers from the window if you can't even drink them outside?

Sure enough, the Gainesville Police are aggressively arrest-ing anyone with an open container. This is the rough equiva-lent of making the speed limit at the Indy 500 ten miles per hour, then arbitrarily pulling over a few cars every now and then. I have no idea why the Gainesville police are spend-ing their time doing this. Couldn't you get elected mayor of Gainesville on a platform of no arrests for open containers on game day?

Neville looks at me and shakes his head. "I don't like the vibe out here," he says, "Everyone seems too quiet. And you're here and I know the Gators aren't going to play as well with you here, for some reason."

We head inside to Gator City (formerly the Purple Por-
poise), a dingy and dark bar with a floor that is already covered
with a dull film of muck, beer, and sundry other fluids, where
we have wings and beer. On the projection screens in front of
us, Georgia is stomping Auburn. Gator fans seem disappointed
by this outcome. The Florida faithful hate Georgia, and many
of them had hoped to get a rematch against Auburn, whom
they lost to on October 14, in the SEC championship game.

After finishing our beer and wings, we walk across campus
and stand in line outside Ben Hill Griffin Stadium waiting to
enter. Neville says, "Jean shorts on girls don't count." Then he
pauses for a few moments and says, "Neither do jean skirts."

Florida football, like everything associated with the state of
Florida, has exploded in recent years. Until 1991, Florida had
never won an SEC title. Since that time, they have won six.
This rise to prominence was helmed by Steve Spurrier, who
returned in 1990 as head football coach and, in addition to
looming as a nightmarish figure in my life, also won Florida's first-ever national football championship in 1996. As if
Florida's football success weren't enough, their long-dormant
basketball program won their first-ever national championship
only seven months ago. So, Florida is the Internet millionaire
in the old money country club of SEC football. The new guy,
whose appearance on the national scene has reshuffled the
pecking order of the SEC. And this, perhaps more than any
other reason, explains why they are hated more by other SEC
schools than any other program. To illustrate this point, as my
friend and Kentucky fan Weatherholt said, "I would pay several
thousand dollars if you guaranteed me that for the next ten
years Florida would have a losing record in both basketball and

football." Not for his own team to win, mind you, but for Florida to lose.

We arrive at our seats around three, twenty minutes or so before kickoff. Somehow, we have ended up in the South Carolina cheering section, which is very disappointing to Neville and Jorge. "This is unfortunate," Neville says.

The playing surface in Ben Hill Griffin is sunken beneath the ground level, which means that the stands don't climb as high into the sky around the field as they do at other stadiums. It also means each Florida opponent begins the game already more than six feet underground.

There are hedges in both end zones of UF but none on the sidelines. It appears that Kentucky's Commonwealth Stadium is going to be the only hedgefree zone of the DDT. I'm halfway wondering whether they're going to import hedges for the indoor SEC championship game in Atlanta.

On the opening drive of the football game, UF's field goal kicker Chris Hetland misses yet again. He's now 2-9 on the season. All the South Carolina fans around us cheer. Neville attempts to do the Gator chomp in response and a portly South Carolina fan in front of us warns, "You better watch it or you won't make it out of here." Neville informs him that this is *his* stadium. He means Florida, I think. The man responds by raising his hands above his head and twirling his fingers. Neville looks at me and I shrug. Eventually, the portly South Carolina man's arms tire and he lowers his spirit fingers.

The sun is setting but, even as the sun lowers, we are all sweating. It's hot and humid and the South Carolina bench remains in the sunlight longer than any other part of the playing surface. We constantly reach up to wipe away the sweat dripping on our foreheads. The portly man in front of us looks like he just jumped into a pool. This is the third South Carolina game I've seen in person in four weeks, and by far the hottest. Throughout the game, I halfway expect to get a telephone call asking me to help break down film.

The main UF scoreboard keeps an updated tally of rushing, passing, total yards, and first downs. I don't understand why every other SEC stadium doesn't do the same.

The Florida student section is directly behind the South Carolina bench and runs all the way up to the top of the stadium. The students are to our right and, when their hands move to do the Gator chomp they move as one. Also, the Gator chomp actually ends in a hand clap that echoes in the stadium. I suppose I should have already known this, but I've never been to a Gator game before. When you watch the game on television, you can't hear it, so I always assumed there was no sound associated with the Gator chomp. This is the kind of incredibly important information I knew the DDT would enable me to soak up and, in turn, share with you.

South Carolina scores first to take a 7–0 lead. All around us, the South Carolina fans cheer wildly. Neville and Jorge shake their heads. Amazingly, the South Carolina fans begin a "Just like last year" chant. Last year, South Carolina beat Florida in Columbia for the first time since 1939. Evidently, last year's victory has sent South Carolina fans' confidence surging to record levels.

Steve Spurrier runs a trick play. Sidney Rice attempts a throwback pass to quarterback Blake Mitchell, and the dreadlocked Reggie Nelson of Florida narrowly misses an interception. This Predator look for members of the secondary, you know, the dreadlocks or hair hanging out of the back of the helmet, has become the newest football trend. I can't believe someone hasn't co-opted the nickname Predator already. "I ain't got time to bleed." Indeed.

Ryan Succop of South Carolina's field goal is good from fifty-five for the second time this season. Unfortunately for South Carolina, the play clock has expired before he can kick. South Carolina is penalized and punts. Neville claps his hands. "Nice break," he says, "nice break."

On the ensuing drive, Florida's Chris Leak underthrows a pass to wide receiver Dallas Baker, but Baker manages to steal the ball away from a South Carolina defender for the Gator touchdown. It's 7–7 and rousing chants of "Gator bait" echo through the stadium. Content with such a close game when his team is a substantial underdog, Spurrier chooses to run out the clock and both teams jog into their locker rooms tied at seven.

During halftime we are entertained by the lowest flyover I've ever seen. Two jets scream by and appear to barely miss the scoreboard. Perhaps Maverick is in one plane? The band had been playing a patriotic medley but there is now a loud buzz in the stadium as everyone considers how happy they are to be alive.

Some guy comes out with a chance to win a Dodge truck if he can throw a football twenty yards through a wooden board with a hole on it. The guy manages to throw the ball only twelve yards. Boos cascade down upon him. Based on my own successful performance during a halftime time contest at a football game I feel comfortable criticizing this guy.

Seriously, how do you not know if you can't throw a football twenty yards? Most guys I know can a throw a football twenty yards underhand. If you don't know how far you can throw a football this seems incredibly easy to test. Go outside. Take twenty large steps and attempt to hit your garage door. If you can't, never throw a football again. You know how fat guys never take their shirts off at the pool? Well, you have to become the football-throwing equivalent. No matter what, you choose not to throw. A midget could be running away with your wife's purse and you could have a clean shot at him with a spear. You should still choose not to throw. And, whatever else, you definitely don't go onto the field at halftime and prove to everyone that you can't throw twenty yards.

Meanwhile, the superhuman Tim Tebow warms up by throwing thirty-five-yard darts into the corner of the end zone. The football seems as if it should be trailing smoke.

The second half commences with a nervous Neville clapping his hands alongside me. "Gators," he says softly to himself, "Go Gators." Jorge is more vocal. "This game is not going well at all," he says. I shrug my shoulders. "At least you're getting to watch your team play like crap surrounded by South Carolina fans," I say.

For most of the third quarter, the teams take turns moving the ball short distances without scoring. Neville and Jorge become increasingly tense. Begging for penalties and criticizing the referees as nervous fans are wont to do. Then, in a still-tied game, Florida blocks a South Carolina field goal with 8:09 remaining in the third quarter. This rouses the Gator faithful from a stillness that had settled upon the crowd. The lights have come on in the stadium, and it's a bit dark in the end zones where there are no lights. Neville and Jorge cheer the blocked field goal loudly, to the consternation of the South

Carolina fans in our section. Unperturbed, Neville begins the Gator Chomp.

The third quarter ends with the score still tied and, at the start of the fourth quarter, the entire stadium sings along to "We Are the Boys from Old Florida." Many people put arms on each other's shoulders and sway. This is the most southern thing I've seen Florida fans do all day. Sure, this song is a hokey tradition that is vaguely bicurious, but it's a tradition and everyone joins in. Except the South Carolina fans in our section. And me. I'm definitely not swaying along to "We Are the Boys from Old Florida."

South Carolina finally breaks the scoreless tie when their field goal kicker, Succop, is good from forty-six. It's 10–7 USC. Then Florida answers by trotting out Chris Hetland for another field goal attempt after Saint Tebow misfires on third-and-goal. The Florida faithful boo this decision. Neville astutely comments, "If this were a video game, Hetland's confidence meter would be zero." Hetland makes the kick and we're tied at ten.

South Carolina drives the field and scores a touchdown to take a 16–10 lead. Beside me, Neville just shakes his head. "It's because you're here," he says, looking at me, "all because you're here." But, then, Florida blocks the extra point. All around us, the South Carolina cheering section is a mob of Gamecocks alternating chants. The clock is dwindling when Florida takes possession. It seems possible that Steve Spurrier is going to beat his former team for the second time in two tries.

On the opposing sideline, Florida's second-year coach Urban Meyer is on the verge of coming in for the harshest criticism of his tenure. Meyer replaced Ron Zook, the coach who had previously replaced Steve Spurrier, in 2004. In his first season, 2005, Meyer led the Gators to a 9–3 record, but all three losses came in SEC games, including last year's loss to Spurrier. Meyer arrived in Gainesville after coaching at Bowling Green and the University of Utah for two years each. He is a forty-two-year-old from Ohio, and the man he is standing on the opposing sideline across from is a Florida legend. As if that doesn't make this game significant enough, Meyer's Gators only have one loss, and remain on the fringes of the national championship picture. So this game is important, exceedingly important, to Meyer and the Gators.

Facing fourth down from their side of the fifty Tim Tebow runs onto the field. Everyone in the entire stadium knows what is coming next. The Tebow quarterback sneak. It is absolutely impossible to describe how delirious the crowd at Florida becomes when Tebow enters the game. It's as if Jesus Christ suddenly alit at midfield. Tebow runs the quarterback sneak for a first down. Ben Hill Griffin stadium exhales as one then cheers madly as a celebrating Tim Tebow morphs into Hacksaw Jim Tebow.

Everyone on both sides is cheering. There's 3:03 remaining and Florida is driving, trailing by six. Before each play as Florida prepares to snap the ball, the South Carolina fans around us scream as loudly as they can. The stadium is so loud right now that I cannot hear either Neville or Jorge. Just when it seems the Gamecocks have victory in their grasp South Carolina gets Tebow'd. On first-and-goal from the Gamecock twelve, Tebow carries the South Carolina defense into the end zone with him. There is no sound, just one loud yell. After trailing for over a quarter, Florida has tied the score at sixteen.

Onto the field jogs Hetland, the field-goal kicker who is now 3–10 on the season. Only the Gamecock fans are screaming now. Every Florida fans is completely silent, willing the ball to split the uprights and give the Gators the lead. And . . . the extra point is good. Florida now leads 17–16. After fify-seven minutes of trailing or being tied. Florida has their first lead of the game.

In the midst of a deafening roar, South Carolina takes possession with a chance to win the game. On play after play, the cheers crest as the ball is snapped. South Carolina advances the ball down the field and Steve Spurrier strides after his new team on the sideline as they drive in the direction of his own name and number on the Florida Ring of Honor above the field. Finally, with eight seconds left, The War of the Visors has come down to a final forty-eight-yard field goal to determine the game. The entire stadium is standing. For the second year in a row, Florida Gator fans know, at long last, what it is like to cheer for the sideline opposite Steve Spurrier.

The ball is snapped and Succop makes solid contact to send the pigskin spiraling over the line of scrimmage in the direction of the distant uprights. But a leaping Florida lineman, Jarvis Moss, has timed the kick and his leap perfectly. His arm meets the ball and the kick ricochets off his hand and comes to rest on the Florida turf. The kick is blocked. It's no good and mayhem reigns in Gainesville.

By the time the ball comes to rest on its final play, over ninety-thousand fans, both Gators and Gamecocks, are completely drained of emotion, their voices are hoarse, and hardly anything seems to separate the two sides. Neville turns to me and shakes his head, "Wow," he says, quite simply. The game is over and Florida has won.

Steve Spurrier jogs off directly beneath us to the cheers of fans from both teams. Both Gators and Gamecocks are applauding the visored one. South Carolina's fans slowly file out of the stadium as the Gator players celebrate in the south end zone, alongside their fans. Finally Urban Meyer leaves the field and the cheers rise anew and bear him along into the tunnel. Meyer raises his right arm and pumps it but once. As if to brush away the overhanging ghost of Steve Spurrier.

Later that night, Gator fans will celebrate not only their win but the Auburn, Texas, and California losses. Talk will turn to a potential national championship and Neville, Jorge and I will find ourselves out at The Swamp (eighteen and up) on University Avenue. First we'll meet Lieutenant Luke Mixon and Lieutenant Nate Lyon, who were two of the pilots of the F/A-18 Hornets that flew over the stadium. I ask them how close they came to the scoreboard. "Not very close at all," they say.

We also run into the South Carolina guys whom I hung out with in Columbia. Even in defeat, they are still wearing their

The fly-over pilots assure us we were nowhere near death, then grudgingly pose for a photo.

visors and praising Steve Spurrier. Unfortunately, Dan Blackmon is not wearing his Gamecock pants. "Too hot for those
here," he says. I tell them I'm ready to put the jean-shorts Gator
fan rumor to bed. "Are you kidding," Bob Cook asks, "they were
everywhere around us." Apparently, jorts are attached to the
Florida fanbase like Al Pacino was attached to the mob in *God-
father*, "Just when I thought I was out, they pull me back in . . ."

I head off to the bathroom at The Swamp to empty my
beer-filled bladder. Before I'm even able to unzip my fly, someone is banging hard on the door. I open the door to see Neville.
"Tebow," he says, eyes aglow, "Tebow is here." Suddenly, there
is a rush from the bottom level of the bar to the top level. The
newest Southern football saint is in the building.

Tebow is wearing a white shirt large enough to clothe an
entire tribe of islanders. He is generously doling out handshakes
and hugs to the onrush of fans. Exclamations of support rain
down upon him from every direction. If there were babies,
Tebow would be kissing them. At no time does he pull out the
patented Tim Tebow elbow or stiff arm a sorority girl to clear
space for himself. Instead, he is all smiles as the entire bar comes
to the upper floor of The Swamp.

It is utterly impossible to explain how much Florida fans
love Tim Tebow. Their adoration defies all comprehension.
Hyperbole can do the Florida love for Tim Tebow no justice.
Ultimately it had to happen: The Swamp has been Tebow'd.

As we walk outside into the late Florida night, it all becomes clear to me: UF fans have traded in the iconic Steve
Spurrier visor for the soon-to-be iconic Tim Tebow stiff arm.
And, in the warm air of Gainesville, on this night, it seems like
a good trade indeed.

THE GREAT BAD PUNTER

As I've spent the season on the road in my favorite conference, thinking about not only the careers of countless SEC heroes, but also that of my grandfather, and my own touch football days in college, I've come to the realization that I need not stand on the college football sidelines for all eternity. For, after all, I could be a bad punter on a college football team. This is the only position that I'm sure I could play. And I have four years of NCAA eligibility left to burn refining my bad punting skills.

At a very young age I realized that my football athletic ability best suited itself to noncompetitive intramural endeavors. And lots of Tecmo Super Bowl, of course. I couldn't play in the secondary (too slow and too white); I couldn't play wide receiver (ditto); I couldn't play quarterback (as noted I can't throw the ball even fifty yards); I couldn't play offensive or defensive line (at six foot, 175 pounds, I would be lineman roadkill); and I couldn't play tight end or linebacker or running back either. Basically, I'm completely worthless to any college football team in America. Except I'd be a really great bad punter. Consistently bad. Yet, effectively bad.

You know how teams consistently have punters who bomb the football into the end zone for a touchback when all that is needed is a little finesse punt from the forty-one or so to pin the opponent inside their own twenty? How many times have you slammed the remote down or stood and cursed your team's coach when some big-legged pantywaist punter sends the football tumbling through the back of the end zone? The worst is when your team decides to punt from the thirty-five-yard line (instead of going for it on fourth down or attempting a long field goal) and the punter kicks the ball into the end zone and only gains fifteen yards in field position. It's downright shameful and inexcusable.

Here's where I come in. See, I could remedy this very situation for any team that is smart enough to add me to the roster as a walk-on bad punter. That's because I don't have a strong enough leg to actually make the kick reach the end zone. But my form is perfect, and I never attempt to kick the ball and miss. I just can't kick it very far. Which is why I'm personally guaranteeing that every kick I attempted from a short distance would not reach the end zone. Ergo, there would never be a touchback. Defensive coordinators would love me. Occasionally full-figured women wearing large full-bodied panties with bad eyesight would mistake me for the starting quarterback and I would have full-fledged groupies. All because I would be a great bad punter.

I'm here offering my services to the right team. SEC, preferred, but really, I'll ply my trade wherever a team needs to pin their opposition inside the ten-yard line. Which, by the way, is every team on earth. All season long, as I traveled on the DDT, I watched SEC punters boom the ball through the back of the end zone. Every team did it at least once. This means I should be in high demand. It's really the only reason I've gone on the entire DDT or written a book at all, so I can end up being a great bad punter for the right football team.

Some people have doubted that I'd be a great bad punter. These people are what I like to call punter player haters. They sicken me. When I share with them my brilliant idea, they respond with comments like, "That is the dumbest idea I have ever heard in my life," and "Do you have an actual vagina?" That's okay though, everyone has haters. Even great men like

Gandhi and Justin Timberlake. I'll use the fuel of my doubters to help power my short punts. When I down the ball inside the five and sprint across the field with my index fingers raised high to the heavens, these punter player haters will be watching me on television, and they will lean over in a fit of fury and jealousy to kick their dogs. Or their cats. It's been my experience that most punter player haters actually live alone at home with their cats. And sometimes those cats are named Lorenzo and those punter player haters are named Neville and graduated from the University of Florida in the class of 2001.

Once, after a particularly horrendous performance by the University of Tennessee of drilling short punts into the end zone, I gathered a collection of practicing attorneys and we went to the Vanderbilt football field. I personally guaranteed that I would punt twenty times from the forty-yard line and that none of my kicks would reach the end zone; instead every single one would be downed inside the twenty. Sure enough, twenty times in a row I went out and did it. Bang, I'm a great bad punter superstar in the making. My punter player haters were so angry. Because I was so damn good at being so damn bad at punting.

It's really only a matter of time until my phone starts ringing with offers from coaches who see that I put the *special* in special teams. Any day now, I'll be asked to put on football pads for the first time in my life, slip on my cleats, and stride onto the grass field of a stadium filled to capacity to watch me perform. For most of the game, I'll stand biding my time on the sideline, until one blessed moment, my name will be called. "Travis!" Tennessee Volunteer Coach Phil Fulmer (or any other coach in need of a great bad punter) will shout. "Get out there and pin the Tide deep." And I'll run out onto the same field my grandfather played on, catch the snap, and pin the Alabama football team inside the five-yard line.

Everyone will love me because I'm the greatest bad punter in the history of the universe. It's going to happen, just you wait. I'm a bad punter legend in the making.

ALABAMA

TUSCALOOSA, ALABAMA
AUBURN UNIVERSITY VS. THE UNIVERSITY OF ALABAMA
NOVEMBER 18, 2006

The Iron Bowl, the annual Auburn-University of Alabama blood feud, is a large collection of well-mannered Alabamians who would just as soon kill each other as say hello. Only it's the South, so everyone is obligated to be friendly. This rivalry is like strychnine in the morning coffee, sending someone upstairs to use your bathroom without warning him that two steps are missing, a pecan pie laced with arsenic, a passive-aggressive research scientist's greatest laboratory. It's the only place on earth where, "Howdy y'all," at a tailgate might be followed by an unfortunate punji stick trap. And if you ever have a chance, you absolutely must go.

What makes this rivalry the best in college football is that no state line divides the two schools, the football teams consistently excel, and the state of Alabama lives and breathes college football with a passion that is unmatched anywhere else in the country. Your wife might be an Auburn grad, your grandfather an Alabama grad. At some point, everyone in Alabama has to pick a side. Abraham Lincoln, a man they still haven't forgiven in Alabama, memorably said that a house divided against itself cannot stand. (Perhaps this is why so many people in Alabama live in mobile homes. Well, I guess that's not altogether fair; after all, some people live in apartments.)

In Alabama, every house is divided. Somehow, someway, if you live in the state your blood seeps across the Auburn-Alabama partition, which means that whatever happens in this game can't be forgotten for an entire year. The sting of defeat is unavoidable, inescapable, since you are surrounded by your gridiron enemies, and cannot help but run into neighbors and family members who will bask in the glory of their win. In Alabama, an Iron Bowl loss stings like a paper cut that is reopened anew each morning for a year. Even worse, on the day after the big game, Alabama and Auburn fans have to come together at church and accidentally touch hands when the offering plate is passed. Even religious life does not allow any measure of avoidance.

So, Ohio State beat Michigan this week in the overrated Big 10? Big deal. I'm heading up to Michigan for Christmas and, while I'm up there, I won't meet a single Ohio State fan. Michigan lost and everyone I celebrate Christmas with share the misery of that defeat. At no point will an Ohio State fan be present to pass the cranberries or excessively dot the "i" on a Christmas card. Not so for Alabama families.

In an effort to convey the subterfuge underlying fan interactions at an Iron Bowl tailgate, here is a typical conversation between an Alabama and Auburn fan. The parenthetical is what everyone wishes they could say:

ALABAMA FAN: *"Hey, good to see y'all again."* (*I wish you'd gotten a flat tire on the way to the game and Tommy Tuberville'd gotten hit by a semi helping you change it.*)

AUBURN FAN: *"Hey, good to see y'all here too. Nice campus."* (*I hate you. Tuscaloosa smells like cat urine.*)

ALABAMA FAN: *"Y'all been deer hunting this year?"* (*If only that orange you're wearing was just a little more understated you might get shot.*)

AUBURN FAN: *"Naw, but man Jimmy's getting big. Pretty soon he's going to be playing for Alabama."* (*Your son is fat and Alabama's team is made up of other fat white boys. In reality I think your son plays the ninth lead in his high school's version of* The Merry Wives of Windsor. *That's real cool.*)

AUBURN FAN: *"Probably so. How's Sarah Beth?"* (*Is your wife still as fat as Al Borges?*)

ALABAMA FAN: *"Oh, she's good. She's in Atlanta . . . Georgia."* (*You know, Georgia. That team that just hung 37 points on you at home. Ring any bells?*)

AUBURN FAN: *"Nice talking with you. Gotta head on now."* (*I hope you noticed that I used my thumb when I gestured we had to leave, you rotten bastard. Yep, count 'em, five in a row coming.*)

With an atmosphere like this, who wouldn't love a chance to check out the Iron Bowl as stop eleven on the DDT?

The Iron Bowl tradition was born on February 22, 1893, when Auburn and Alabama met in Lakeview Park in Birmingham, Alabama. The name Iron Bowl derives from the city of Birmingham's prominence as an iron and steel production capital. Discord commenced with the rivalry's inception, which Auburn considered the first game of the 1893 campaign while

Alabama considered it the last of the 1892 season. After a contentious beginning, the rivalry was suspended in 1907 because the schools could not agree on where the officials should come from. After forty-one years of suspended rivalry, the series began anew in 1948, and Alabama celebrated by waxing Auburn 55–0 at Birmingham's Legion Field. For the next forty years, each game between Alabama and Auburn was played at the supposedly neutral Legion Field. In 1989, the Iron Bowl traveled 110 miles to Auburn's Jordan-Hare Stadium. Alabama continued to play their home games in the series at Legion Field until 2000, when they also moved the Iron Bowl to their Tuscaloosa campus. If anything, moving the games to campus stadiums has made the rivalry between the two schools even more heated.

Yet despite their intense rivalry, in a strange way, Alabama and Auburn manage to keep each other afloat; in the entire history of their programs Auburn and Alabama have never had losing seasons in the same year.

On the way to the University of Alabama campus in Tuscaloosa, I stop in Birmingham, where my cousin Brooke takes me to meet with James H. Watkins, a forty-one-year-old autistic Alabama fan who has an encyclopedic knowledge of all things Alabama.

Inside Watkins's apartment, the walls are plastered with Crimson Tide paraphernalia—posters, a bedspread, several old media guides, and an Alabama T-shirt draped over the chair.

While we are there Watkins does the following: Correctly recites Alabama's record from 1981 to 1992; discusses the longest winning streaks in Alabama-Auburn history ("Oh, no," he says, "Auburn has never beaten Alabama six times in a row. Just five times from 1954 to 1958"); and upon hearing my street address correctly tells me that my Nashville zip code is 37212. According to Brooke, Watkins took a job sorting mail in Birmingham and was paid per item of mail he could correctly distribute. Based on his unbelievable recall of zip codes, Watkins could sort mail at lightning speed. Typically, at that time, salaries topped out at $15,000 a year for this sorting job. Watkins made $60,000 his first year. Even now, you can name any city in America, and Watkins can tell you the zip code for the town. To test him I throw out St. Thomas, Virgin Islands, and Bloomfield Hills, Michigan (my wife's hometown). Watkins nails both.

Astounded, I begin to pepper Watkins with questions from Alabama's past seasons that I have no knowledge of. "What was Alabama's record in 1938 and who was the coach?" "Frank Thomas and Alabama was 7-1-1," replies Watkins without pause. When I get to a computer the next day, I look up the information and find that every bit of it is true.

James Watkins, the greatest statistician of Alabama football.

Watkins then asks what my birthday is. "April 6, 1979," I tell him. "You were born on a Friday," says Watkins. Later I ask my mom about this. Not surprisingly, Watkins is correct.

"Do you think Auburn's going to beat Alabama for a fifth consecutive time?" I ask Watkins. There is a prolonged silence. Then my cousin Brooke speaks. "He doesn't like to talk about Auburn winning," Brooke says.

Having met the unsung prodigy of Alabama football history, I attend my friend Kelly's law firm holiday party, which falls a mere six weeks before Christmas. Previously on the DDT, Kelly accompanied me to the LSU game and hosted me the night before I went to the Auburn game. While at the law firm party I come face to face with several associate lawyers, and at least one partner, who are rocking 'Bama Bangs. Yep, the "largest law firm between Atlanta and Dallas" has partners sporting 'Bama Bangs. Also, I love the fact that they are the self-appointed largest firm between Atlanta and Dallas. Because this area encapsulates the following cities: Jackson, Mississippi, and New Orleans, Louisiana. Coincidentally the new tagline for the DDT book is: "The best SEC sports book written by a man who lives between Jackson, Tennessee, and Chattanooga, Tennessee."*

While at the law firm Christmas party, one of Kelly's friends, Trevor, arrives dressed as Santa Claus. Shortly thereafter, Santa is drinking a whiskey and water at the bar when kids materialize from nowhere and start telling him what they want for Christmas. Santa makes several drunken promises.

Once the party is over we head out to a bar in downtown Birmingham. Immediately upon entering the place, a group of at least six girls swarm Santa. I've never seen anything like it. If Florida quarterback Tim Tebow had walked in beside the guy in the Santa outfit, the girls still would have gone to Santa. Every single one of them asks to sit on Santa's lap and in turn requests

* According to Clay's mom.

gifts that are staples of every *Penthouse* letters section while slapping and pinching Santa's butt. One girl actually whispers into Trevor's ear, "I want a big fat vibrator for Christmas, Santa."

Meanwhile, Kelly turns to me and announces, "This is why we're renting a limo and going out with a group of guys dressed in Santa suits in two weeks. You should come back down." Evidently, drunk Santa parties are hugely popular in New Orleans and this trend has slowly worked its way north. This is a trend that needs to spread. It's like the exact opposite of 'Bama Bangs.

The next day, Kelly and I take I-20 West to Tuscaloosa from Birmingham, leaving at around ten in the morning. Traffic is bad. Made even worse when a semi swerves onto the side of the road to allow an Auburn fan to retrieve the flag that had blown off his car window. On some level, risking death for a ten dollar flag seems excessive. Especially when you still have a flag left. On another level, though, everyone knows it's really lame to only have one team flag blowing in the wind. Real fans have at least two.

While en route, I share with Kelly my favorite SEC football quote. As soon as he took the job as Auburn football coach, Pat Dye was asked how long it would take him to beat Alabama. Without skipping a beat Dye replied, "Sixty minutes." I have no rooting interest in Alabama-Auburn one way or the other and that quote still gives me chills. Even Kelly is impressed. "Yeah," he says, "that's not bad."

My wife calls while we are driving, and I tell her about the traffic. "Oh, man, you have to drive all the way to the coast, right?" Evidently, my wife believed that the Crimson Tide must, you know, be near a place where a tide actually exists. When I explain that the University of Alabama is not, in fact, particularly close to any body of water that has a tide, she replies, "This whole Crimson Tide business is just so ridiculous. Especially when you combine it with the elephant mascot."

As soon as Kelly and I arrive in Tuscaloosa and find a parking spot, we begin the 'Bama Bangs counting. We spot lots of 'Bama Bangs hidden beneath baseball caps. This is throwing off our counting. Near Denny Chimes, which is a bell tower near the quad with twenty-five bells, but is arrogantly described as a "campanile with a 25-bell carillon," we get on a roll. "Bangs, bangs, bangs," we count out loud as we point. We planned on buying a clicker somewhere to keep a more scientific tally, but I didn't manage to find one prior to arriving at the game. Even still, I imagine this is how endangered species are also tracked, by pointing and counting aloud. Unfortunately, 'Bama Bangs aren't endangered, they are thriving and expanding. They're the kudzu of hair.

We also spot a number of Alabama band members walking to the stadium carrying their instruments. In particular, the guys with the tubas seem to be really struggling. Unfortunately, I don't see anyone carrying cymbals. Without their slamming punctuation, is any band complete? As we are contemplating this, we find a baby's shoe abandoned near the stadium. Luckily for the father who is responsible for this (the father is definitely responsible), it's still warm outside.

The Alabama quad is filled with games for kids to play, and children and families are everywhere. This is the best setup for children I have seen on any SEC campus on the DDT thus far. Kelly and I are both envious because we can't play the games ourselves. "I think we're too old," Kelly says, "and we don't have any kids."

While Kelly and I stand on the outskirts of the quad, watching with envy as children play Wiffle Ball, compete in field-goal-kicking contests, and even a game of quarterback passing accuracy, we meet Chad and Brooke Hopper. Chad is an Alabama grad and his wife Brooke is an Auburn graduate. Today, they'll be sitting together in Bryant-Denny Stadium. Chad tells me they started dating in 1999. "After Alabama won that year, she started crying and wouldn't talk to me. I knew then I had a good girl."

Then, Brooke steps in, "If possible, we don't sit together. In 2004, I was eight months pregnant and, after Auburn won, he left me in the stadium and made me walk back to the car alone." Chad nods his head, "That's true. I can't stay in the stadium and listen to their fans when they win."

Brooke continues, "three hundred sixty-four days he's the love of my life but for this one day . . ." She pauses, and Chad interjects, "I'd say it's more like the month of November." Discussion ensues, and eventually the couple reaches a compromise. "Okay, the week of the game," Brooke admits.

I ask how Alabama's own Civil War is going to be resolved in their son. "He's two. He says Go Auba and Roll Tide now," Brooke says. Perhaps he has a future in Alabama politics. "I think I should get the firstborn," says the father, "I have season tickets already. You can have the next one." This sounds like a debate that is just beginning.

The couple keeps pictures of Auburn's Samford Hall, the tallest building on the campus, constructed in 1888, and of Alabama's Denny Chimes bell tower hanging in their house. Whoever wins in any given year, gets to hang their picture higher for the next 364 days. My friend Kelly speaks up, "Why don't you just keep both pictures at the same level?"

Chad looks dismissively at him, "There's no fun in that," he replies. Welcome to Alabama-Auburn where equality makes everyone angry.

At no point since I've been on campus, has there been a moment when I couldn't complete a pass to someone with 'Bama Bangs. And we're not talking fly pattern or Hail Mary passes. It would be an easy screen completion. Actually, there might not have been a moment when I couldn't have run the option alongside a guy with 'Bama Bangs.

Kelly and I tally 237 instances of 'Bama Bangs during admittedly haphazard counting for an hour near the quad. Being idiots when it comes to math, we have no idea how to extrapolate this data to any purpose. Fortunately my friend Shaw, who came with me on the Mississippi State trip, is soon to be a PhD in mathematics. During college, he occasionally tried to impress women by having them recite their Social Security Number and then correctly repeating it to them several weeks later. Currently he knows my social security number, three of my credit card numbers, and remembers every phone number I had in college.

Later, when I describe my wish to quantify and catalog the 'Bama Bangs in attendance, Shaw sends me a lengthy report to help me in my calculations: "You said you saw 237 instances of 'Bama Bangs in the quad. Given the fact that you were there for about a half hour counting, let's assume that you saw a total of 3,000 people. That makes 7.9 percent of the people on the quad with 'Bama Bangs. But you have to consider that you probably saw some of the same people a few times. If you saw everyone on the quad twice, and with an error allowance for observation of 0.1 percent, that puts the total number of 'Bama Bangs safely

between 230 and 244. Then, given the proliferation of caps being worn by the SEC crowd, you have to consider that some of
the people you saw were hiding their 'Bama Bangs under their
hats. We can just add this to the uncertainty folded into the
observation error, and adjust the number to 250, which gives us
a comfortable 8.3 percent of all people on the quad sporting
'Bama Bangs. Now, the stadium seats 92,138, and since this
game was the biggest of the year for Alabama it's safe to assume
that the game was sold out. Including peripheral employees,
perpetual tailgaters, and other sundry ne'erdowells who don't
actually enter the stadium, there were probably a total of about
100,000 people in a small radius about Bryant-Denny Stadium
on game day (which is statistically pretty convenient!), and
thus, there were probably about 8,300 'Bama Bangs haircuts.

"To determine the real 'Bama Bangs quotient (BBQ), you
want to look at the eligibility of the crowd for 'Bama Bangs. For
instance, in a sample space of 100 attendees on Saturday, probably thirty are women, twelve of the remaining men are bald,
hence unable to grow any kind of bangs at all, two would be
children too young to have hair that long, and (rounding up)
one would be a transvestite, which, for some reason, seems like
it shouldn't count. Hence, the eligible population is really fifty-
five out of every hundred. Since we determined before that 8.3
out of every hundred people had 'Bama Bangs, this means that
your BBQ is 8.3/55, or 15.1 percent."

Every time I read this I get more amazed. Shaw deserves the
Nobel. Or at least a free meal at Dreamland in Tuscaloosa.

We walk around Denny Chimes and pause where the captains
of Alabama football teams past are memorialized with stones
surrounding the bell tower. I take a picture of quarterback Jay

Barker's stone. Primarily because Jay Barker made my Octobers miserable from 1992 to 1994. Barker simply didn't lose, winning a National Championship for Alabama in 1992 and then in 1993 bringing Alabama back for a miraculous 17–17 tie against my beloved Vols in a game that I'm convinced shortened my life by several years. To this day the very mention of that game makes me angry. Furious, even.

Dear Jay Barker, I still hate you. Love, Clay Travis

We make our way to Bryant-Denny Stadium, where statues of former Alabama national championship winning coaches Wade Wallace, Frank Thomas, Gene Stallings, and Bear Bryant stand guard. Three of the statues are relatively uncrowded. Guess which one isn't. Yep, Bear Bryant. His statute is swarmed.

Thanks to Bear Bryant, Alabama fans will wear anything if you make it in houndstooth. Here are a collection of clothing items I saw in houndstooth on game day: women's skirts, baseball caps, women's pants, fedoras, men's pants, blankets, men's shirts, shawls, suit coats, belts, winter coats, scarves, and dresses. Items that I presume come in houndstooth but did not see: thongs.

Alabama has left an open space for the statue of their next coach who wins a national championship. (Insert Mike Shula joke here; I don't have the heart.)

I think it's a rule that if you are an Alabama coed and you're going to a football game, you have to wear heels. Otherwise, I don't think they let you in. Kelly sums up the women, "Even the really ugly girls (trust me, there weren't many) are doing everything they can to make themselves attractive. They all try really hard." Indeed.

Bryant-Denny Stadium is in the middle of campus. It towers over the other nearby buildings including the president's palatial residence. From the main strip of bars in Tuscaloosa the stadium vaguely resembles an alien spacecraft looming in the distance.

We meet Auburn fans Charles and Alex Wellman with whom we'll be sitting for the game. Charles reports that he just ran into infamous Auburn grad Charles Barkley outside the stadium. "He told me, 'War Eagle, my brother.'"

Inside the stadium, we make our way to our seats in time to see Alabama's star wide receiver Tyrone Prothro introduced to start the game. He's wearing a full uniform and limping badly. He was injured almost fourteen months ago, late in a Florida game that Alabama would go on to win 31–3. Since that single play, in which he fractured both his tibia and his fibula, Prothro has been unable even to walk normally. Prothro's a tremendous example of how fickle football fate can be. I don't know a single SEC fan who isn't rooting for him to come back for the 2007 season.

Auburn fans in Tuscaloosa have been holding up their thumbs on every occasion. That's because Auburn is attempting to win for the fifth consecutive time over Alabama. As the Auburn team charges onto the field, many in orange raise only their thumbs. "Fear the thumb" is, for the moment, giving "War Eagle" a run for the money as the verbal currency of choice for Tiger fans. There's a large collection of Auburn fans in the recently completed north end zone upper deck. Bryant-Denny has been remodeled, and now features three Jumbotrons, lots of new luxury suites, and scrolling scoreboards on the façade of the upper decks on the east and west sides of the stadium. Seating capacity has expanded to 92,138, and, if anything, Bryant-Denny seems far too nice to be a college football stadium.

For the record Bryant-Denny makes it ten out of eleven SEC stadiums with hedges. They run along both sidelines behind the benches. There are none in the end zones, although Alabama's student section is in the south end zone and some students dangle their legs over the wall as they watch the game. It's very loud, and fans in the Alabama student section are shaking their pompons in time to the Go Alabama, cheer.

The sun has not dropped behind the stadium yet, and I'm ruing the fact that I've forgotten my ninety-nine cent Sunclassic sunglasses. I knew it was going to happen at some point, but, even still, grief isn't easy.

On the positive side, our seats are awesome, fourteenth row at the forty-yard line behind the Auburn bench. On the negative side, I realize my pen is lost for the second time on the DDT. No one around me has a pen but, eventually, we manage to find one down the row a bit. And then I end up keeping it. Fortunately, there is a name on the pen, which enables me to now thank its giver, Sherry Benson, whom I've never met, but who managed to loan her pen to the cause of the DDT.

One of my seat companions, Charles Wellman, tells me he and his brother rode down from Birmingham on a bus with Auburn running back Kenny Irons' parents. "Kenny's dad," Wellman tell us, "was saying the simplest things, like, 'I told him to hang on tight to the ball' and Auburn fans were standing around him just nodding and gobbling up everything he could say."

On the first possession of the Iron Bowl, Alabama drives inside the ten against Auburn, then Mike Shula calls three consecutive running plays into the center of the Auburn defensive line. Each play is unsuccessful. Alabama's field-goal kicker, Jamie Christensen, trots on the field and his field goal gives 'Bama a 3–0 lead. "Everybody in the whole damn stadium knew we were going to run Castillo," says an Alabama fan behind me, a blatant indictment of Shula's conservative play calling.

Mike Shula is in his fourth year as head coach of Alabama's football team. He is the son of legendary Dolphins coach Don Shula, and was the starting quarterback for the Crimson Tide from 1984 to 1986. After two losing seasons at Alabama to begin his coaching career, Shula won ten games in 2005 and appeared to have secured his job. But his failure to win close games, seeming uncertainty on the sideline, and general inability to win games against Alabama's biggest rivals Auburn, Tennessee, and LSU has left him desperately in need of a win over Auburn today. Especially because Shula is currently 0-3 against Tuberville and Auburn.

Remember my question about whether a decapitated head could still see, even for a split second, following its severing? After Auburn decks Alabama quarterback John Parker Wilson, I thought we might have a test case on the football field. Somehow, Auburn's Kevin Sears manages to pick up the football and not Wilson's rolling head. Shortly thereafter, Auburn scores on a lightning quick run by their sophomore tailback Brad Lester to take a 7–3 lead.

I think Auburn head coach Tommy Tuberville has gotten into the Alabama fans' heads. The guys behind me have called Tuberville a riverboat gambler approximately fifteen times already, and we're only in the second quarter. They've screamed this mantra on kickoffs, punts from inside his own territory, second-and-short yardage for Auburn, third-and-long for 'Bama. Name any play, and Alabama fans are leery of what Tommy Tuberville might do. Basically, Alabama fans feel about Tommy Tuberville the way I used to feel about Steve Spurrier when he was at Florida.

But how does calling someone a riverboat gambler have staying power when it comes to present-day football anyway? Weren't riverboat gamblers popular in the mid-1800s? Especially now, when it's almost impossible to find a southern person who hasn't gambled on a riverboat, this cliché makes even less sense. Anachronistically this is like calling a college football coach a gold prospector or moonshine smuggler or a beaver pelt trader.

Meanwhile, back on the field, Alabama quarterback John Parker Wilson fumbles on another quarterback sack and Auburn recovers. On the next play, Kenny Irons scores a touchdown standing up. On the drive back to Birmingham, Irons' father is going to say something akin to, "I told him, if he can score a touchdown, that's a good play." It's 14–3 Auburn and the entire stadium seems to be nervously shifting in their seats.

Then, with 1:23 remaining in the half, beaver pelt trader Tommy Tuberville brings a blitz and gets burned. Alabama completes a fifty-two-yard touchdown pass to Nikita Stover, whose name sounds like that of a Russian mail-order bride, and suddenly Bryant-Denny is alive. On the play, Wilson is hit after the pass and Shula elects to accept the penalty and go for two. The two-point conversion attempt fails and, at the half, the score is 14–9 Auburn.

Going for two here, is the quintessential Shula move. It's

being aggressive for aggression's sake because you think that's what people want you to do. Classic overcoaching. Shula's like the guy who goes to a dance club, doesn't dance for two hours, and then, inexplicably, is seen furiously doing the running man on the stage by himself.

Both Alabama and Auburn fans have their ears perked for the outcome of Ohio State-Michigan and the other SEC games. The Alabama scoreboard people actually do a good job displaying up-to-date scores on other games around the country. They're like the antithesis of Jefferson-Pilot-Lincoln Financial. That's because people in the state of Alabama are college football fans. Period. They care about their own teams, but they also know a ton about your team. Probably more than you do, as a matter of fact.

On the opening drive of the second half, 'Bama scores a touchdown and then unsuccessfully goes for two again. It's 15–14 'Bama midway through the third quarter, and the stadium has just gotten really, really loud. Deafening even, as Auburn takes possession.

Incidentally, the Alabama students are separated from the regular fans by a chain-link fence. This makes zero sense. Unless the students are still smuggling in mountain lions. Or alums are trying to get back to college by climbing into the student section. Then, I might see the need for the fence.

It's dark now, and rapidly becoming cooler. Somewhere in the stadium, a father has just noticed that his son is missing a shoe and is trying to hide that fact from his wife. On the new screens on the upper-deck facades before kickoffs, the word ROOOLLLL actually rolls along the screen. Pretty cool. The pompons are up and waving at record levels in Bryant-Denny. Not cool.

We have been standing for the entire game. From what I can see, it appears that the entire stadium is standing. If you didn't know any better, you'd get the feeling that the outcome of this game is sort of important.

Auburn answers Alabama's score on a high-arching third-and-fifteen touchdown pass from quarterback Brandon Cox to wide receiver Prechae Rodriguez. It's 22–15, Auburn after a fullback pass for a successful two-point conversion. Oh, that beaver pelt trader Tuberville.

At the end of the third quarter, two of the approximately forty-eight current or former members of Lynyrd Skynyrd come on the field as "Sweet Home Alabama" is played. One of the guys appears to have a beret on. I'm just going to pretend I didn't see this.

Midway through the fourth quarter with Auburn appearing to be in control of the game, running back Kenny Irons inexplicably fumbles in the open field, and Alabama recovers the ball. Bryant-Denny explodes. On the next play, Alabama is stripped of the ball, and Auburn recovers. At least it appears that Auburn recovers. We have to wait for an instant-replay review.

While awaiting the instant replay, I get very frustrated trying to figure out why the SEC doesn't allow the replays to be shown in the stadium once a play is under review? Isn't it ridiculous to assume that a referee wearing headphones is going to be influenced by what clearly biased fans think? Even if the footage obviously favors the visiting team, it's not like home team fans are going to think the correct call is being made. At the very least, when it comes to controversial plays, if people viewing the game on television are able to see the plays, fans in the stadium should be able to see them too. Thanks to the current nonsensical system, the fans in the stadium are the most clueless about what's going on when instant-replay challenges occur. If you're anything like me, at games you really care about, you end up calling your friends at home and seeing what they can tell from the television replays. Does this make any sense at all?

Just as my inner turmoil is beginning to get the better of me, the official announces that the Alabama fumble stands and Auburn takes possession. Alabama's fans, predictably, boo the call.

Alabama regains possession after an Auburn punt and, with 5:19 remaining, faces a fourth-and-fifteen at the Auburn nineteen-yard line. First, Shula spends too long making a decision about what to do, then he rushes his field goal team onto the field. Second, this delayed decision necessitates that the team take a timeout, because they don't have time to get the field goal off properly. This sets the Alabama crowd into a fit of indignation. Up until now, the crowd has been almost entirely supportive of their idiotic coach. But now, Alabama only has one timeout left and the crowd knows how important that is.

After the timeout, Shula sends his offense back onto the field, where they fail to gain the first down. It is the penultimate possession of the game, when victory or defeat hangs in the balance, and Shula seems to have altered his decision at least three times. Go for it, kick a field goal, and then back to go for it. All spliced around a timeout that didn't need to be taken, and all making the odds of his eventual success even lower. I don't think Alabama fans would be entirely uncomfortable with either decision, but it's Shula's inability to make any decision at all that truly drives them crazy. "You had a third-and-fifteen on the play just before this one," groans a man behind me. I know what this fan means. It's not like this fourth-and-fifteen situation is completely unprecedented in the annals of coaching. "Make a choice and go with it," another shouts.

Unable to get a first down and end the game, Auburn punts to Alabama, and, on his final opportunity to salvage victory, Alabama's Wilson throws another interception to end the game. Immediately, several Auburn players rush to the benches on their sideline, climb on top of them, and begin flashing their thumbs and their entire hands to the Alabama student section. This is Auburn's fifth win in a row over Alabama and, not surprisingly, this move by the Auburn team members is not favorably received by the Alabama students. Curses and objects fly.

For the next thirty minutes chants of "We love Shula" echo throughout Bryant-Denny. Only Auburn fans are the ones doing the chanting. Already, the thumb is in ascendance and questions are brewing about whether "fear the index finger" has the same ring or if, when they go for six in a row next year in 2007, Auburn fans will adopt the European tradition, and begin counting with the other thumb on the new hand. Questions abound. But, from my seat, I can't even see the Alabama players slinking off the field on the other sideline, only the jubilant celebration of the Auburn fans and their players.

After the game, we eat dinner in the Alabama student dining hall with Kelly's younger brother Corey, who is a freshman. Students are constantly filing in to replenish themselves after an afternoon spent drinking. I regale Corey with all sorts of college lessons. Such as: You'll never regret sleeping with any woman in college if you wear a condom. And, never miss any sporting event in favor of studying. I'm a great influence.

Later that night, at a bar called The Booth on the Tuscaloosa strip, I will talk with an Alabama undergrad named Maggie

and ask her to sum up the differences between being an Alabama and Auburn student, "At Auburn you'll smoke a lot of
pot and you might go to the bars," she says, pausing contempla-
tively. "At Alabama you'll smoke a lot of pot, but go to bars all
the time." Somewhere the president of the Alabama Southern
Baptist Convention just started crying.

By the end of the night, Alabama and Auburn fans have
come together in the bars of Tuscaloosa. I don't see any fights or
near fights. Everyone seems content to drink beers, listen to
music, chase women, and admire each other's bangs. The anger, aggression, and distaste have been washed away and, at
least for one night, the two warring armies of Alabama fandom
have lain down their weapons. By the end of the night, the
state of Alabama is once more one nation, under God, undi-
vided by bare foreheads. Long live 'Bama Bangs.

WOMEN OF THE SEC

For as long as I can remember, SEC football and beautiful women have gone hand in hand.

In the 1980s and very early 1990s, getting a *Playboy* magazine was the ten- to thirteen-year-old boy's equivalent of splitting the atom and, for me, this quest was inextricably linked with University of Tennessee football. That's because, on our trips to Knoxville, the naked female breast became the brass ring of our preadolescent minds. There was no scheme too outlandish, no brainstorm too far-fetched, no obstacle that our minds could not overcome. We were too young to know that Malcolm X had advocated black power by any means necessary. But we knew the feeling, even if we were white kids from Nashville.

By any means necessary, to us, usually meant via the gift shop in the Holiday Inn World's Fair. Yes, Knoxville actually hosted the World's Fair—in 1982, as a matter of fact. And they built a Holiday Inn for it. Our focus was the Holiday Inn World's Fair gift shop because we knew that *Playboy* magazines were available there. Tantalizingly close. Just above the football magazines on the back row, only a thin veneer of plastic foil separating us from boobs, glorious boobs. Each week, we would go to the gift shop and feign interest in the latest *Big Bopper* (insert photos of Candace Cameron, yes!!!!) or *Sports Illustrated*. We would stand there forever, thinking of something, anything, that might enable us to walk out of the gift shop, newer men, older men, men who had seen bare breasts.

We were aided in this daydream by the fact that, at the age of ten, we got our own hotel room. My next-door neighbor Matt, his cousin Johnny, me, and whoever else was our age and might be traveling with us. Of course, the first year we'd gotten our own room we'd received a stern warning from Matt's father, "Remember boys," he'd said, "no matter what you think about doing, we'll know. Every bit of trouble you could possibly get into, we've already gotten in, and we'll know." We'd nodded. Said we understood. And immediately raced back to our hotel room with our own key and our own beds and our own television and our own bathroom and jumped from one bed to another while we set about implementing new schemes to get a *Playboy*.

Then, we'd gone downstairs, passed the gift shop with longing eyes and walked out into the fields surrounding the Sunsphere, a large golden orb that, for some reason, was the focal point of the 1982 World's Fair, and tossed a football while contemplating ways to get our hands on a *Playboy*.

Maybe an older sister's boyfriend who was a freshman at the school? Rejected. Maybe an older man who had too much to drink at the bar and would be sympathetic to our plight? Rejected. Maybe a kindly worker in the gift shop if we claimed we were buying it for our handicapped father? Rejected. Maybe we could charge the magazine to our room and claim it was Mello Yellos we'd purchased, not pornography? Rejected. The roster of our rejected plans knew no bounds. And our progress was nonexistent.

Nowadays, kids can find pornography in mere seconds on the Internet. Milliseconds even. I'm convinced this will eventually ruin our country. Not because of the negative impact of pornography on your youth, but rather because kids today take bare breasts for granted. They don't have to work for them. They're just there. Easily accessible. Available. Bare breasts are like Topps baseball cards now. In my day, you had to work to see the naked female form, send your brain cells racing into one dark alleyway ending in one metaphorical brick wall after another, pound the pavement, beg, problem solve, create hypotheses, cope with failure, and embrace risk with the faint possibility of a tantalizing reward. I'm convinced that just about every single male CEO of a major American corporation was the kid who was smart enough to scheme to get his hands on a *Playboy* by the time he was thirteen. Now, we've just got a generation of fat, lazy kids who have no respect for how difficult it used to be to see a naked female breast. They sicken me. (These kids, not the breasts.)

So, we didn't get a *Playboy*. But, in our own hotel room, we discovered SpectraVision. Glorious SpectraVision. With the five-minute free previews and all the boobs you could possibly want in a lifetime. Or so it seemed. Boobs that were bigger than a football, boobs that were smaller than a football, boobs that made you forget about football altogether. We were so smart. Setting the alarm clock in the room so that we could get our five minute previews, then shutting it off before the time ran out and we were billed. It was brilliant. Spectacular. With SpectraVision, not only had we split the atom, we'd cured cancer, and this newfangled thing called AIDS. Life, quite simply, could get no better.

Until we accidentally went over five minutes on the free preview one Saturday night after a game.

Uh-oh.

All night we lay in bed staring at the ceiling. We were so nervous we didn't even want to open the window to our hotel room and throw ice out at people in the parking lot. Maybe the SpectraVision hadn't registered our movie, we hoped. Maybe our dads wouldn't notice when we checked out. After all, we could have been watching a normal movie. Except the prices were different. All through the night we thought of excuses. And we debated whether we should come clean. In the end, we embraced the tried and true method of felons and ne'er-do-wells across the centuries, and said nothing at all.

After a fitful night's sleep, we gathered our bags and walked downstairs. My stomach felt like it did when I'd loaded too much syrup on my pancakes. Heavy and thick. I felt like my football team had lost ten games in a row, all rolled together at once. Matt and I sat down in the lobby and waited.

Matt's father, Tim, returned from the checkout desk. The computer printout in his hand seemed to glow. "Did you boys get a movie?" he asked. Matt and I looked at one another with eyebrows raised. As if the very question itself was overwhelmingly ridiculous. A movie? Us, a movie? I opened my mouth. Matt opened his mouth. Yet we both stayed silent. Tim peered at us over his glasses.

"A naked movie?" he asked, piercing us with his owlish gaze. I was sure my eyes were as wide as they had been when I saw the bare breasts for the first time on the television. Then, out of our silence, Tim smiled. His smile was like rain falling on the parched Saharan desert. He left and talked to my dad. I thought I saw them both smile. "Let's go," they said, and we went.

The movie was not mentioned during our car ride from Knoxville to the outskirts of Nashville. Matt and I could not believe our good fortune. We talked about the UT football game we had seen, and UT football games to come later that season. Tim let us both call our moms on his brand-new car phone that was larger than a football. We talked about school and homework and major league baseball and everything on earth but naked women in naked movies that we shouldn't have ordered. Then, it happened.

Only a few miles from our houses, Tim cleared his throat.

"Boys," he said, "we know about the movie. And I told you we would know about everything you did in your room."

Matt and I were both quiet. Here came the hammer. I could feel my heart beating through my shirt. Envisioned that the cotton was actually rising.

"And we think," at this point Tim paused to nod to my dad, "that there's probably a few things it's okay to keep from your mommas." Matt and I exhaled. "So, if you don't say anything, we won't say anything."

We quickly agreed to the deal. We were men. Benighted fellows of the silent-breast roundtable. I leaned my head back comfortably into the rear seat. Took a deep breath. And that's how football and beautiful women became inextricably intertwined in my life. And I'm going to be completely honest, it's still a pretty damn good combination.

Which is why there absolutely had to be a ranking of SEC girls from the DDT.

Of course rating the girls of the SEC is a bit like choosing your favorite child. You like them all and they each have their own particular charms, unusual traits, and annoying tendencies that somehow make them even more endearing. To be clear, you really can't go wrong when it comes to the women of the SEC. In fact, the quality of the women in the SEC might be the only thing more competitive than the football games.

It's altogether possible that, if you took any of these twelve SEC schools and put their girls up against any other school in the country, the SEC would win. But that doesn't eliminate the need for the SEC Girls Power Rankings. So, here we go:*

12. Mississippi State: Maybe it was the eleven-thirty morning start, or perhaps it was because the best-looking girls in Starkville don't even go to the actual games, but my friends from George Washington and I were severely disappointed by the quality of the girls. When guys come down from the East Coast and aren't impressed with SEC girls, it's an indictment of epic proportions. I actually found myself apologizing to them. This, the dreaded number twelve ranking, is my revenge.

11. Florida: It all comes back to the extra six to eight pounds of weight on the back of the arms. The pork-loined shoulders factor. The best thing that can be said for Florida girls is that Erin Andrews once went there. The second best thing is that they are doubtlessly always carrying snacks in their oversized purses. Then again, winning two national championships in nine months probably eases the pain of making out with a fat girl, as long as your fingers don't get lost in the arm fat, of course. Gross. Having said all this, if Tim Tebow were a woman, I'd rank them number one.

10. Arkansas: I regret to inform you that hairspray seemed very popular in Arkansas, as did dressing up and going out like you didn't go to school in the South. The whole scene just reeked of trying too hard. Look, your campus is in the middle of the Ozarks, in a town several hundred miles from anywhere; don't try and be something you're not. Yet, head out in Arkansas and every bar

---

* I should note that the only adjustment these results have received is based on the benefit of the weather. That is, I've never met or seen a girl who didn't look better in the sunshine than she did in the cold or the rain. So, all things being equal, there was a clear advantage conveyed for games that were on campus in September or October. I've done my best to take this into account.

has a trendy one-word name (think: Stir) and girls who try to pretend they're Carrie Bradshaw and her loathsome *Sex and the City* friends. Here's a newsflash ladies: You aren't thirty-something Manhattanites out sipping cosmopolitans. Embrace your Southerness. Or just stay lame.

9. Kentucky: This was one of the games where I fear that my judging ability really was constrained by the weather. It was freezing at the time of the tailgate and every girl was wearing enough clothes to be a Boise State cheerleader. I did manage to spot a few real diamonds in the rough, but not enough to place Kentucky higher than ninth in the ratings.

8. Alabama: Alabama falls to number eight because the girls were the most Ole Miss-like of the other SEC schools. All of the girls here were also dressed up in heels and sundresses, only they were just a little bit worse in every category than the females at Ole Miss. Don't get me wrong, Alabama girls are hot, but hot in that way that Ashlee Simpson is in comparison to Jessica Simpson. You know, if you saw Ashlee out by herself you'd probably think she was pretty good looking. (My wife excluded. She hates Ashlee Simpson with an outrageous degree of passion.) But put her next to Jessica and you don't even notice Ashlee. Yep, the Simpson sister syndrome has struck Alabama and Ole Miss.

7. Tennessee: I live in Nashville. I've been a UT fan all my life and I know a lot of hot women who went to UT. Having said that, number seven is an accurate ranking. As a group, UT girls are too fond of makeup, an unfortunate trend that leaves many of them looking like Joan Rivers. Tennessee women are hot enough without the excessive accoutrements. But until they give them up, number seven is as high as you're going to get, ladies.

6. LSU: My friend Kerry endorsed LSU games as being the hottest gathering of women over thirty on earth. I think there's some

truth to this. In addition, there is just something about LSU girls that seems naughty. Maybe it's the prevalence of Mardi Gras beads or the fact that, per capita, the girls consume more alcohol here than anywhere else I visited. But you get the idea that things go on in the dorm rooms and off-campus apartments here that would make Caligula blush. Add in the Golden Girls, who basically exist solely to be hot girls on the football field, and we're talking a collection of women that probably beats every other school not in the SEC hands down.

5. South Carolina: My mom pointed out how attractive the girls on this campus were. When your retired mother who otherwise makes no comments about the attractiveness of women feels compelled to acknowledge how attractive the women are, this really counts for something. Plus, I saw several hot girls in heels and dresses breaking into oysters. This is the kind of spirit you like to see.

4. Auburn: These girls are just plain hot. Aside from nonfunctional belts, there didn't seem to be any one particular type of style that was popular here. Girls were in sweatpants, jeans, khaki shorts, pants, jerseys, sundresses. It didn't matter what they were wearing, they were gorgeous. And, if I didn't know better, I'd think some of the Hope Scholarship money is getting covertly funneled into Auburn. In fact, it's altogether possible there is a secret tunnel of hotness somehow connecting both Athens and Auburn. This place was number two on the cleavage meter.

3. Vanderbilt: Per capita, an absolute gold mine. Top four Vanderbilt Law School oft-repeated sentences:
   1. You get this round.
   2. Oh my God, did you see that girl?
   3. Your team sucks.
   4. Oh, my God, did you see that girl?

Plus, every Vandy girl I've ever met could actually carry on a conversation without a nonsensical giggle by the third sentence. Not to say that Vandy girls are completely bereft of the nonsensically giggling contingent, just that it is much reduced. Also, Vandy is a much smaller school than the others, so there's much less of a barrier between the largest male dork on campus and the hottest girl. You can imagine why this might appeal to me. Don't get me wrong, Vandy isn't a campus where *Lucas* wannabes come to find fulfillment, but it's closer to it than any other school in the SEC.

2. Georgia: A weekend in Athens is, quite simply, jaw-dropping; everywhere you look there's another gorgeous girl with a plunging neckline in a black or red dress. Maybe this is partly thanks to the Hope Scholarship. Rumor has it, thanks to the Hope making college funds go unused, ultimately these college funds end up financing fake breasts. But as my anonymous friend who refuses to acknowledge the legitimacy of the term *fake breasts* argues, "If it's inside the skin then it isn't fake. I mean, you don't run around pointing to people with new hearts or new hips or new knees and talk about how those are fake hearts or fake knees or fake hips. They're just breasts, glorious, under-the-skin breasts." I'm persuaded by this logic and am happy to name Athens the Cleavage Capital of America, and also number two on this list.

1. Ole Miss: Put any man in the Grove for more than an hour, give him legitimate openness of opinion (e.g., his wife can't be a graduate of a competing school and threaten withholding sex if his vote doesn't comport with her own vote), and I personally guarantee he will be blown away by the beauty. Put it this way, if you clubbed a guy in the head, dragged him to the Grove, woke him up, and told him that he was dead and now in Heaven, he'd probably believe you.

OLE MISS

If I absolutely had to be a male cheerleader, Ole Miss would be my choice. That's because I could end up a United States senator like current Mississippi politicians Thad Cochran and Trent Lott. Either that, or I could end up a member of the so-called world famous Bud Light Daredevils, like Ty and Gus Cobb. These are evidently the four most famous alumni of Ole Miss cheerleading, at least according to Ole Miss cheerleading fun facts online. So, basically, no matter what, I'm going to end up pretty cool. Either doing backflips off trampolines and dunking the basketball for thousands of disinterested halftime fans or giving incendiary speeches on C-SPAN about the need for a bridge in Yalobusha County.

But, think about this, what are the odds that both a state's senators would have served as cheerleaders for the state university? Even more amazing, imagine you are Thad Cochran; it's 1978, and you have just been elected senator. You're thinking you pretty much have the Ole Miss cheerleading achievement honor locked down. Maybe the current cheerleaders will hold your name up when they build a pyramid during halftime or do a basket toss, or maybe they'll even chant your name while they layer the hairspray into their hair. And then, suddenly, your old cheerleading buddy Trent Lott arrives in Washington and gets elected senate majority leader. And Lott's hair never moves, which means no one is chanting your name anymore while they hairspray each other down pregame. Welcome to Ole Miss, where even the cheerleaders are members of the good ole boy's network. It's a bona fide southern-fried cheerleading mafia.

When I tell Lara about both Trent Lott and Thad Cochran being senators after serving as Ole Miss cheerleaders, she responds, "It's well-known that being a cheerleader is important for your political career." I take the bait and ask why. "Because it gives you a leg up," she says with a straight face. This joke absolutely kills at eight-year-old cheerleading camp.

So, with visions of cheerleaders past tumbling (I originally wrote cartwheeling and my former professional cheerleader wife said, "If their cheerleaders are just doing cartwheels they're really lame cheerleaders,") through my consciousness, I head to Oxford for stop twelve of the DDT, at the Egg Bowl, the annual game between Mississippi State and Ole Miss. Accompanying me are my wife, her father, and his fiancée. This means, as always, I will be on my best behavior.

We arrive in Oxford, Mississippi, several hours before kickoff and park near the Lafayette Courthouse in the center of downtown Oxford. If you've never been to Oxford, go. It's spectacular. The town square is worth the trip alone. All around us, Ole Miss and Mississippi State fans are streaming by on the sidewalks. It seems possible that everyone in the town is smiling. Kickoff is several hours away but, until then, everyone wants to enjoy Oxford Square.

Founded in 1848, Ole Miss wears the colors crimson and blue to mirror the school colors of Harvard and Yale, respectively. The town of Oxford features red double-decker buses imported from England, and red phone booths are peppered around the Square. Mississippi State fans would call all of these gestures pretentious.

My wife, who has heard rumors about the riches of some nearby shops, leaves me, and I wander into Square Books which has not one, not two, but three different bookstores all located within a post pattern of one another. Even if you didn't already know it, seeing these three bookstores so close together would probably serve as pretty good evidence that you were standing on hallowed literary ground. Leaving the bookstore I make my way to J. E. Neilson, Co., which is located on the southeast corner of the square and is the South's oldest documented store in continuous use. Having originally opened as a trading post in 1839, it existed for nine years before Ole Miss was even founded.

I'll confess that I've been partial to Oxford ever since I traveled down at age fifteen to visit William Faulkner's home, Rowan Oak, located just a half mile from Oxford Square. Add the fact that I then spent the entire next summer reading everything William Faulkner had ever written, and you've got yourself one biased writer. I also met the now-deceased Larry Brown, a former firefighter from Mississippi whose novels of the South are amazingly evocative, signing copies of one of his books in Square Books that same visit, which only boosted my love for this landmark Southern town. I can't imagine anyone not being impressed by a visit to Oxford.

With a population of around fourteen thousand nestled about eighty-five miles from Memphis, Tennessee, in north Mississippi, Oxford is a jewel of the South, evoking the timeless rhythms of the past while embracing the advances of the twenty-first century. The entire city seems steeped in history despite having been burned on August 22, 1864 during the Civil War. In spite of this, the latter-day residents of Oxford are so friendly they even smile at Yankees. Of course they haven't forgiven the Yankees for their incendiary excesses, but they're at least cordial.

Not everyone, however, finds Oxford as spectacular as I do. I meet an Ole Miss graduate and current fan by the Lafayette Courthouse and our discussion immediately centers on what Oxford is currently like. "It's the three O's," he says, frowning. "Overpriced, overrated, and overcrowded. These out-of-towners come in here and they don't have any idea what things should cost. A 1,300 square foot house just sold for $350,000." He shakes his head, "All these stores are expensive here." Suddenly, leaving my wife to shop seems like a bad idea.

I leave one of Oxford's few detractors and head over to visit Oxford's most famous resident, William Faulkner, whose bronzed likeness sits forever on a bench on the Town Square. I leap a fence and sit down beside the Faulkner statue. It's a beautiful fall morning without a single cloud in the sky. Or, as someone writing bad Faulkner might describe it, "The pulchritudinous and ponderous autumnal sun, which sun had not and would not ever stop rising above the temporal and tumescent day, could not, nay would not stop; it was indefatigable, reigning triumphant, the very apotheosis of life come, springing forth verdant and bounteous on the myriad prisms of indomitable and incandescent rays, until the primordial, iniquitous and querulous night should come stealing, vulpine and sinister, over the rolling hills of the town."

After I tire of waxing poetic and sitting next to my literary idol, I hustle back toward LeShea's, where my wife is shopping but, before I can even get to her, she has found me on the square. "I need the credit card," she says. I shake my head and cough it up. Inside the store I sit down on an antique bench. Somehow, I always end up on antique benches whenever my wife is shopping. Once, I spent a long time wondering why all the places to sit are so uncomfortable in trendy women's shops. Then,

Faulkner and Clay.

I realized that I had never seen a woman sitting down in these stores. Ever. These chairs/settees/Mediterranean divans/couches/Saharan stools exist solely for decoration. Men are the only people to ever sit on them. Somehow, this makes the money being spent even more painful. "Look," my wife says to placate me, "they have free Mountain Dew."

My mini-Mountain Dew costs me eighty dollars. I feel lucky. A year ago, my wife bought a beige ottoman to put in front of our couch. (For the record, I just had to ask my wife what the thing is called. Her reply: "An ottoman, you ask me that at least once a month.") It cost me something like four hundred dollars. It replaced a trashy brown table that I could always eat on and put my feet on. Now, I can't eat on the ottoman or put my feet on it. Worse, I had to spend more than a day practicing law to buy it. I love this. Because if, when my alarm had gone off that morning, someone had knocked on the door and said, "You better get moving to the office or you won't get this beige ottoman at the end of the day," I would have just gone back to sleep. Something I've learned over the years is that, if you can look around your home, without moving, and point to at least five things that you can't name or wouldn't be willing to receive in lieu of a day or week's pay, then you're married. This canon is undefeated. I can walk into any man's house and tell whether he's married or not two steps into the doorway. Another test could be even simpler: Walk up to any man on the street and say, "Spell and define ottoman." If he can do both, he's married.

Outside on the square my father-in-law, Patrick, and his fiancée, Carol from Michigan, are also enjoying their time in Oxford. "It's beautiful here," Carol says. "I feel so bad that we burned it down." Patrick is wearing a tie because I told him that people dressed up for Ole Miss games. Only very few men his age are wearing ties. "I think I'm going to take my tie off," he says.

After Lara's shopping, we immerse ourselves in the Grove, a ten-acre tailgating expanse near the center of campus filled with towering oak trees and tailgate after tailgate, stretching as far as the eye can see. There are kids everywhere. Blue, red, and white tents cover the grounds. Above us the leaves are still hanging in the oak trees yet below us the ground is covered with leaves as well. Young girls race around in their Ole Miss cheerleading outfits. Almost all the women wear high heels. Most people seem unable to walk fifty yards without stopping to talk with someone they know at least twice.

In every direction you look, you can see children tossing footballs, practicing their spirals with determined expressions on their faces. In fact, there are more kids throwing footballs in the Grove than anywhere else I've been thus far. I'm attributing this to the Manning Factor, that is, every kid here knows that Peyton and Eli Manning used to run around throwing football passes in the Grove when they were young, and now their dads are even more likely to bring along footballs for the kids and let them do the same. Who knows, maybe the Manning magic is contagious? Or maybe the Grove itself is a magic elixir for young boys from the South. To an outsider, it seems possible that the people hanging out in the Grove are all related to one another. Later, at the game, I will talk with a fourteen-year-old who is sitting beside her dad. When I ask her how long she has been tailgating at the Grove, she will think for a long time and then reply, "I can't remember when I didn't." Exactly. This is Ole Miss football in a sentence. You get the idea that no one can remember when he or she didn't go to the Grove.

Hardly any televisions are hooked up in the Grove, because there is no electricity to speak of. After the mad rush in the morning to set up the tents, the cars are abandoned and so are the electrical outlets. There are many places for candlesticks and I'm told that, at night, candles will light the Grove. Somehow, even in the sunlight, the Grove seems steeped in the candlelit shadows of the past.

My wife is taken by the number of women wearing belts. "I don't understand why all these women have on big belts on top of their dresses when the belts don't do anything." It's always ironic to hear a woman criticize any element of fashion for its lack of functionality. This is like me criticizing a guy's beer choice. Although, for the record, I do hate guys who drink Michelob Ultra.

We meet Charlie and Jane Farris, a married couple from Holly Springs, Mississippi. They have a large chandelier in their tent, draped in Mardi Gras beads and stuffed animal mascots of their opponents, including Gators, Gamecocks, Demon Deacons, and the mascots of any other team that Ole Miss has played in the past five years. I ask if they leave their chandelier in the tent during the game. "Oh, yes," Jane says, "but we have to put a lock on the cooler with the beer. The Diet Coke not so much, but the beer . . . well, people will get into the beer." I ask them how long they will stay after the game. "Well, they try to kick us out by eleven but we usually last until midnight. By the morning, everything will be perfectly clean under here."

I should remind you that Ole Miss and Mississippi State fans hate each other with an unparalleled passion. The general consensus among Ole Miss fans is that Mississippi State fans are illiterate rednecks, while the general consensus of Mississippi State fans is that Ole Miss fans are arrogant and pretentious pansies. This divergence of opinion is interesting because the general consensus of the rest of the country is that all Mississippians, Rebels or Bulldogs, are illiterate rednecks.

There aren't as many Confederate flags as I expected. More than any other SEC school, Ole Miss has wrestled with the demons of its Southern past. The lyrics of Dixie have been modified, Colonel Reb, Ole Miss's former sideline mascot whose cane, tophat, white mustache and goatee evoked memories of an antebellum plantation owner, was excised in 2003, and sticks are now forbidden on the entry to Vaught-Hemingway Stadium, to keep the Confederate flag from being carried inside. Since Colonel Reb's removal in 2003, Ole Miss has been without an official mascot.

All these changes pale in comparison to those that have swept through the Ole Miss campus since the James Meredith riots in 1962, which were caused when Meredith became the first black student to enroll in Ole Miss. Two people were killed, forty-eight were injured, and thirty U.S. marshalls received gunshot wounds. And this all happened just a little over forty-four years ago. Amazing. Today minorities make up almost twenty-percent of the student body.

Oftentimes, critics rightfully ridicule the South for being resistant to change. But I think, often, the flip side of this issue is not examined. The South has changed more in the past twenty-five years than any other region of the country. Some of the same men and women who rioted against desegregation in 1962 are the same men and women who are embracing Ole Miss's progressive changes in the twenty-first century. That's a pretty amazing transformation and it speaks well for the future of Ole Miss as a university.

In the present-day Grove, you can drink anything at Ole Miss so long as it is in a party cup. You know, the red plastic cups that were probably the last thing you remember seeing several times in college. These things are everywhere at the Egg Bowl. The only thing that unites Ole Miss and Mississippi State fans on this day is the color of their plastic cups.

It's official, every woman of child-bearing age is wearing high heels. This is proven when we head to the stadium behind a girl wearing a walking boot on one foot and a high heel on the other. Even the Ole Miss women play hurt. Actu-

Ole Miss women play hurt.

ally, I'm a bit surprised they don't make walking boots with heels in Mississippi.

Tickets are available at the box office as it's not a sellout. Patrick and Carol buy tickets for forty-five dollars each. Lara and I already have tickets, which I bought from a devoted reader of my column, John Windsor. John's primary concerns could be summed up in this question: "Seriously, man, no one is going to be wearing Mississippi State colors in these seats, right?"

Playing the Egg Bowl on campus is a relatively new aspect of the rivalry, as the game relocated to the respective campuses of the two schools beginning in 1991. Prior to 1991, all the games were played in Jackson, Mississippi. The Egg Bowl name comes from the shape of the bronze football atop the trophy that is awarded to the winning team at the end of the game. The historical football on the trophy looked more like an egg than the current version and, so, the name has endured. This will be the 103rd meeting of the two schools.

My wife and I are seated in section NN in the Rebel Club. Surprisingly, the Rebel Club is the least rebellious section of the stadium. Everyone is quiet and genteel around us. In fact, most people in our section are not even seated by the time the game starts. Instead, they are watching from the inside concourse where tables, chairs, and food offer enticements. This is the first SEC game I have ever watched from the club seats. I feel like I should tell a story about firing a lazy employee at my company so I fit in. Unfortunately, I am both the laziest person at my company, and the only employee.

On the opening drive of the game, Ole Miss is sacked on third down to force a long field goal. But Ole Miss receives a false start penalty, so they are penalized five yards and the down is replayed. On the next play, shockingly, Ole Miss quarterback Brent Shaeffer throws a touchdown pass. It's 7–0 Ole Miss.

In our effort to continue the hedge watch on the DDT, I am happy to report that Ole Miss has hedges behind both benches but not in the end zones. Ole Miss, therefore, represents eleven out of twelve SEC stadiums with hedges of some sort. The only place without them is Kentucky. And, as we learned a couple of weeks ago, that's because commonwealths such as Kentucky, Pennsylvania, and Virginia constitutionally forbid the construction of hedges at football stadiums.

The food in the Rebel Club is free. This makes the game even better, although I'm trying hard not to overdo it. I have nachos, barbecue, chicken tenders, an ice-cream bar, three drinks, a brownie, a pecan tart, popcorn, and, to be healthy, three grapes. A couple of years ago, my dad went to a minor-league baseball game, where he had a ticket that entitled him to as much free concession food as he wished. He came home after the game sick as a dog, having consumed half the stadium's offerings. I should mention that my dad was fifty-five at this point. Evidently, when the excess is free, Travis men are eternally eight years old.

While I am binging, I think to myself, wouldn't it be cool if instead of continuing to pine for the return of the Colonel Reb mascot, Ole Miss had William Faulkner as a sideline mascot instead? Has this ever been considered? If not, it should be. Can't you just see a gray-haired mascot Faulkner striding along the sidelines in a tweed coat with a walking stick? Maybe carrying a copy of *Absalom, Absalom!* and occasionally pausing to taunt opponents in virtually indecipherable strings of adjective-laden insults—especially since Faulkner was the quarterback on his high school football team. Of course, he quit school after he broke his nose, but these are just minor details. Personally, I think it's about time I spread the rumor that Faulkner quit playing football because he wasn't allowed to play quarterback while smoking his pipe.

Incidentally, John T. Cosser, who liked the Faulkner suggestion, is going to bring up my idea that William Faulkner be selected as the university's sideline mascot at the next meeting of the Ole Miss Athletic Committee. I can't wait to hear the outcome on this. Also, William Faulkner's niece, Dean Faulkner Wells, has endorsed the idea. If Ole Miss would do the right thing and select Faulkner as their mascot, it would make the entire DDT worthwhile. How many other schools on earth could claim to have a bona fide Nobel Prize winner on the sideline? And, just think, once Ole Miss football coach Ed Orgeron wins the Nobel Peace Prize, Ole Miss would have *two* prize winners.

Ole Miss has banners on the west end zone that say they won national championships in 1959, 1960, and 1962. If we think the Bowl Championship Series national championship selection is a mess, in 1960 Ole Miss could claim a national championship along with Iowa, Minnesota, Missouri, and Washington. In fact, if you really want to rack up winnable wagers, go on the NCAA Web site and check out how many college football champions they list for each year. Yep, according to the NCAA data, Southern Miss won back-to-back football national championships in 1981 and 1982.

Unfortunately for Ole Miss, they have only won a single SEC Championship since 1963. That was a tie for the Western Division title in Eli Manning's senior year, 2003. And LSU won the western division tiebreaker over them that year. So, really, Ole Miss didn't win anything at all. And, since football success in the past two decades has been largely predicated on either Archie or Eli Manning, Ole Miss fans are already rooting for the Manning sons to start procreating so they can look forward to more gridiron glory.

Earlier this year, Ole Miss retired former cornerback Chucky Mullins' number thirty-eight jersey, and unveiled a bust in his honor in the corner where the team enters the field. I was ten years old in 1989, when Mullins tackled Vanderbilt's Brad Gaines and shattered four vertebrae in his cervical spine causing instant paralysis. This was a huge story in the South, made even more tragic when Mullins died of complications from his injury, less than two years later. Each year, on May 6 (the anniversary of Mullins' death), October 28 (the anniversary of the hit), and Christmas day, Gaines visits and maintains Mullins' gravesite. Prior to the hit, the two men had not known each other.

The Mullins bust is inscribed with only two words: NEVER QUIT.

Mullins' number thirty-eight is only the second in Ole Miss history to be retired.

Back on the field, after trading field goals, MSU scores a touchdown to tie the score at ten and the smuggled cowbells in Vaught-Hemingway Stadium come alive for the first time.

From experience, I salute all the Mississippi State fans who hid cowbells in their pants and snuck them into the stadium.

At halftime, the MSU band plays the theme song to both *Super Mario Brothers* and *The Legend of Zelda*. I have no idea why they did this but, when I closed my eyes, it was like I was in third grade all over again. I'll say this much, the guys playing cymbals were spectacular.

The sound effects in this stadium are really something. Half an hour later, during a break in the third quarter, they play the Al Pacino "inch-by-inch" speech from *Any Given Sunday*, spliced with footage from Ole Miss football games. The crowd goes crazy. If only Ole Miss could get Coach Ed Orgeron to actually give this speech instead of Pacino. Listening to Orgeron hit all of Pacino's high notes in his strangled diction would be like listening to dolphins squealing for fish at the aquarium.

With 2:57 remaining in the third quarter, Ole Miss kicks a field goal to take a 13–10 lead. Not to be outdone the MSU fans start up a "maroon" and "white" alternating cheer. "Maroon is not really a color you can cheer for," my wife comments. She's right. Together, we brainstorm some other colors that might make for awkward cheering: burnt sienna, gray; mustard, blue; chartreuse, red.

There are 57,658 people in attendance today. Of this number, approximately 15,376 are women who are so attractive they'd be worth losing a finger to have sex with. Of course, since I've traveled to the game with my father-in-law, perhaps I'd better keep these thoughts to myself. But, hey, we're all friends here, right? After all, I'm married. I have the ottoman to prove it.

The Ole Miss band plays "Dixie" just as the third quarter

ends. Many people sing along. This might not be the first time
they've played it, but it's the first time I've noticed. Isn't it
ironic that the only people who sing, "I wish I was in Dixie,"
are always in Dixie? Seriously, think about this yourself, how
many times have you actually sung this song or heard it sung
and not been somewhere in the South? I'd bet one hundred
dollars your answer is never.

At the start of the fourth quarter, Ole Miss picks off MSU's
quarterback, Omar Conner, at midfield for the first turnover of
the game, but is unable to do anything on offense. The crowd
boos when the punt team comes on. "This is just like last week,"
says a man behind me, "all we need is one first down and we
win." Last week, Ole Miss lost an absolutely heartbreaking
game, in overtime, to LSU, 26–23.

But, unlike last week, after stopping MSU, Ole Miss returns
the ensuing punt over fifty yards for a touchdown. The stadium
stands as one, women are raised into the sky by their dates, red
pompons twirl across the sunlit afternoon sky, and strident
cheers echo across Vaught-Hemingway as, suddenly, Ole Miss
leads 20–10, with only 3:30 remaining in the football game.
"We gonna get that Egg," screams a man near me. A man in the
front row of section NN leads the Hotty Toddy cheer, Ole
Miss's signature cheer, which definitely sounds like it was written by white flappers in the 1920s, for the Rebel Club. He
screams, "Are you ready?" And, in turn, the responsive cheer:

> HELL YES! DAMN RIGHT!
> HOTTY TODDY, GOSH ALMIGHTY
> WHO THE HELL ARE WE? HEY
> FLIM FAM BIM BAM
> OLE MISS BY DAMN!!!!

Somewhere, right now, Trent Lott and Thad Cochran are drying their eyes. Either that, or J. K. Rowling is constructing a new cheer for Gryffindor.

In the wake of the punt return touchdown, some of the State fans begin to file out of the stadium. They leave too soon. In less than a minute, MSU goes the length of the field and scores a touchdown. Suddenly it's 20–17 Ole Miss, with 2:20 remaining. The Ole Miss fans around me are shaking their heads. They are still recovering from their near win last week at LSU and, once more, they're in a tight game.

The Ole Miss Pride of the South band does their best to rouse the anxious Rebel fans by playing "Dixie" again. My wife turns to me, "I thought UT was the Pride of the South band," she says. "No, they're the Pride of the Southland," I say. This raises an intriguing question about who copied whom, the age-old which came first, the chicken or the egg. Except with bands. Also, is there a Pride of the Southlands?

The sun is shining on our section and Ole Miss fans are suddenly seeing red. Especially after Ed "Colonel Reb is Crying" Orgeron goes for it on fourth down on the Mississippi State thirty-seven and gets stopped. Over/under on the amount of things Orgeron breaks if he loses this game? Four hundred sixty-seven. Odds on one of them being the Jumbotron? 13 to 1.

And, as if getting stopped on the fourth-down play isn't bad enough, Ole Miss gets called for a fifteen-yard personal foul penalty. Suddenly, MSU has the ball on the Rebel side of the field and is driving. I keep expecting to see Orgeron just rip his shirt off on the sideline and start waving it above his head.

With six seconds left, MSU lines up to attempt a fifty-one-yard field goal to tie the game. From where we are sitting, the

angle allows us to watch only the reaction of the fans and players. I can tell the kick is long enough but, until the Ole Miss
fans begin dancing in the aisles, I'm unsure of the result.

It's no good. Bedlam ensues. Ed Orgeron has his inch. I can
neither confirm nor deny that Orgeron took a bite of the
Golden Egg Trophy.

All around us, the dignified crowd in the Rebel Club for-
sakes all dignity. They scream, they yell, they dance, and they
make plans to move the party from the Rebel Club back to the
Grove. Lara and I step onto the elevators and are whisked
downstairs where we immediately walk outside. It's the fastest
I've ever exited a football stadium in my life. This club seat
football is pretty nice.

Outside the stadium, we meet up with Lara's father and his
fiancée again. Their seats have been equally good and their
faces are tanned from an afternoon spent in the southern sun.
"What a game that was," says Patrick. "From where I was sitting I thought that kick was good." We head back to our car
through the throngs of cheering Ole Miss fans.

Behind us, a huge procession of revelers leads the way to
the Grove, chanting the Hotty Toddy cheer the entire way,
where Ole Miss fans will party until candlelight overtakes the
night. Where the ghost of William Faulkner will doubtless be
sitting in the branches of the live oak trees trading invectives
with the ghost of Colonel Reb. And where, beneath the
branches of these trees, somewhere amidst the revelers, Senator Trent Lott and Senator Thad Cochran are doing cartwheels
and leading cheers. Hotty Toddy indeed.

LESSONS FROM THE DDT

Now that the campus visits of the DDT are complete, and I have traveled from Gainesville to Fayetteville, Lexington to Baton Rouge, I'd like to share a few of the many lessons I learned along the way. Some are practical, some are worthless, and a few might help you avoid felony convictions. So, here we go.

Despite the stories you've heard, no SEC stadium is dangerous to visit as an opposing team's fan. It's a rumor that just won't die. I don't know how many times I heard, "Don't go to (insert city or stadium here), they'll punch you for doing nothing." By the time I arrived in Gainesville, I expected to see opposing team fans being roasted on a spit fire, while Gators fans danced with glee. But this danger is completely an urban legend. If you remember nothing else from the DDT, this is the lesson I'd like you to take with you.

When I was in college, I wanted to go to a Tennessee Titans game in Philadelphia, and was told by several buddies from Philadelphia that it would be fine so long as I didn't cheer for the Titans or wear anything with Titans colors. "Huh?" I asked, as I did a double take. It seems to me that, if you aren't willing to welcome fans who are just like yourself, only clad in different colors, then there's something really wrong with your fandom. I'm proud to say that while SEC fans are the most passionate in the country, they're also, in my experience, the friendliest.

Along with that lesson encouraging attendance, I also bring you seventeen other things I learned on the DDT this fall:

1. No matter what fan base you're a part of, at least 15 percent of your fans suck. Really suck. Think Camryn Manheim in a leotard. They fulfill every stereotype anyone has about the South and illiterate rednecks. They drink heavily without becoming funnier, never say anything that makes listening to them better than complete silence, insult everyone, have no concept of terms like irony and satire, and talk loudly and more frequently than anyone in the general area. At any moment, you hope that they're going to trip and fall into the path of an oncoming truck that is moving too fast to slow down. Inevitably this would be too late, however, because they have been married since they were fourteen and have already spawned nine children. But, and this is key, every team has them. They aren't only clad in Alabama Crimson or Volunteer Orange. They aren't all from North Florida and they don't all bark like bulldogs for fun. These guys suck, and they are pretty equally distributed across the SEC. Trust me, no fan base is immune. Actually, Vandy might be immune.

2. If you go to an SEC stadium without a ticket, you can get in for a decent price. Period. The most I paid was one hundred dollars. Now, I didn't always have great seats—in fact, more often than not, I had among the worst seats in the stadium—but I had seats. So, if you've been concerned about showing up without a ticket, don't be. And if you end up not finding any for a decent price, isn't hanging out on a college campus and watching the game in a local bar with other fans infinitely better than sitting alone by yourself drinking warm Natty Light? Don't answer, that was a rhetorical question.

3. The Tickle Me Elmo market, as it turns out, really isn't that strong. You may recall that earlier this fall, my ever-scheming friend Kumar had hatched a plan to scalp Tickle Me Elmo dolls

on eBay. Well, two months after the market's initial surge, and a roller-coaster ride of emotions later, Kumar reports on the devastating financial losses, not to mention emotional humiliation, he is suffering: "In general, I made a gross miscalculation. The prices have been plummeting, and I ended up having to do the worst imaginable thing, I returned seven of them to Target. See, I thought buying twenty-five Elmos was embarrassing, but it turned out to be even more embarrassing to have to fill up a shopping cart and return them. People thought I had decided not to give my kids one. They're going for fifty dollars now on eBay, and it isn't even worth my time to package them up and mail them out."

4. University of Georgia girls have bigger breasts thanks to the Hope Scholarship. With other Southern states like Tennessee and South Carolina adopting lottery-funded scholarships, I expect this trend to spread even faster. It used to be the sentence, "Susie got a scholarship and she's getting D-cups," was a non sequitur. Now, it's a fact of life.

5. If you're planning on flying into Fayetteville, Arkansas, you better have an expense account. Or make your reservations for next season now. Alternatively, if you're planning on driving to Fayetteville from anywhere not already inside the state of Arkansas, take my advice and request an expense account now.

6. Calling someone a Yankee is still considered an insult in the twenty-first century South. At least half the people who disagreed with me about anything I wrote in my columns about the DDT e-mailed and accused me of being a Yankee. Along with being called a plain old Yankee, I was also called a dumb Yankee, a damn Yankee, a fool Yankee, and a stupid-ass Yankee. First, I thought this pejorative had all but vanished in the one hundred forty-one years since the War of Northern Aggression ended. It

was one thing when my ninety-year-old grandmother, then suffering from Alzheimer's, met my wife for the first time and heard her speak, only to wrinkle her face, and spit out, "You're a Yankee," before shaking her head as if this was the most remarkable thing on earth, then scooting away on her walker. However, I didn't think people with e-mail addresses would still use this insult. And in response, I'm not a Yankee. I was born and raised in Nashville. And my parents, grandparents, great-grandparents, and great-great grandparents were all born in the South, too. Also, how many people north of Kentucky are named Clay Travis? Isn't this a dead giveaway? I might as well be named Robert E. Lee, for Chrissakes.

7. Tim Tebow has a chance to become both the most hated and beloved player in SEC history. He's like the Bill Clinton of SEC football. Halfway through the football season, I turned to my Florida friend Neville, and said, "You do realize that about half of our conversations between now and 2010 are going to center around Tim Tebow in some fashion or another?" Neville's response: "Tim Tebow is a god." Case closed.

8. SEC football crowds are moving beyond Southern white people. This was encouraging to see. I like to think that as the South continues to grow we can keep the best aspects of Southern culture while embracing some of the best aspects of other cultures as well. Based on what I've seen this fall from Indian immigrants at South Carolina who are huge Tennessee fans, to Northern executives relocated to the South with season tickets to Ole Miss football games, the expansion of the SEC fan base is happening. I think it bodes well for the future of the SEC that some of the most passionate fans of Southern football aren't members of the Sons of Confederate Veterans, and might not even have parents who were born in this country.

9. The way to keep old folks in the South healthy is to offer them tickets to an SEC football game. Every time I sat in the upper deck at a stadium, I was out of breath by the time I got even remotely near my seats. Then, I would walk out onto the concourse and see a near-perpendicular stairway leading even higher into the sky. I would trudge up the steps breathing hard and notice that row after row I was passing dozens of people who appeared to be at least seventy. Often a decade or two older. It was uncanny. People with oxygen tanks thrown over their shoulders, some who had stepped out of their wheelchairs and carried them thrust forward on the stairs like old muskets fixed with bayonets. I am now convinced that seats to an SEC football game offer the best way to stave off mortality.

10. More people care about whether guillotined people can see afterward than you can possibly imagine. I thought I was alone in this. Yet, all fall, people from across the South, and, indeed, the world, have been weighing in on the debate. Here's the deal: If I ever get decapitated and someone is filming me, I promise you guys that I'm going to blink my left eye to prove that I can still see. I'd like everyone reading this book right now to raise your right hands and solemnly swear to the same thing. While getting decapitated is probably a pretty horrible way to die, at least we could all advance science should it happen.

11. LSU running back Justin Vincent is the Rosa Parks of boat shoes, breaking down the horrible racial footwear barriers that have divided us all for decades. Just when you thought only white people were going to be able to walk around in boat shoes, Justin Vincent stood up for footwear equality. I understand that OutKast's next album will be titled *Justin Vincent Wears Boat Shoes*. I'm putting in my order now.

12. LSU fans do not smell like corn dogs and, this insult, as brilliantly original as it seemed, actually derives from the Big 12. After diligent research, I was able to trace it to an Oklahoma message board referring to Oklahoma State fans, circa 2001. Evidently, the offending name caller at Oklahoma originally alleged that Oklahoma State fans were "carnies" (people who travel around with carnivals, traveling circuses, or state fairs). Since people at said events eat lots of corn dogs, logic dictated that they would thus reek of this most foul species of carnival food. Auburn fans then appropriated this, the greatest college football insult of all time, for their own devices.

13. Not only can dolphins live in fresh water but pink dolphins exist and live in the Amazon. I'll be shocked if this report doesn't lead the evening newscast for at least two weeks following the publication of this book. This fact is absolutely astounding and definitely one of the most important things I gleaned from the DDT.

14. Meeting CBS Sports announcer Verne Lundquist requires real negotiating skills. I made a request via CBS media relations to hang out with Verne at the SEC championship game. After a week, I got a telephone call saying that Verne was going to be too busy for me to follow him around for the entire weekend. Seems there were lots of banquets and whatnot beginning on Thursday of SEC championship week, and Verne thought it would be too difficult to have me around all the time for three days in a row. This was awesome, because I love the idea that me following around Verne for three days in a row was even considered. Was there a meeting where this was debated? My wife wouldn't even let me follow her around for three days in a row. I'm not sure there's anyone on earth I'd let follow me around for three days in a row. Okay, I might bend the rules and let Jessica Biel. In any

event, I was unable to meet Verne Lundquist, but one of his staffers did send me the following e-mail, "Clay, Verne wants you to know that he now knows you exist." Which, you know, is something.

15. Nonfunctional belts on girls are rad. Even though my wife finds them objectionable, I'm thinking it's just a way for girls who are hot to do ridiculous things just because they can. It's the sports equivalent of when Vince Carter, the world's greatest dunker at the time, decided to do a layup on a breakaway in Toronto. I'm hoping that at some point in the future guys will start their own trend that is equally absurd, like wearing cartridge belts over their shoulders. Probably the cartridge belts would have to be empty (unless you go to Mississippi State), but I like the idea.

16. Cheering with pompons is extremely effeminate. So effeminate that men who cheer with pompons will threaten to kill you when you make fun of them for this. Sounds like somebody is trying to make up for the fact that he secretly likes to wear panties.

17. Finally, 'Bama Bangs are here to stay. You really didn't think I'd forget about this, did you? Thanks to our scientific study and reports from coast to coast, we've identified them in twenty-eight of the fifty states. And in Italy. They're coming to a town near you. Be afraid, be very afraid.

SEC CHAMPIONSHIP GAME

ATLANTA, GEORGIA
THE UNIVERSITY OF ARKANSAS VS. THE UNIVERSITY OF FLORIDA
DECEMBER 2, 2006

In the past thirteen weeks of the DDT, I've traveled 8,382.5 miles. I've been to eleven Southern states and I've seen every team in the SEC play at its home stadium. I've seen blowouts and overtime games, SEC contenders and bottom-tier hopefuls, hot girls and hot girls. I've hung out with SEC fans of all races and creeds and, if you live in the South, there's probably a good chance I've come close to your home during my road trips. At long last, after a season spent driving through fall, the DDT reached its final destination, Atlanta, Georgia, for the crowning of the SEC champion. This year's game is a faceoff between Florida, representing the eastern division and currently sitting at 11–1 (7–1 in the SEC, with their only loss to Auburn), and Arkansas at 10–2 (7–1 in the SEC, with their only conference loss to LSU) from the conference's western division.

During the Civil War, it was a truism that all Southern trains eventually led to Atlanta. When Atlanta fell to the

North in 1864, its defeat guaranteed Abraham Lincoln his second term as president. When the city hosted the 1996 Olympics, generations of Southerners at long last gained the confidence that the South had truly risen again. As a child Atlanta loomed so large in the Southern consciousness that, each time we drove through the city en route to Florida, my mom would comment, "If Sherman saw Atlanta now, he'd say, 'Hey, I thought I burned this place down.'" I've heard this joke, conservatively, five thousand times. Mom's Sherman-channeling was always one of the highlights of the Florida trip. And now, fans from across the SEC spend their falls hoping that their teams can reach the city come December. So it was that I embarked upon the final stop of the DDT.

Each time I visit Atlanta the city seems more overwhelming. Whenever I go out, I feel lost. You know how they say that kudzu grows an inch every day no matter what happens? I feel like Atlanta grows ten square miles every day no matter what happens. If you had an aerial view of the city of Atlanta it would look like those time-lapse photographs that demographers and engineers always use to show great change in a certain place. Only the time-lapse photograph would be in real time when it comes to Atlanta. Things really do seem to change that rapidly. At some point in the next century, I firmly believe that every city in Georgia will be considered an Atlanta suburb.

On my 250-mile, three-plus-hour drive to Atlanta, I do an interview with a Birmingham, Alabama, radio station that is broadcasting from an Atlanta strip club, the Cheetah. During this interview, I discuss Alabama's search for a new coach in the wake of Mike Shula's firing. I crack a few jokes about

Alabama's top two coaching candidates, the electroshocked and exhumed corpse of Bear Bryant, and Jesus. Later the host of the show, Lance Taylor, e-mails me, "We have never received more angry callers in the history of the program." So, you know, I accomplished a ton on my solo drive to Atlanta.

After Friday night out with several friends now practicing law in Atlanta, I end up at three in the morning at the Majestic Diner, where I find myself amidst a large collection of intoxicated people, small-time felons, and SEC football fans. Perhaps these groupings overlap. Several Gator fans are doing the Gator chomp, and a couple of Arkansas fans are calling the Hogs. Kickoff is fifteen hours away.

Thirteen hours after my late-night diner experience, I'm outside the Georgia Dome in downtown Atlanta and fans are still doing the Gator chomp and calling the Hogs. I was concerned about what the ticket market would be like outside the stadium but a few minutes of scouting erases those concerns. Face value on an SEC championship game ticket is sixty dollars. Several blocks away from the stadium, I buy a ticket in the upper deck for forty dollars. The young guy who sells me the ticket says, "Man, I'm gonna end up sitting beside you. I'm getting killed out here."

I make my way over to the Georgia World Congress Center, an enormous convention center filled with fans that is located next door to the Georgia Dome. At the entrance to the SEC corporate hospitality tent, I meet Nathan Ealy, a huge Auburn fan and also a fan of the column, who has a corporate hospitality pass for me, thanks to the fact that he does various on-air production for ISP Sports and Auburn. Nathan has agreed to take the risk of being my chaperone amidst the corporate bigwigs of the SEC. Unfortunately, Verne Lundquist, who now knows that I exist, is nowhere to be found. We walk inside. The seating area is cavernous and there are more men in suits than I've ever seen at a football game. Seriously, who are these guys that wear suits to a football game? If I had to do business with either a guy who wore a suit to a football game or a guy who dressed like a normal person, I'd pick the unpretentious, normal-looking person, no two ways about it. Who wouldn't? Vanderbilt fans, that's who.

There are two huge projection screen televisions flanking the band. Each screen features the ACC championship game between Wake Forest and Georgia Tech. When Wake wins 9–6 and is crowned 2006 ACC champion, everyone watching the game cheers. Southerners are known for holding their grudges, and it seems that nobody in the center has forgiven Georgia Tech for defecting from the SEC in 1964 in order to ultimately end up in the significantly inferior ACC football conference.

The band is playing "Wonderful Tonight" by Eric Clapton. I'll tell you, nothing gets my blood boiling for a championship game like a soulful rendition of "Wonderful Tonight." If they could have added "Tears in Heaven" to the song lineup, I think people would have formed a mosh pit in front of the stage.

There is ample food, and Nathan and I sit down to eat with his coworkers, Jay McPhillips and Krissy Ellis. There are, however, no Golden Flake potato chips to be seen in the corporate area, which is both shocking and disappointing to me.

The UCLA-USC game comes on next on the big screens, causing all the Florida fans in the area to flock to the televisions. I have little interest in watching the first quarter of this game, and thus decide to head down to the SEC FanFare, a large collection of activities, exhibits, and games set up each year at the championship game for fans. Before I leave, Nathan tells me that you have to pay to get in, so Krissy offers her wristband, which is fastened, a little too snugly, around her arm. Both of us struggle to get the band off her and onto me without ripping it too noticeably. "I used to be much better at this in college," Krissy says. Weren't we all, Krissy, weren't we all?

My refashioned band works fine and I arrive at FanFare, downstairs in a cavernous convention center room, to see games aplenty. Unfortunately, there are also lots of kids monopolizing said games. There's a quarterback accuracy challenge, a kicking challenge, and a large flag football field. The kicking game features participants attempting to drill a football through blown-up uprights. I'm sure there is no truth to the rumors that Florida coach Urban Meyer was scouting field-goal-kicking talent here for the championship game. None at all.

There are also tons of flat-screen televisions showing highlights from each SEC football team. During my entire time in the FanFare area, I don't spot a single person actually watching these highlights.

Adults are dealing with the pain of not being able to play any of the games by drinking beer. Lots of beer. Apropos of absolutely nothing adult fans start "Woo pig sooie cheers" or alternating orange-and-blue chants in the Conference Center. It's never the college kids who start these cheers. Always some drunk cell-phone dealer from the Ozarks or Ocala.

Dr. Pepper is sort of a big deal when it comes to college football championship games. This has always surprised me. Why is it Dr. Pepper decides to spend all its marketing money on college football games? That and men dancing in tight jeans and plain white T-shirts. Regardless, the soft-drink corporation is caffeinating every kid in sight with paper shot glasses of Dr.

Pepper. Kids are standing around slamming down shot after shot of Dr. Pepper as rapidly as the glasses get filled up.

In the back of the convention hall, is a large flat-screen television showing the USC-UCLA game. I hear yelling and go back to see what everyone is cheering about. UCLA appears to have scored to take a 7–0 lead on a quarterback sneak, although the play is being reviewed. "Oh, he was definitely in, no doubt about it," says an impartial man wearing an alligator hat.

So, remember when I said that Florida girls carry six to eight extra pounds on the backs of their arms? Well, I seem to have also mentioned this in my CBS SportsLine column, which some of these ladies apparently read. A few of them recognize me, and have things that aren't that nice to say to me. The situation is only made worse when I ask if they would like me more if I were carrying milkshakes and cheese fries. Fortunately, our confrontation ends near the face-painting area, which is swarmed by fans of both Arkansas and Florida and features signs that say GET YOURSELF AIRBRUSHED (presumably not the same kind of airbrushing that happens at Fantasy Fest in Key West). As the girls go off in search of land to graze on, pork-loined shoulders bouncing, I let loose a long sigh of relief.

Incidentally, does anyone else remember when airbrushed shirts were extremely popular back in like 1990? It seemed like every school trip we took, the coolest kids would all get airbrushed T-shirts. I think they peaked during Desert Storm. I remember one kid had an airbrushed rendering of Bart Simpson in fatigues on a T-shirt that said I HATE YOU SO DAMN INSANE. This was, of course, a clever play on Saddam Hussein's name. It was the sixth-grade airbrushed-shirt equivalent of splitting the atom. And the best-looking girl in sixth grade liked him for it. Not that I was bitter or anything, but I'm pretty sure I hated that guy.

Upon leaving FanFare I head across the walkway to the Georgia Dome. My seat is in the twenty-second row, above the Arkansas end zone. There are only twenty-six rows in the upper deck of the entire stadium, so there are maybe five hundred people in the entire stadium who have as bad or worse seats than I do. Make that zero. As I soon learn that my seat is conveniently wedged between a fat Arkansas fan and a fat Florida fan. I'm like the SEC's own version of the Maginot Line. I can report that both stink equally bad.

Florida fans appear to outnumber Arkansas fans about 65 percent to 35 percent. This has something to do with the fact that Fayetteville, Arkansas, is roughly 4,826 miles from Atlanta.

Just before the game starts, I head to the bathroom. It's packed, primarily because Florida fans are all gathered around the televisions watching USC and UCLA play. If Florida beats Arkansas and UCLA retains their lead over USC, Florida fans believe they'll be playing for the national championship. That's because, right now, Ohio State is definitely one of the two teams slotted to play in the BCS Championship but USC has to defeat UCLA to ensure their place. I pull out my camera and consider taking a picture of the Florida fans huddled around in the bathroom. Then I think better of it. Somehow, this seems like the kind of thing a person could get arrested for. And there doesn't seem to be an easy way to explain away taking pictures in the men's bathroom.

Back in my upper deck seat, after a slow offensive start, Florida's Chris Hetland ends the scoring drought by making a thirty-five-yard field goal. Florida fans go crazy. You would have thought Hetland had just made a game-winning kick. A girl in front of me screams, "Oh, my God, we made a field goal!" The first quarter is nearly complete and it's 3–0 Florida.

The Georgia Dome is a very antiseptic and almost formal setting for an SEC football game. It lacks the rigid iron seats, concrete steps poured during the Hoover administration, tiny foot and seat spaces, and the vibrancy of on-campus tradition that make visiting an SEC stadium unique. All the edges of the Dome are ironed out so that you feel like you could be anywhere in the country. There's no real character to the place. And there are definitely no hedges. After watching every game outdoors all season long in old stadiums with a ton of individuality, the Georgia Dome just doesn't feel right to me. It's like showing up to a football game in a suit.

Meanwhile, the guys who actually did show up to the game in suits are noshing on brie and wine in the luxury suites. They love the Georgia Dome, and have no idea what the score of the game is. Too busy making moves and closing deals. The first quarter ends with a missed Arkansas field goal. It's still 3–0 Florida.

No television cameras are going to put the camera on me and my neighbors in our nosebleed seats, a mere four rows from the roof of the stadium, and yet, all around me are optimistic fans who have made witty and original signs featuring the letters CBS. My favorite is COACH URBAN OWNS. The meaning of this trifecta of words eludes me; it sounds like the first part of a sentence. Or a line from Terrell Owens's new children's book. Second, could they have at least come up with three words that started with C, B, and S, respectively? This is the best they could come up with? I guess *owns* makes more sense than oc-cludes, owes, obviates, occupies, ossifies, or oozes, but still.

The stadium announcer gives the first score of the day for USC-UCLA. It's 13–9 UCLA and the Florida fans explode in cheers. A few plays after this announcement, Florida blocks Arkansas's yogic punter and on the shortened field scores a touchdown. 10–0, Florida.

Every ten minutes or so, my friend, and Florida grad, Nev-ille, has been sending me trash-talking text messages from his suburban home, where he is watching the SEC championship game alone, save for the company of Lorenzo the Cat. Such messages include "Leak just Tebow'd *you*," sent after I evidently missed a tackle on Leak's second quarter bootleg touchdown, and "Urban! Believe," after Florida's successful field goal. This is irritating on several levels. Among them a. my team isn't even playing, and b. I get charged ten cents every time he texts me, thanks to the fact that I have the worst texting cell-phone plan on earth. For the first time in my life, Neville's trash talk actually exerts a tangible financial cost on me.

With 5:20 remaining in the first half, Tim Tebow enters the game for the first time, and Florida fans go crazy. I find myself wondering if Florida fans will cheer as deliriously for Tebow next year, when he's the presumptive starter and plays every snap. Will Tebow get tired of running around and pumping his arms after every first down? Even more important, if Florida fans do cheer just as crazily, how many are going to overheat and die in early season games from heat stroke? These are very important questions that have yet to be resolved.

Florida quarterback Chris Leak hits freshman wide receiver Percy Harvin streaking down the sideline for a touchdown and it's 17–0 Florida. The smelly Arkansas fan sitting next to me turns to me and says, "Ball game." Neville hits me with a series of text insults. The biggest winners out of Percy Harvin becoming an offensive force are younger kids also named Percy. Up until now, it's been a tough existence, but Harvin has just legitimized the name, and potentially made it, well, cool. Actually, this may be why Percy Harvin is so fast. He got a lot of experience running from people making fun of his name. The ever-fickle Florida fans react to the score by forgetting about the current game taking place before them and begin screaming for the people at the Georgia Dome to give them an updated USC-UCLA score.

While the Florida fans are clamoring for news on their to-be rivals, Arkansas' unfortunately named Casey Dick answers with a fifty-yard touchdown pass to wide-receiver Marcus Monk. It's 17–7 Florida and, for the first time all day, Arkansas fans have something to cheer about.

During halftime, the Dr. Pepper fan contest goes down. If a contestant is able to throw eleven footballs through a hole he or she will win a million dollars. Ten of these passes are from five yards away and you receive ten thousand dollars for each successful pass, then you make ten times your earnings if you can make the final throw from twenty yards away. The announcers always ask the contestants how often they've practiced. The answer is always something like, "Oh, I went out and practiced a few throws." The most I've ever heard anyone commit to is eight–ten throws a day. This is ridiculous, and total BS. If I were a contestant, I would practice these throws at least an hour a day. Probably two hours. I might cease all other work. This is a million dollars, people, and most of us will never have another (legal) chance to make this much dough in one night.

Equally irritating is the fact that no one can make any calls on their cell phones due to a signal overload. Perhaps this is because every group of Florida fans I can see has at least one member trying madly to get in touch with an outside source for an update on the USC game.

Just as the Florida band is about to take the field, a huge cheer begins in the Florida section and works its way, like the wave itself, among the orange-and-blue clad fans. USC has lost. All of a sudden, the stakes of the SEC Championship Game just got raised. Big time. If Florida can manage to beat Arkansas, they stand a very real chance of advancing to play Ohio State for the National Championship in the BCS title game. Neville texts me, "The national championship bakeoff is under way."

Two minutes later: "Come on," Neville pleads via text message, suddenly giving up his trash talk, "pull for UF." I inform him that my journalistic integrity forbids me from taking sides. Also, that I hate Florida. But this hate was much easier to countenance when I didn't have so many Florida fans as friends. Plus, I'm duty bound at this point, now that my own team is eliminated from competition, to root for an SEC team to win the national championship. My situation is painful. Very painful. And, yet, I persevere.

The USC-UCLA score is officially announced in the Georgia Dome. Arkansas fans shake their heads. Florida fans enter into an ecstasy of cheering, flailing limbs, the odd pompon, even. There has never been a better nine-month period in Florida athletics history than that which has stretched from March 2006 to this moment. The camera finds a Florida fan holding a sign: HEY USC FANS, AT LEAST FLORIDA LOST TO A RANKED TEAM. It seems like every SEC fan in the building cheers. This is the kind of strained logic that the BCS inspires. Imagine if this same fan held up a similar sign at a college basketball game. He'd be pelted with jeers. Yet, put him on the sideline of a college football game and, suddenly, he's Socrates.

Soon after this, both teams begin the second half by lining up on the wrong side of the field. As omens go, I'm not sure what this portends.

In life there are certain immutable truths: the sun rises in the east, water freezes at thirty-two degrees, if you are famous and you ride in a sports car without panties people will take your picture as you exit, and Chris Leak will throw an interception during a football game. As soon as the second half begins, the Leak interception truth renews itself again. Arkansas has great field position.

A few plays later, Arkansas stud running back Darren McFadden throws a dart for a touchdown to Felix Jones. I love McFadden's pass here. He literally looks like he is throwing a pass on the goal line in Madden. The receiver hardly even moves and he's already hit the x button. It's 17–14 Florida, and the Arkansas fans are calling the hogs with fervent passion.

The hitting in this game is ridiculous. There's 11:55 remaining in the third quarter and, already, more players have been injured and carried off the field than I've seen all fall. The tension in the Georgia Dome is palpable.

Adding to the tension, Antwain Robinson of Arkansas suddenly intercepts a Chris Leak shovel pass and takes it back for a touchdown. The Arkansas fans are going crazy while the Florida fans are stunned into silence. Except, that is, for the Florida fan behind me who screams at Chris Leak from the rafters, "I'm glad you're a fuckin' senior, dickhead." With friends like these . . .

It's 21–17 Arkansas, with 8:33 left in the third quarter. The Razorbacks have scored three unanswered touchdowns and the smelly Arkansas fan in front of me is clapping as loudly as he can.

You can tell college football momentum by the animal sounds in ascendance. Right now, the hogs are getting called to the high heavens and the Gator chomp is nowhere to be heard. One of the reasons I like college football more than any other sport is because the momentum swings are so drastic. Most games you watch take you on an emotional roller-coaster ride, not unlike an eighth-grade relationship.

Arkansas and Florida might be the two most dissimilar schools in the SEC. Arkansas is the farthest west (by at least two hundred miles) and has a very insular culture. You get the idea that most people in Arkansas not only know you, they know your daddy and your granddaddy too. For instance, when I went to the Wal-Mart in Arkansas at two in the morning back in September, I met Mitch Mustain's high school classmate. Florida's different. Some sort of odd amalgamation of the rest of the country yet with more hair gel. I'm certain that Florida has more fans not from the South and more fans whose parents have no affiliation with the state or the school than any other SEC fan base. Yet they've embraced the Gators as their own team. From the Ozarks to Ocala, Fayetteville to Gainesville, the roads of SEC football have all led to this moment. And, despite these differences between Arkansas and Florida fans, they're all together now lined up around one hundred yards of artificial turf. And they're all loud; the Georgia Dome is absolutely deafening.

With five minutes or thereabouts left in the third quarter, Urban Meyer runs a fake punt on fourth-and-ten from his own fifteen. I'm not sure if this is brilliant or desperate. It's probably both. Sort of the Robespierre of fake punts. If Meyer gets stopped here, and Arkansas scores to go up ten he'll spend the next year of his life reliving this exact decision. But the fake works. Unfortunately for Meyer, Florida is stopped again and forced to punt.

The Arkansas fans have traveled a long way and, right now, at this very moment, they have not been louder all night. Florida is forced to call their final timeout with 3:58 remaining in the third quarter. The balance of the game seems to have shifted firmly into Arkansas's corner. Then . . . the inexplicable happens.

In the dumbest play of the SEC season, Arkansas's punt returner attempts a fair catch on a great punt by Florida's Eric Wilbur. While running backward full speed . . . over his shoulder . . . at his own three-yard line. He fumbles the ball into the end zone and Florida recovers for a touchdown. For a moment the Florida fans around me are stunned. Then they explode. Amazingly, Florida has regained the lead, 24–21. Maybe I'd also fit right in on the SEC gridiron, as a really great bad punt returner?

It's the fourth quarter now, and the attendance in the Georgia Dome is announced with great fanfare. "75,374," proclaims the announcer, taking at least a second to enunciate every number he speaks. Fans of both teams shrug their shoulders. This is a pedestrian number. If only seventy-five thousand people showed up for a home game at Florida the coach would get fired. If only seventy-five thousand people showed up for a football game at Tennessee, the Rapture would have actually occurred.

Back on the field, lightning strikes, via Percy Harvin. He makes one cut on a running play and is gone. Sixty-seven yards later, Florida has extended their lead to 31–21. The Gator chomp is once again ascendant and, as I look around the stadium, I marvel at the number of momentum shifts that have occurred so far during this game.

I've moved back a row now, so I can breathe clean air. Sitting beside me are Jonathan and Carissa Bellflowers, who live in Valdosta, Georgia. They're a mixed couple; Carissa's a Razorback and Jonathan is a Gator. I ask Jonathan how the week has gone. "There was a whole lot of trash talk," he admits, giving his wife a fake glare. Hopefully, unlike my own, this trash talk has not cost him money.

As I'm talking to the mixed Razorback-Florida couple, Arkansas's Cedric Washington throws a pass for a touchdown on a trick play. It's 31–28 Florida. Not to be outdone Andre Caldwell, of Florida throws a touchdown pass on the next drive to give Florida a 38–28 lead. It's late in the fourth quarter now, and Florida has reclaimed their ten-point lead. This is the fifth different player to throw a touchdown pass in the game. Five different players throwing touchdown passes is an SEC championship game record that will stand for a long time. The playbooks are getting exhausted here. Pretty soon, I think Verne Lundquist is going to come down from the CBS announcing booth and run a reverse sweep with sideline reporter Tracy Wolfson as lead blocker.

We get the jumping hip bump between two Florida players after their most recent touchdown. This particularly bicurious celebratory dance has taken over. And I wonder how. It's the only time one man can ever touch another man's hip and not be considered extremely effeminate. Think about this. If you were doing anything other than getting fitted for a tuxedo and another man touched your hip, how uncomfortable would you be? Yet, get on a football field and score a touchdown and the first thing anyone wants to do is jump and bump hips with another man. I'm halfway expecting Tim Tebow to start doing spirit fingers and high kicks after each touchdown next year.

Before I can recover from my hip-bump ruminations, Arkansas's Darren McFadden, the best running back in the SEC, gets cocky and throws a pick to Reggie Nelson of Florida on yet another halfback pass. Prior to this pick I think McFadden had a quarterback rating of one gazillion. It's almost gotten to the point now where Florida is calling defenses predicated on trick plays requiring McFadden to pass. Also, if you're McFadden, doesn't it really suck that you absolutely have to come back for your junior year? Even though you'd undoubtedly be a top-ten NFL pick. If I were McFadden, I'd stay in Fayetteville, hang out, and not play football for a year. Maybe design some really cool airbrushed shirts. You know, just chill. And that's even though McFadden will be the Heisman Trophy front-runner for the 2007 football season. Regardless, his interception here essentially ends the game.

After the interception, Florida runs several plays to help drain the clock, then punts the ball back to Arkansas. Shortly thereafter, Florida picks off a Hail Mary pass from Casey Dick in the end zone to end Arkansas's chances, and the SEC chant begins to rain down upon the field. Amid the raucous celebration of the Gator fans, Florida takes a knee. The game is over. Accompanying this SEC cheer from Florida fans, a glittery device explodes on both sidelines that is layering the field in high-tech confetti.

For the first time since 2000, and for the first time in the history of Florida football, the Gators have won an SEC Championship without Steve Spurrier as their head coach. Incredibly, Florida has now won their seventh SEC Championship since 1991.

And now, even more incredibly after a season of having their national championship contention ridiculed by the national media, the USC loss has just thrust Florida to the precipice of the BCS championship game against Ohio State.

I stand and watch the Gators crowned champs. Although, from my position in the upper reaches of the Georgia Dome it is difficult to tell what is transpiring. I can make out Urban Meyer holding the championship trophy but this is about as much Florida Gator fan celebration as I, a Tennessee fan, can stomach. So, I walk down to the bathroom and throw up. Okay, not really. Instead I look down at my phone, "Does it hurt?" Neville has texted me. At least ten cents worth it does.

That night, I meet up with law school friends and plunge once more into the Atlanta night. The SEC football season is over and Gators and Razorbacks, Dawgs and Volunteers, all the fandoms of the South come together to drink beers and pine for the return of SEC football. As I stand holding a beer, my friend Rowder, from Auburn, approaches me, "Be honest," he says, "you wish the whole DDT was starting all over again tomorrow, don't you?" Even after an entire autumn on the roads of the South, the answer is a resounding yes.

The morning after the seventy-third SEC champion has been crowned, I climb out of bed and sit staring at the sunshine filtering through the window of my buddies Rowder and Glidewell's Atlanta home where I have spent the night. For the first time all fall, I have no upcoming destination for a football game. Another season of SEC football has come and gone, the thirteenth football season I've watched without my grandfather. I look down at the wedding ring on my finger, the same wedding ring that he wore after he left the University of Tennessee without graduating.

Twelve years before, when I was fifteen, my grandfather entered the hospital to have elective surgery on his left knee. His cartilage was long gone from a football injury he suffered in 1933, which now caused him a great deal of pain as his bones rubbed against each other when he walked. It was an old football injury, affecting him at eighty-one in a way it had not at thirty-one or fifty-one. And it affected his ability to get around the rose garden outside his home and assist my grandmother in her mobility. So, on July 13, 1994 he entered Memorial Hospital in Chattanooga, Tennessee, for elective surgery to have his left knee replaced. Eighteen days later he was dead. The victim of inattentive doctors, bad timing, and a football afternoon in the fall sixty-one years before.

As I leave Atlanta, I think about all the people who have shared the football season with me this fall. My family, my friends, and countless people I didn't know until I arrived on campuses across the South.

When I was sixteen, my father took me on a trip to Mississippi to visit the town of Vicksburg. I was learning how to drive and, thanks to my Civil War nerddom, I wanted to visit the city that had been called the Gibraltar of the West until it fell to General Grant on July 4, 1863. So, we did.

After a few wrong turns in the old city my father and I were lost amidst the crumbling buildings of another era. We didn't know which way to go. Out of nowhere, an elderly black woman appeared on a sidewalk, stopped, and talked with us for several minutes. Her directions were impeccable. When we got back to the car my dad, a lifelong Southerner, had tears in his eyes.

"You can go a lot of places in this world, Clay," he said, "but no one is ever going to treat you better than the people do in the South." At the time, I shook off my father's comments. After all, I was a teenager and ready to leave Vicksburg. Now that I've spent 8,382.5 miles traversing the length and breadth of the South, and lived and traveled lots of other places in the world, I can say without reservation that my father was absolutely right.

On my drive back to Nashville, I get off the interstate in Chattanooga, Tennessee, and go north through the city and on out into the suburbs where my mom and her parents lived in Red Bank. I get off on Dayton Boulevard and drive along the street that carried me to my grandparents' house countless times as a child. Past Red Bank Elementary where my grandfather took me to the playground, past the Baskin-Robbins where we would go for ice cream, and on up to 8 Trenton Street where my grandparents lived throughout my entire childhood. I park on the side of the road and for a moment I close my eyes, and it is the third Saturday in October and once again my grandfather and I are about to watch the University of Tennessee play Alabama. No one has lost, time is still, and I'm certain that inside the walls of the house the multiple clocks are all set to chime. That it's eternally football time in Tennessee.

But now, someone new lives in my grandparents' old home so I turn the car around and drive on down Dayton Boulevard until I come to Hamilton Memorial Gardens. I turn into the cemetery, park, and walk to the vicinity of my grandparents' headstone. After a time, I find it amidst the thousands of other markers. I stand for some time in the cool December afternoon, then I leave my grandfather Richard K. Fox's final resting place.

In 1933, my grandfather played in the first SEC football season, and now the champion of the seventy-third has been crowned. Another season is over, and so is my fall journey, and I feel certain somehow my grandfather knows this.

I climb back into my car and begin the final leg of the DDT, 120 miles from Chattanooga to Nashville. Outside Chattanooga, I notice that, according to the compass on my car, I am traveling south even though I'm actually heading north. For a time, I watch the dashboard indicator to make certain that the compass doesn't correct itself. By the time I reach I-24 I realize that my Dixieland Delight Tour has finally overtaken my car. No matter which direction I'm headed, all roads are leading me south.

EPILOGUE

I realize that due to relatively unimportant things such as jobs, children, money, and spouses, most people can't manage to hit all twelve SEC stadiums in a single fall. However, I would imagine that many of you are wondering which one school I would suggest you go to, if you can attend only one game at an SEC university other than your own. My predictable response to this question: Go to them all. It might take you eleven years, if you pick them off one by one, visiting a different stadium each season, but I assure you it will be worth the journey.

Now, you're probably thinking, "Yeah, but really, where should I go? Which is truly the best?" This is a difficult question, primarily because there are so many factors to consider. There's the stadium, the idiot redneck quotient, the surroundings, the friendliness of the fans, the likelihood of being arrested despite doing nothing improper, and just something I'll call the *vibe factor*. And yet, it seems to me that my book on the

DDT would be incomplete without one final ranking: the schools themselves, and so I embrace this duty with Solomonic wisdom.

Going from worst to best, I give you, after 8,382.5 miles and fourteen weeks on the road, the SEC schools in the order in which I would rank them if you had but one weekend to live and wanted to spend it on an SEC campus watching a football game.

12. Vanderbilt: Nashville is the best city in the SEC by far, but Vandy offers the worst football environment hands down. Who can blame them, really? Their team never wins and the students are all smart enough to know that football success doesn't legitimately affect their own lives. In fact, if you stood in the Vanderbilt student section and saw the women Vandy men attend school alongside you'd never feel sorry for Vandy's football team ever again. I'm serious. The best part about going to a Vandy football game is seeing the drunk girls in their sundresses. Of course lots of these girls don't arrive until almost halftime and then leave by the end of the third quarter, but still, what fifteen minutes of third-quarter glory.

11. Mississippi State: Once this book is published, I'm going to become the only person in Starkville less popular than Ole Miss coach Ed Orgeron, which is a shame, because the people I met at State were as nice or nicer than the people I met anywhere else. But State is just not a wild football environment. The stadium is relatively small and, chances are, the home team is going to lose. Having said that, if you go, buy a cowbell. I guarantee you when the entire crowd is ringing the cowbells in tandem, it's pretty cool.

10. Kentucky: It's tough for me to rank Kentucky so low, because I

have more friends and family from Kentucky than any other SEC state outside Tennessee. In fact, the name Clay even comes (via my paternal grandfather Henry Clay Travis) from Kentucky politician Henry Clay (1777–1852). And my paternal grandfather came down from Muhlenberg County, Kentucky, to Tennessee in the 1930s. But Kentucky is just not a football school; it puts and, probably always will put, basketball before all else. If you go, keep in mind that Lexington is a great town and plan on a September or October game. Otherwise, we're talking cold. Serious cold. Also, I promise to Kentucky fans that next time I come to a game, I'm also going to a horse race at Keeneland.

9. South Carolina: Williams-Brice Stadium is two miles from South Carolina's campus, amid railroad tracks, the State Fairgrounds, and what appears to be industrial wasteland. As the only SEC stadium not located within close walking distance of the actual campus, this is a major indictment. While the Cockabooses, the passion of the fans that is second to none, and the fact that oysters are probably going to be available at tailgates, makes the environment pretty cool, you lose a lot of the flavor of the SEC college experience by setting up to tailgate two miles from campus. And the parking? My God, the parking. Be ready to sit in traffic for hours after the game is over.

8. Arkansas: The surrounding hillsides of Fayetteville are breathtaking. And the town of Fayetteville is incredibly cool. But Arkansas is just too recent an addition to the SEC to stand as the best representative of SEC football. Plus, no matter where you're coming from in the South (or in the country for that matter) chances are getting to Fayetteville is going to tax all your planning and resources. Having said that, once you get there, it's an amazingly unique and hidden gem of a town.

7. Alabama: If you have a family this is probably the easiest and

best game to take them to. When I was there, the entire quad was given over to games for kids. It was relaxed and less intense than lots of other SEC tailgating scenes. Maybe this had something to do with Mike Shula being the head coach; perhaps things will change with Nick Saban. But the environment just didn't seem that electric. Even with Auburn in town.

6. Florida: If I absolutely had to attend an SEC school outside Tennessee, Florida would be my choice. The weather is great, the academics are the best of any state school in the SEC, and the campus is flat and easy to traverse. The only downside to Florida really is the arm fat on all the girls and the fact that Florida has more fans who aren't actually Southern than any SEC school. It's also the only SEC campus you'll visit where gelled hair is a prerequisite for coolness or where a night out clubbing in a brand new silk shirt (with the mandatory three buttons undone) seems like a good idea. Also, and this is key, Florida fans are sort of clueless and completely impatient with anything less than immediate success. Even in the wake of a 2006 national championship, I guarantee they'll boo their team at home for a halftime deficit this season.

5. Ole Miss: If I allow myself to include William Faulkner's Rowan Oak home, Oxford is the number-one destination for me. But the actual football game environment moves it down a few notches. The stadium is not as loud or spirited, and the game-day atmosphere is not as fevered as it is at other SEC schools. Having said that, once you reach the top five of SEC schools on game day, you really can't lose. Outside of Nashville, Oxford is the best town in the SEC to take your wife or girlfriend along. Trust me, she'll love it. And with the Ole Miss women there, so will you.

4. Auburn: Attending a game at Auburn is the quintessential SEC experience. Or at least what I think most people who have never

been to an SEC football game expect the games to be like. You're driving through the middle of Alabama and haven't really seen anything for quite a while. Then, you make a few turns and all of a sudden traffic is at a standstill and people are tailgating everywhere you look. You still can't see anything but gradually, as you get closer to the town of Auburn, you notice that the hair on the back of your arms is standing up. It's as if you can literally feel the excitement percolating in the environment. And then, you pull into Auburn and the entire small town seems to exist solely for the football game. No building is taller than four stories high and, as you walk around, all you can think is, where in the world did all these people come from?

3. Georgia: Athens is about as close to Southern heaven as you're going to get. Abundant bars and restaurants, friendly people, girls with enough cleavage to stay afloat in pools for days, and rabid barking men clad in red pants . . . some with dog bones around their necks. It's enough to make anyone excited, even if they don't like football. The campus is gorgeous, huge oak trees rising into the sunshine, sun-drenched tailgates, beer pong in the shade of tulip poplars. It's hard to get much better than this.

2. Tennessee: When 106,000 people stand and scream as Tennessee splits the T and comes rushing onto the field, I guarantee that, even if you hate the University of Tennessee with complete and utter passion, your jaw will drop and your heart rate will begin to race. Then, wait until the entire crowd rises to its feet and screams on the opening possession of the visiting team. Your ears will ring and the sheer spectacle of over one hundred thousand people clad in orange will overwhelm your senses.

1. LSU: Make it a night game and come prepared to drink until you can barely stand. It's Mardi Gras meets football on the bayou. You'll see things you haven't ever seen before—yellow snakes, a

multimillion dollar home for an actual tiger; eat food you've never tasted before—boudin, pralines, and the like; and be welcomed with open arms by Cajuns dancing with zeal to zydeco bands. By the time the game starts, the purple and gold uniforms of LSU's football players at night will resemble colorful stars shooting across the southern sky.

But no matter which SEC stadium you visit, I guarantee you'll have a good time. And as you pop open a beer, toss a hot dog on the grill, and sit down in the sunshine to prepare for a football game, be sure to take a moment to breathe deeply and enjoy it all. Quite simply, life doesn't get much better than this.

ACKNOWLEDGMENTS

There were many people who made both this book and the DDT journey a great experience. First, my wife, who somehow puts up with me and actually responded, when I told her about my idea of spending thirteen weeks on the road watching football games across the South, "You're not going to the world's largest cocktail party, too?" And then insisted that we go watch Vanderbilt play Temple when I didn't really want to go on my DDT bye week. I'm a very lucky man.

Second, thanks to the members of the Vanderbilt Law School class of 2004 who hosted me or went along to the games or just sent e-mails all fall ridiculing my team. I'm asked frequently whether law school was worth it. The answer is yes. Not really because upon graduating I was able to practice law but because, for three years, I was around such a great group of people. I am tremendously grateful. And the 2007 SEC football beers are on me. Same goes for my George Washington University classmates from 2001 who went on the DDT trip to Mississippi State with me, and for those who played football alongside me every Sunday during college.

Third, tremendous thanks to my agent Byrd Leavell, who took this book and ran with it. His only real flaw is having chosen to attend the University of Virginia, as opposed to an SEC school. And that's not much of a flaw. At least not once football season is over.

Fourth, Kate Hamill at HarperCollins, who was quick to respond to every e-mail from me, no matter how absurd the topic, and provided sage advice even to questions like, "Does this paragraph make me look like too much of a pervert?" She made stellar edits, dove right into the SEC experience, and was such an absolute joy to work with that she is even my friend on facebook.com. Also tremendous thanks to Brian Grogan, vice president of sales at HarperCollins, a Florida fan who can trace his Floridian roots back several generations. He immediately latched on and supported this book even though it was written by a Vol fan. He's also the only man in world history to celebrate winning a college football bet with a Pac-10 colleague by presenting a cake to his vanquished foe with this inscription: *SEC Rules Pac-10 drools*.

Fifth, thanks to my editor at CBS SportsLine, Roland Liwag. Despite being a Gator grad, Roland has been a great help during two years of the ClayNation column. Also thanks to Bill Ruhl, Greg Bromberg, Craig Stanke, Joe Ferreira, and everyone else at SportsLine who has helped with the column.

Sixth, I'd like to give thanks to several journalists, radio hosts, sports bloggers and other general ne'er do wells who offered support and assistance on my journey: Mark Nagi, Geoff Calkins, George Lapides, Will Leitch, Orson Swindle, Lance

Taylor, and Bud Ford at UT Sports Information. All of whom kept me entertained throughout the fall, offered assistance on the book in various degrees, and helped make the DDT a truly rewarding journey.

Seventh, to everyone who read any version of this book and offered feedback and support: several members of Vandy Law class of 2004, my wife, my parents, several members of the GW class of 2001, Lisa Travis Blomquist, Kenneth and Hester Fox, Chad Messier, Terry Taylor, Tony Earley, and others whom I'm sure I'm missing. You all made invaluable contributions, and the parts of this book that suck are entirely my own creation.

And, finally, to the fans across the South who welcomed me to your tailgates, sold me cheaper tickets than you needed to, tossed me a cold beer, and kept me entertained all football season, tremendous thanks. The ultimate reason SEC football is the best in the country is because SEC football fans are the best in the country. I owe you all a tremendous debt of gratitude.